WHEN
WORLD VIEWS
COLLIDE

WHEN WORLD VIEWS COLLIDE

A Study in Imagination and Evolution

JOHN J. PIERCE

Foreword by Lester del Rey

CONTRIBUTIONS TO THE STUDY OF
SCIENCE FICTION AND FANTASY, NUMBER 37

Greenwood Press
NEW YORK • WESTPORT, CONNECTICUT • LONDON

Library of Congress Cataloging-in-Publication Data

Pierce, John J.
    When world views collide : a study in imagination and evolution /
John J. Pierce ; foreword by Lester del Rey.
        p.   cm.—(Contributions to the study of science fiction and
fantasy, ISSN 0193–6875 ; no. 37)
    Bibliography: p.
    Includes index.
    ISBN 0–313–25457–5 (lib. bdg. : alk. paper)
    1. Science fiction—History and criticism.   I. Title.
II. Series.
PN3433.8.P55 1989
809.3'876—dc19   88–7708

British Library Cataloguing in Publication Data is available.

Library of Congress Catalog Card Number: 88–7708
ISBN: 0–313–25457–5
ISSN: 0193–6875

First published in 1989

Greenwood Press, Inc.
88 Post Road West, Westport, Connecticut   06881

Printed in the United States of America

The paper used in this book complies with the
Permanent Paper Standard issued by the National
Information Standards Organization (Z39.48–1984).

10 9 8 7 6 5 4 3 2 1

88 - 9426

To a redoubtable dinosaur, Sam Moskowitz;
and a delightful mammal, Sandra Miesel

Contents

Foreword

Some fifty years ago, when I first began writing science fiction, there were only a few magazines where that type of literature appeared. Very few new books of science fiction were published, and even the reprints of the classics by Wells and Verne were not easy to find. Science fiction wasn't even thought of as a category, and the word "genre" was yet to be applied, since scholarship neglected it almost completely. In fact, the idea that it was "ghetto" hadn't been given expression, though a later generation insisted that it had been exiled into one.

At that time, it was still possible to read everything that was being published in the field; indeed, secondhand magazine stores and used book outlets made it possible for a reader to become familiar with much that had been published before. Most of the small group of devoted fans and many of the writers in the field were familiar with all the current works and an extensive body of previous science fiction. Some were already beginning to make collections that would preserve the ephemeral magazines for the future.

Already, however, there had begun an evolution in the nature and ethos of science fiction, led by such early writers as Stanley G. Weinbaum and Raymond Z. Gallun. The simple gadget story was giving way to fiction with a more complex view of the attitudes behind science.

Women, though hardly liberated or given fair treatment, were no longer mere objects to be rescued by male heroes from the clutches of monsters. Sentient beings in alien form or from some nonhuman world were not automatically evil and about to invade earth. There was at least the beginning of an end to the xenophobia and chauvinism all too common earlier. The style of writing was beginning to improve, and the emphasis was shifting from mechanism toward a greater interest in the human ways and values as they were exposed to the changing society caused by the spread of new frontiers and new technologies.

Some older readers resented that change bitterly and talked endlessly of the "good old days." But the few hundred known fans and writers still regarded themselves generally as part of a sort of extended family, despite their often bitter arguments about the true place and purpose of science fiction. That remained true in large degree through World War II and into the early 1950s.

Now, however, another generation has passed, and each decade seems to bring more changes than the one before. Some magazines survive, but the torch has passed to books. A myriad of books comes yearly from the publishers—most still in paperbacks, but with a growing percentage in hardcover format. Science fiction today appears with some frequency in *The New York Times* best-seller lists, and it is possible for a successful book to earn its writer half a million dollars or more as an advance. Academia has discovered science fiction; most of the modern fans have probably gone through college, where science fiction is now often studied as a genre of general literature to which it must be related.

Science fiction has evolved and diverged into many ways and moods. There seems to be a type of science fiction for every taste, and followers of one type frequently know little and care less for other types. The Hugo awards given by the fans at the annual world science-fiction conventions and the Nebula awards given by the SFWA professional writers often bear no similarity in choice. And neither bears much relationship to the sales figures for the books, which are determined largely by general reader preference.

With such a large body of past and present science fiction, it seems impossible for any one man to have read all available kinds of science fiction. Indeed, with such divergence in style, taste, intent, and basic nature as now exists in science fiction, it would seem that no man would want to.

And yet that is the task that John J. Pierce has set for himself—a task in which he has succeeded. For more than fifteen years, I have followed his attempts to master the entire field, from its first beginnings to its latest publication—not just as it has appeared in America but its international spread as well.

He has read, researched, made notes, and *thought*. Above all, he has thought, searching for trends, meanings, and all that lies behind the seemingly hopeless confusion of science fiction. He has read carefully those fields of science fiction to which at one time he objected strongly, pursuing insights into their intent as keenly as those works he might have preferred.

As I write this, two of the volumes in his monumental *Imagination and Evolution* trilogy have been published, and this, the third, brings his insights into science fiction up to the present. I had read none of this before the first book appeared, despite my interest in what I knew of his work and purpose. Having finished reading this volume, I am forced to a feeling of awe at what Pierce has accomplished.

This doesn't mean that I always agree with his evaluation of the works covered, nor that I can always accept every one of his attempts to gain full insight into the intents and place in the field of any particular writer or movement. That doesn't matter.

What does matter is that he has done something unique in attempting such a formidable study and in gaining such insights. He has spread science fiction out before us and traced relationships as no one has even attempted before. He has given us a way to relate what we may have read to what we have not, and he has furnished an enormous framework from which future scholars can go on in their efforts to place the works and the fields in the totality of literature.

The volumes in Pierce's *Imagination and Evolution* trilogy cover the field in depth and scope far greater than has been done before. I hope that future scholarship will build upon this foundation. Am I am grateful that I have been given the chance to read them and have been forced to think even more deeply about the field that has been my life's work.

Lester del Rey

Preface

When World Views Collide is the third volume in a history of science fiction that began with *Foundations of Science Fiction* and continued in *Great Themes of Science Fiction*, both published by Greenwood Press in 1987. Like the other volumes, *When World Views Collide* is subtitled, *A Study in Imagination and Evolution*—*Imagination and Evolution* was the working title of this history when it was first conceived as a single volume.

Imagination and Evolution had been in gestation for a long time—since 1971, in fact. Science fiction wasn't as popular then as now, nor was it the subject of as much academic scrutiny. It was before the *Star Wars* phenomenon, before the phenomenal advances for new novels by Robert A. Heinlein or Arthur C. Clarke, before *Science Fiction Studies*, before the proliferation of ponies on sf authors like the Starmont series. In those days, sf novels did not appear on best-seller lists, nor were sf authors featured in the *Washington Post* or the *Village Voice*. Most of the scholarship still originated with sf, from serious fans—some would say the best still does, but the contents pages of today's scholarly journals at least show the extent of professional academic involvement—and those fans were just beginning to hear of cognitive estrangement, semiotics, or deconstruction.

In those days, sf was just emerging from the divisive controversy of the New Wave. The bitter polemics of that controversy, in which the invective was both personal and ideological, had gone on for close to seven years. More recent controversies, such as those centered on feminist sf or cyberpunk, seem almost tame by comparison—although they too have inspired bitter invective. Long before the New Wave feud, however, sf had been the arena of other controversies. Science fiction didn't even have an agreed-upon name when the literary humanists such as E. M. Forster began to take on H. G. Wells with their anti-utopian works. The quasi-Marxist Futurians battled conservative fans just before World War II, although that feud remained in fandom. The bitingly satirical sf of the Pohl-Kornbluth school, which found a home in *Galaxy* in the 1950s, was a challenge to the dominant school of hard-headed technological and social extrapolation which flowered in *Astounding* in the 1940s. A storm of controversy arose over Heinlein's *Starship Troopers* (1959), with its determined assault on the consensus liberalism of its day.

Science fiction is widely regarded as just another form of popular entertainment—like mysteries, spy thrillers, Westerns, and romances: Isn't *Star Wars* just the traditional Hollywood Western in new trappings? Science fiction is also widely regarded as conventional in its values— even pathetic in its conservatism—compared to the modern literature of stylistic invention or psychological insight, moral depth, social relevance, or political commitment: the works of James Joyce, Marcel Proust, Jean-Paul Sartre, Doris Lessing, Joseph Heller, Gabriel García Marquez, and others. Yet if science fiction can't be taken seriously, why should its debates be so intense? Was the controversy *that* bitter between the advocates of the hard-boiled detective novel and the traditional British school? Do the authors or fans of Regency romances and bodice-rippers vilify each other from the housetops? Sometimes, perhaps. But such disputes are uncommon compared to those in science fiction. Even in histories and encyclopedias of the genre, the language is often far from dispassionate, and the issues seem to be taken as seriously as classical literary debates on the merits of romanticism vs. naturalism, symbolism vs. neorealism, modernism vs. postmodernism, and so on.

In all of this, there is a sense that science fiction is important. *Imagination and Evolution* began with that sense, born of the controversy over the New Wave. It is only fair to confess that the author himself was one of the polemicists of that period, the self-proclaimed spokesman of a Second Foundation that sought to defend the cause of traditional science fiction through a fanzine called *Renaissance* and other media. *Towards a Theory of Science Fiction* (1971) was his/its definitive position paper; David G. Hartwell has even quoted from it in *Age of Wonders* (1985) as an example of the temper of the time. At last word, British sf fan Chris R. Tame intended to reissue the manifesto, arguing that it is still much in demand and still relevant. Be that as it may, a history of sf must not be a mere exercise in polemics; but there are bound to be those who will find a bias in this history, especially as it relates to the New Wave. Well, there are other histories, biased in their own ways; if there is a fault here, it is more than compensated elsewhere. Although the author considers himself a revisionist Wellsian humanist and a pluralistic libertarian, the intent of *When World Views Collide* is, as much as possible, to present each world view on its own terms, as expressed in the works of its partisans.

Although the main concern of *Foundations of Science Fiction* was the evolution of literary traditions as such, the volume suggested the significance of world views; those fundamental beliefs about the nature of man, of the universe, and of man's place in the universe, by which we seem to interpret the meaning of existence. *Great Themes of Science Fiction,* which focuses on the evolution of specific themes in sf, touched on world views again in relation to their influence on the treatment of those specific themes. But the conflicts about science fiction itself, such as that surrounding the New Wave, are largely conflicts about world views themselves—however much they may be masked as conflicts over literary quality or literary taste. Much more could be said, and perhaps will be in a further volume, about the purely literary evolution of sf, and the contemporary quest for the great science fiction novel by writers such as Gregory Benford, Gene Wolfe, Robert Silverberg, Kim Stanley Robinson, and others. *When World Views Collide* is about science fiction as a way of defining and delimiting humanity and human values, which may well be the most important aspect of the genre today—yet one that has never before been treated comprehensively.

Thanks are in order for Sam Moskowitz, Alexei Kondratiev, Dwight Decker, Patrick McGuire, and John Andrews for their assistance in research and translation. But, most of all, profound gratitude is in order to all sf writers whose labors have made science fiction as important as it is.

WHEN
WORLD VIEWS
COLLIDE

Introduction

A GLOBAL CIVIL WAR

Then came the Global Civil War, a rapid spiraling of diverse conflicts that, by 1994, was well on its way to becoming a full-scale worldwide struggle. . . . The World Unification Alliance came into existence because it seemed the best hope for human survival. But its well-meaning reformers found that a hundred predators rose up to savage them: from supranational conglomerates, religious extremists, and followers of hundred different ideologies to racists and bigots of every stripe.[1]

This passage is not from a classic of world literature, not even from a classic of science fiction. It is part of the stage setting in Jack McKinney's *Genesis* (1987), a novelization of several episodes of the animated Television series *Robotech* (1985), which is, in turn, an adaptation of the Japanese *anime* series *Super Dimension Fortress Macross* (1982). Although much has been changed in the English-language version, the vision of a Global Civil War is true to the Japanese original—and true to the perspective of science fiction itself. If we are all children of a common evolution, sharing a world in common, how else can we see the contemporary conflict of nations and ideologies than as a civil war? The Japanese have a word for it, *sengoku*, but the concept is hardly theirs alone. The astronauts in Edgar Pangborn's *West of the Sun* (1953), for example, are haunted by "the horrors of the Civil War of 2010–13,"[2] as they seek to establish a humane society in harmony with the natives of a distant world on which they have been marooned.

Pangborn's civil war is between the forces of the Collectivist Party and those of the liberal humanist democracy. It is a familiar scenario, an extension of the on-again, off-again Cold War that has been part of our history for more than forty years. But in Pangborn's imagined future, the civil war appears to be civil in the classic sense: a bitter struggle of partisan against partisan—no doubt of brother against brother—rather than of nation-state against nation-state. Perhaps we must think of the Thirty Years' War in Europe after the Reformation to envision an adequate parallel. James Clavell's film *The Last Valley* (1971) takes that conflict for its setting, and while it offers only brief glimpses of the war itself, they are harrowing enough to convince us that there has been none crueler. Omar Sharif's portrayal of a tortured intellectual's striving to protect the villagers of an idyllic Alpine valley from the worst excesses of Michael Caine's mercenary force must strike a responsive chord among those who have witnessed the cruelty of our own ideological conflicts. Then, as now, passions of belief not only excused countless barbarities, but also served as a convenient cover for baser motives.

The Protestant and Catholic zealots of the seventeenth century, and those who used the cover of their zealotry, never had the capacity, however, to destroy the world that nuclear weapons had given their latter-day counterparts. As Walter M. Miller, Jr., points out in a "forewarning" to *Beyond Armageddon* (1985), an anthology of post-holocaust sf, what makes the confrontation of nuclear superpowers so frightening is that:

The Marxist ideologue in the Kremlin and the Christian Fundamentalist ideologue here at home share a passion and an apocalyptic expectation of the other's impending extinction or damnation according to two oddly symmetrical scenarios for the end of the world.[3]

And, as Miller also points out, the confrontation of the superpowers is aggravated by the growing number of actual and potential "nuclear jihad states and atomic banana republics."[4] To the passions of West and East are added those of Islamic fundamentalism, Arab and Israeli zealots, and a Third World seeking vengeance against Western imperialism. Even if world leaders achieve nuclear disarmament, the passions of rival faiths and ideologies will remain. We could still suffer another Thiry Years' War; perhaps civilization will collapse in fratricidal war of the sort that now afflicts Lebanon and Northern Ireland, or in "little" wars like the desultory conflict between Iran and Iraq. There could well be another religious holocaust in the Middle East, or a racial holocaust in South Africa. Nor are such openly violent conflicts the only aspects of the developing global civil war. There is the estrangement of what novelist C. P. Snow called the Two Cultures: "Literary intellectuals at one pole— at the other scientists.... Between the two a gulf of mutual incomprehension."[5] There is the conflict between secular and religious ethical and social values. There is even the growing alienation between intellectual and popular cultures.

Karel Capek (1890–1938) is known as the father of robots in science fiction—he introduced the word in his play *R.U.R.* (1921)—but Capek should also be known for his insight into the theme of the global civil war, which is actually the underlying theme of that play. In what he called a "comedy of truth," each of the characters in *R.U.R.* represents an ideological viewpoint, and each of them has some claim to the truth:

Be these people either Conservatives or Socialists, Yellows or Reds, the most important thing is—and this is the point I wish particularly to stress—that all of them are right in the plain and moral sense of the word. ... I ask whether it is not possible to see in the present social conflict of the world an analogous struggle between two, three, five equally serious verities and equally generous idealisms? I think it is possible, and this is the most dramatic element in modern civilization, that a human truth is opposed to another truth no less human, ideal against ideal, positive worth against worth no less positive, instead of the struggle being, as we are so often told it is, one between noble truth and vile selfish error.[6]

Capek seems hopelessly naive today. Since 1921, we have seen the Nazi death camps, the Soviet gulags, Hiroshima, and too many other atrocities. Nothing seems as fatuous as the idea that there is good in every person or institution; we have seen too much raw evil. Yet perhaps Capek, even today, is right in another sense: Perhaps there is more than one *kind* of good and more than one *kind* of evil. Perhaps the claim that each creed or system makes that its truth is the only truth, its good the only good, is itself the source of the untruths each preaches and the evils each perpetrates—for that matter, of those each excuses.

Commentators of the Right have often complained lately about the "selective indignation" of the Left; yet their own indignation seems to be equally selective. There is more than enough hypocrisy to go around. Or perhaps it isn't hypocrisy; perhaps it is true ideological blindness. Even in their celebrated conversions, such partisans of the global civil war remain true to type: Conservatives are radicalized and become Marxist zealots; Marxist dropouts turn to dogmatic neoconservatism. If one of the prevailing orthodoxies is discredited, the other must be altogether valid. If both fail, the only alternative is some new fanaticism. To any dispassionate observer, the faith of the partisans seems absurd—how can they *not* know that they serve half-truths at best, or total lies at worst? Yet the global civil war is not only between, but *within* men. For those not blindly committed, it is hard to avoid feeling torn between conflicting moral and cultural values. Perhaps they somehow sense what the partisans have missed: that each faith or ideology making a claim to their allegiance is true *and* false in its own way. Each defends some sacred principle, only to betray one equally sacred. Each demands, in the name of one human need or ideal, that we sacrifice a complementary need or ideal: the dignity of the individual or the welfare of society, material progress or spiritual fulfillment, science and civilization or art and respect for nature. Surely there must be some way for us to strike a balance, to seek a reconciliation, to feel *whole* again.

"Poets are the unacknowledged legislators of the world,"[7] declared Percy Bysshe Shelley, and ever since it has been a recurrent conceit of literary intellectuals that they hold the salvation of mankind in their hands. Charles Dickens and Victor Hugo saw themselves as moral teachers as well as novelists. Émile Zola and Upton Sinclair were social critics in their fiction and political activists in their lives. Arthur Miller and Norman Mailer are known almost as much for their political activism as for their plays and novels, and Jean-Paul Sartre is probably better known for his philosophy of existentialism than for any of the fictional works in which it is expressed. We look to men of letters for the sort of wisdom we once sought from priests or philosophers; but in setting them up as wise men, we expect too much of them. We would have our wise men be wise in all things, forgetting that each can be wise in some things and foolish in others. We may even expect too much of wisdom itself. The estrangement of the Two Cultures, science and literature, has warped our understanding of the relationship between knowledge and wisdom. It is as if they had nothing to do with one another. On the one hand, we have the image of the walking encyclopedia, crammed with facts but devoid of vision; on the other, that of the creative artist whose wisdom is the revelation of his muse, beyond dependence on knowledge.

Arthur Koestler, in *The Act of Creation* (1964) points toward the true source of wisdom. Creative insight, he suggests, arises from a sudden perception of the link between frames of reference that had previously seemed unconnected. Insights are not the same as mere facts, yet they are dependent on a knowledge of facts. Wisdom can be seen as the cumulative series of insights into the nature of man and the nature of the universe that is the basis of both the scientific and literary cultures. But the cumulative growth of wisdom thus depends on the cumulative growth of knowledge. According to Koestler's theory, a false insight should feel just like a true one. Much, perhaps most, of that which is destructive in our contending faiths and ideologies may well derive from insights that were flawed by lack of knowledge, but seemed true from the sheer emotional force of revelation. Even when they were meant to liberate or ennoble mankind, they have thus often become instruments of oppression. Even when they were not fatally flawed to begin with, their essence has often been lost sight of, or perhaps simply outlived its usefulness.

Ian Watson's *The Martian Inca* (1977) offers a vivid illustration of this phenomenon. A Soviet space probe, returning from Mars, bears an alien virus—a virus which, although usually fatal, can confer the gift of prophetic insight. Julio Capac, the sole survivor of an outbreak that has wiped out a village in the Peruvian Andes, thus finds himself filled with wisdom overnight: "the way of his Thought . . . a huge quipu made up of stars, of knots of energy."[8] Suddenly, it appears that he can perceive the relations of all things, reality is like a quipu:

Yet he saw how the knot was tied, as he dreamt the tying of it. He saw how all such knots were tied and might be untied, retied in many other ways. He saw how strings might be attached to other strings.[9]

Preaching his revelation, Capac soon galvanizes the Incan people into a revolution. The revolution ultimately fails, however, because its revelation is as limited as Capac's knowledge; even as he sees his utopian dream crumble, he cannot quite grasp *why*. Lest Western man feel smug in his greater knowledge, however, Watson puts an astronaut, Eugene Silverman, who lands on Mars through the same experience. Silverman just brims with insights, which he attempts to share with a fellow spaceman:

Shall I tell you what consciousness is, Wally? Or rather, what it's always been till now? Each thought in our minds is the arc of a circle. There are so many, many arcs: as many as the thoughts that our minds can possibly think. And these all co-exist in n-space—a super-space that no thought alone can record by itself.[10]

It sounds just barely plausible, but only because Western man has become used to ideas like "n-space," as opposed to the patterns of knots in quipu. As Silverman rambles on about his insights into consciousness and evolution, he sounds more and more like Timothy Leary on LSD. Convinced that the salvation of mankind lies in the virus, he infects Wally Oates, who awakens to a hallucinatory vision of his mistress, Milly-Kim—and both become so wrapped up in their visions that they bring disaster on themselves and the expedition. Of course, the virus serves a natural function on Mars, where it is the basis of sentience in aggregates of organisms that must "evolve" all over again after each millenial "winter." Perhaps it can be of benefit to mankind in the long run, if properly understood. But a dying Oates, through "Milly-Kim," comes to realize the fallacy of seeking instant wisdom from the insights of the virus: "Connections will connect. But what will they connect? Only what is there already."[11]

Watson's novel is a brilliant example of the insight peculiar to science fiction. At its best, sf shares the knowledge and perspectives of both the sciences and the humanities. Yet any attempt to discuss sf as a literature of ideas, and especially as a literature of *great* ideas that might bear upon our present world conflict, is almost doomed to appear pretentious. For science fiction, more than any other genre, has gained a reputation over the years—unfortunately, often deserved—for its pretentiousness. One could cite any number of examples, but surely the most embarrassing is the life and career of L. Ron Hubbard (1911–1986). A quintessential pulp writer of the 1940s, Hubbard was renowned for crude but powerful sf and fantasy novels like *Final Blackout* and *Typewriter in the Sky* (both 1940). Pulp fiction was not enough for Hubbard; he started a "science" of the mind called Dianetics, which was introduced in the pages of John W. Campbell, Jr.'s *Astounding Science Fiction* in 1950, and he won a number of converts—most notably A. E. Van Vogt. Most people in the sf community soon came to their senses, and Hubbard departed from the genre. Dianetics evolved into a religion called Scientology, which attracted a devoted cult following and made millions for Hubbard, which may have been his intention in the first place. Veteran sf fans Sam Moskowitz and Lloyd Arthur Eshbach recall that Hubbard had opined (several years before the birth of Dianetics) that the way to get rich was to start a religion.[12] Whatever the case, the origin of a pernicious cult was indelibly linked to science fiction. When the sf community felt it had finally lived down the dubious honor of having unleashed Hubbard on the world, he returned to the genre like the prodigal son with *Battlefield Earth* (1983), a pulp-style epic running to more than 800 pages. At the time of his death, he had completed the even more monumental *Mission Earth* dekalogy (a series of ten novels) in a style few contemporary writers in the field could emulate, or would want to. But how they sell!

Compared to Hubbard, science fiction's other embarrassments, such as the tedious philosophizing of Frank Herbert's *Dune* sequels or the bondage and discipline syndrome of John Norman's Gor novels, seem trivial. Nevertheless, they reinforce an impression that sf in general must be trivial at best, malignant at worst. Critics of the genre seem to expect the worst: Robert A. Heinlein's *Stranger in a Strange Land* (1961) won unwanted notoriety when news reports linked it to the cult of Charles Manson. Although the definitive account of Manson's cult, Vincent Bugliosi and Curt Gentry's *Helter Skelter* (1974), does not substantiate any such connection, there are probably still those who believe in it and judge Heinlein accordingly. Those who do judge sf on such grounds, and find it wanting, are applying a double standard. Does anyone hold J. D. Salinger responsible for the murder of John Lennon? More to the point, the so-called mainstream has real embarrassments, too. Ezra Pound and Louis-Ferdinand Celine were shameless fascists and anti-Semites; George Bernard Shaw and Lillian Hellman were apologists for Joseph Stalin's bloody purges. On the strictly literary level, can Doris Lessing's Canopus in Argos novels, with their turn to pretentious mysticism, be taken more seriously than Herbert's *Dune* sequels? It is a myth that literary people are necessarily more rational, virtuous, or wise than the rest of mankind.

One can argue endlessly about the literary significance of science fiction, which ranges from such abysmal space opera as the Perry Rhodan series in Germany (1961–) to such classics as Alfred Bester's *The Stars My Destination* (1956) or Gene Wolfe's The Book of the New Sun (1980–87). But an equally important issue in the evolution of sf as a genre is its literary mythology, which Donald A. Wollheim outlined as the "Cosmogony of the Future"[13] in *The Universe Makers* (1971). It is the collective elaboration of ideas and images inspired by the evolutionary humanist philosophy that C. S. Lewis once called "Wellsianity"[14] because of its association with H. G. Wells. Because myths are the literary expression of fundamental beliefs—the concretization of ideas about the good, the true, and the beautiful, about the meaning and purpose of human existence—they are taken very seriously. Our deepest emotions, even our sense of identity, can be bound up with them. Science fiction is a microcosm of all the conflicts and issues of the global civil war—individualism vs. collectivism, science vs. faith, and all the rest. But the peculiar form that the global civil war takes in sf begins with with the genre's formative myth, and with the flawed genius who did the most to create and propagate that myth.

A FIELD OF BATTLE

H. G. Wells was science fiction's archetypical wise man. Like so many of our wise men, he was also a fool. Much, perhaps most, of what both readers and critics find either wise or foolish in sf has its roots in Wells. One can find any number of issues that have nothing to do with him, of course, but all the really important ones are part of his legacy to the genre.

It was Wells who taught us to think, and feel, about time and space in the cosmic sense. It was Wells who made evolution an emotional as well as an intellectual reality. It was Wells who led us to see ourselves as a species, sharing a world in common. It was Wells who popularized a stark, existential confrontation between the human sense of purpose and a cosmos cold, indifferent, or even hostile. And it was Wells who tried to see the entire meaning of existence in that confrontation, summoning mankind to challenge the cosmos and to impose purpose upon it, to seek an evolutionary destiny of becoming rather than of being. The Wellsian vision, expressed in the climactic scenes of *The Food of the Gods* (1903–4) and *Things to Come* (1936) became one of the foundations of modern science fiction.

Consider "Scientifiction, Searchlight of Science," an exuberant and, to our more cynical generation, naive guest editorial by the young Jack Williamson, which appeared in *Amazing Stories* in 1928:

Science has found a million new worlds, and lost itself in them. Earth has become a cosmic mote; man, utterly ephemeral and insignificant. *Science* and *Intelligence* alone remain considerable quantities. Then, if the life of the earth is the briefest instant in Time, a question rises: Must man pass with the earth, or will *Human intelligence* rule on, a new factor in the universe? The idea is stupendous. . . .

Here is the picture, if we can but see it: a universe ruled by the human mind. A new Golden Age of fair cities, of new laws and new machines of human capabilities undreamed of, of a civilization that has conquered matter and Nature, distance and time, disease and death. A glorious picture of an empire that lies away past a million flaming suns until it reaches the black infinity of unknown space, and extends beyond.[15]

Wells is nowhere mentioned in Williamson's editorial, yet it is filled with the Wellsian vision. It begins on the same note of cosmic pessimism, of mankind lost and insignificant in the vastness of the uncaring cosmos of space and time, as Wells' early masterpieces *The Time Machine* (1895) and "The Star" (1897), and it goes on to invoke the same faith in the potential of science and intelligence as Wells' *A Modern Utopia* (1904–5) in its vision of "a new Golden Age." Furthermore, its ultimate dream of an empire lying "past a million flaming suns" recalls the challenge to infinity of the Giant Children in *The Food of the Gods*:

"We fight not for ourselves but for growth, growth that goes on for ever. . . . That is the law of the spirit for evermore. To grow according to the will of God! To grow out of these crooks and crannies, out of these shadows and darknesses, into greatness and the light! . . . Till the earth is no more than a footstool. . . . Till the spirit shall have driven fear into nothingness, and spread. . . . " He swung his arms heavenward—"*There!*"[16]

Williamson went on to make his mark on science fiction with such classics of cosmic adventure as *The Legion of Space* (1935) and later with more cerebral works like "Breakdown" (1942). Space opera is not the sort of sf most critics would call Wellsian, and yet the evolutionary vision of Wells is essential to the background of *The Legion of Space*, as expounded in a prologue to the 1947 hardcover edition, "The Man Who Remembered Tomorrow." It is just as essential to the climactic finale of "Breakdown," in which the dissident idealists fleeing the collapse of the old order on earth dream of forging a new civilization beyond: "Ahead were the stars."[17] Williamson has become a scholar and critic of sf, and he has even published a revisionist study of Wells, *H. G. Wells: Critic of Progress* (1973). Still, even in such contemporary sf novels as *Manseed* (1982), where the cyborg Defender of a newly seeded human colony on a distant world sees the colonists as "infants still, just awaking in their cradle" yet takes "human pride in their cosmic promise,"[18] Williamson keeps alive the Wellsian dream of that long-ago editorial.

That same dream has long been vital to the appeal of sf. It is a mistake, although an understandable one, to assume that readers were drawn to the early science fiction pulps solely by lurid covers and the promise of action and adventure. Action and adventure could be found in mainstream fiction, and such mainstream adventure writers as Sax Rohmer, John Buchan, and Talbot Mundy were better at their craft than any of the newcomers *Amazing* or *Astounding* had to offer. The emotional appeal that attracted readers to science fiction from the first was the same as that which attracted a later generation of fans to *Star Trek:* "To boldly go where no man has gone before."[19] And *"There!"* for *Star Trek*, as it was before for Williamson's generation and even earlier for those inspired by the vision of the Giant Children in *The Food of the Gods*, was not any particular place or event but was rather the Future, the Universe, a dream.

If the Wellsian spirit of modern science fiction is not obvious to critics, it would be even less obvious to Wells himself. Wells may have been a romantic in his own way, but he would never have admitted it. In his time, romanticism was associated with Rudyard Kipling at best; with post-Victorian costume drama or thud-and-blunder adventure at worst. In any case, it was the stuff of comforting illusions about reality and a prop for conventional morality and social injustice. In "A Story of the Days to Come" (1897), Wells' dystopian vision of the future, Victorian popular fiction has given way to popular audio melodrama, but the social significance of mass entertainment remains unchanged, as a commercial braying from one of the Babble Machines of London reveals:

If you love Swagger Literature, put your telephone on to Bruggles, the Greatest Author of all Time. The Greatest Thinker of all Time. Teaches you Morals up to your Scalp! The very image of Socrates, except the back of his head, which is like Shakespeare. He has six toes, dresses in red, and never cleans his teeth. Hear HIM![20]

Nor do we have to guess what Wells would think about most modern science fiction. In *The Shape of Things to Come* (1933), his historian of the future offers a retrospective commentary on Michael Arlen's *Man's Mortality* (1933), "an amusing fantasy of the world dominated by an air-transport syndicate":

It is still a very readable book and interesting in showing the limitations of the educated imagination at that time. The belief in the possibilities of invention is unbounded; air velocities and air fighting are described on a scale that still seems preposterously exaggerated to-day; while on the other hand. . . . In a world of incredible metals, explosives and swiftness, the Stock Exchange, the Bourses, still survive. And there are still Power and Foreign Policies! . . . For some obscure reason, mental and moral progress and institutional invention seemed absolutely impossible to [people at that time].[21]

By "mental and moral progress and institutional invention," Wells meant, of course, the theory and practice of the World-State. *The Shape of Things to Come* is his most detailed exposition of the theme—it is airmen and engineers like Arlen's, ironically, who are the midwives to the World-State that emerges from a destructive world war. Little read now, the book is filled with the sorts of ideas that have enraged generations of literary intellectuals, and with good reason. Wells is blind to the dangers of concentration of power, as for example, when his historian remarks:

The Soviet system certainly anticipated many of the features of our present order in its profession of internationalism, its very real socialism, and particularly in the presence of a devoted controlling organisation, the Communist Party, which foreshadowed our Modern State Fellowship.[22]

Elsewhere, Wells uses *The Shape of Things to Come* to denounce the "estrangement of literature from the Modern State"[23] (such estranged literature is later suppressed) and to warn against the destructive emotions of romantic love (an atavistic affair, which briefly troubles the leadership of the new order, is dismissed by Wells' historian as "elementary in its crudity . . . out of key with all that precedes it and all that follows."[24]). Nor were these only the ideas of the older and embittered Wells. In "A Dream of Armageddon" (1901), his protagonist is a world leader of the near future whose obsession with the love of a woman blinds him to his duty and condemns the world to a cataclysmic war. Long before his swipes at the generation of James Joyce, Wells incurred the enmity of literary intellectuals with his caricature of Henry James and the Jamesian esthetic ideal in *Boon* (1915):

It is like a church lit but without a congregation to distract you, with every light and line focused on the high altar. And on the altar, very reverently placed, intensely there, is a dead kitten, an egg-shell, a bit of string.[25]

Boon was enough to give Wells a reputation as a philistine, even among later generations of novelists who doubtless considered James as stuffy and irrelevant as Wells had. Mark Hillegas has chronicled the reaction of literary intellectuals to Wells and Wellsian thought in *The Future as Nightmare: H. G. Wells and the Anti-Utopians* (1967), and the virtual un-animity of their revulsion is remarkable. The same sort of revulsion is common in criticism of science fiction generally, as one can see in two examples: one is directed broadly against the genre, the other is directed specifically against Wells:

These prophets [science fiction writers] often foretell (and many seem to yearn for) a world like one big glass-roofed railway station. But from them it is as a rule very hard to gather what men in such a world-town will *do*. They may abandon the 'full Victorian panoply' for loose garments (with zip-fasteners) but will use this freedom mainly, it would appear, in order to play with mechanical toys in the soon-cloying game of moving at high speed . . . the ideals of their idealists hardly reach farther than the splendid notion of building more towns of the same sort on other planets.[26]

The second example:

Barring wars and unforeseen disasters, the future is envisaged as an ever more rapid march of mechanical progress; machines to save work, machines to save thought, machines to save pain, hygiene, efficiency, organisation, more hygiene, more efficiency, more organisation, more machines—until you finally land up in the by now familiar Wellsian utopia, aptly caricatured by Huxley in *Brave New World.* . . .

   Mr. Wells would probably retort that the world can never become foolproof, because, however high a standard of efficiency you have reached, there is always some greater difficulty ahead. For example (this is Mr. Wells' favourite idea—he has used it in goodness knows how many perorations), when you have got this planet of ours perfectly into trim, you start upon the enormous task of reaching and colonizing another. But this is merely to push the objective further into the future; the objective remains the same.[27]

The first example comes from J. R. R. Tolkien; the second, from George Orwell. It is hard to imagine Tolkien and Orwell as allies, yet, in this case, they are. Science fiction seems the apotheosis of a crude materialistic philosophy, and Wells the chief prophet of that philosophy. As Hillegas remarks, "it is not the originality of Wells' vision, but its overwhelming vigor, vitality and comprehensiveness that make it a chief target of twentieth century anti-utopians."[28] Hillegas also touches on the basic beliefs of the literary intellectuals who have assailed Wells. Whereas Wells envisioned an essentially amoral universe, in which man-kind must struggle against the blind forces of nature, "most of the anti-utopians tend to hold the quite antithetical view that man tampers with nature only at great risk since there is some kind of higher wisdom in the order of the universe—in God, or in nature itself."[29] This is a world view often called Faustian or, in science fiction, gothic, from its long association with Mary Shelley's *Frankenstein* (1818) and the school of sf inspired by *Frankenstein*. Along with a reverence for nature, Hillegas observes, most of the anti-utopian literary intellectuals share a reverence for the individual as opposed to the collective. "I have no mystic faith in the people," he quotes E. M. Forster, whose "The Machine Stops" (1909) was the first of the great anti-Wellsian anti-utopias. "I have in the individual. He seems to me a divine achievement and I mistrust any view which belittles him."[30]

In anti-utopian fiction, then, the Wellsian vision has been damned again and again for a vulgar, mechanistic idea of "progress" that leaves no room for nature and an equally vulgar collectivism that leaves no room for the individual. Hillegas shows how these critical themes have recurred in the works of Forster, Orwell, Aldous Huxley, and others; and how the anti-utopians have cleverly exploited Wells' own imagery, from both his early dystopian works like *When the Sleeper Wakes* (1898–9) and his later blueprints for progress like *A Modern Utopia*. For Hillegas, however, the story of H. G. Wells and the anti-utopians is *the* story of Wells' impact on literature and culture. It is a story of estrangement without hope of reconciliation; Wells remains the antithesis. In science fiction, it is almost the opposite: Wells has become the thesis, or at least the predominant thesis. In part, this reflects the very innocence of the genre, which began as a popular literature blissfully unaware of the values of "serious" literature. For Jules Verne and his generations of readers, science and technology were in themselves romantic—never mind the romantic poets with their love of untrammeled nature. It was an attitude that carried over into pulp science fiction, as expressed by Delos David Harriman, protagonist of Robert A. Heinlein's "Requiem" (1940), who is the father of space travel in Heinlien's future history. "I believed. I read Verne, and Wells, and [Edward E.] Smith,"[31] he tells the pilots he wants to take him to the moon, when he has been forbidden his heart's desire on the grounds of age and ill health. He was one of "the kind of boys who thought there was more romance in one issue of the *Electrical Experimenter* than in all the books Dumas ever wrote."[32] For Heinlein's generation, the Wellsian vision was something, not cold and mechanistic and inhuman, but warm and romantic and awe-in-spiring. It was rude awakening for Arthur C. Clarke, for example, when—during the planning for the film *2001* (1968)—he discovered that

Stanley Kubrick did not share Clarke's enthusiam for his own favorite sf film. "Stanley calls after screening H. G. Wells' *Things to Come*, and says he'll never see another movie I recommend,"[33] Clarke recorded in his diary.

It all seemed much simpler then. Readers were unsophisticated, even naive: Lester del Rey recalls that some of them misread *Brave New World* (1932), taking Huxley's satirical jape of Wellsian utopias for "a vision of some of the wonders of the future—babies born without pain, drugs to ease all worries, gadgets and machines to take care of most needs."[34] Writers, too, hardly seemed to know what they were doing: in Edmond Hamilton's Interstellar Patrol stories, like "Within the Nebula" (1929), there is a crude sense of the Wellsian vision; yet, in "The Man Who Evolved" (1931), Hamilton is as gothic as Shelley in his suspicion of tampering with nature and is cynical toward the evolutionary dream. One could find all sorts of viewpoints in the pulp magazines, from the stuffy poetic humanism of Stanton A. Coblentz' *The Sunken World* (1928) to the crudely evangelical technocracy of Nat Schachner's "Revolt of the Scientists" (1933). For the most part, however, science fiction hardly seems to have been touched by the sense of irreconcilable conflicts and contradictions so obvious among literary intellectuals. Edward E. Smith could make a Wellsian world-state part of the social background in his *Spacehounds of IPC* (1931), an interplanetary novel otherwise devoted to rugged individualism and old-fashioned romance; Smith was too innocent to realize that both Wells and his critics would have scorned him.

Innocence, of course, has its price. Science fiction could also be incredibly thoughtless in what it took from the past, including the racial and sexual stereotypes common in other pulp fiction, even as it made extravagant claims about its prophetic value. It could indulge in crude xenophobic violence, justified by appeals to social Darwinism. All its intellectual arguments, indeed, whether progressive or conservative in purport, were shallow in substance. But science fiction's ambiguous innocence could not last. By proclaiming itself "a new type of literary art,"[35] a literature of important ideas, it had challenged itself to live up to its boast. And there were other challenges: Olaf Stapledon's *Last and First Men* (1931), which added an entirely new dimension to the vision of the future and in which Wells' positivistic faith in science and technology seemed an inadequate answer to the moral, even spiritual questions facing mankind; Huxley's *Brave New World*, which revealed, to perceptive readers, at least, that Wells' vision was not, after all, shared by the intelligentsia. All was not as simple as it had seemed; what had been a naive acceptance of the Wellsian vision, especially the vulgarization of that vision in space opera, began to yield to a more searching Wellsian *consciousness*. In John W. Campbell, Jr.'s "Twilight" (1934), for example, there is a stark confrontation with the same issue that haunted

Wells in *The Time Machine*: if science and technology make the world too perfect, mankind risks decline and extinction for lack of any challenge. Campbell's time-travelling narrator is at a loss for any answer; he can express only his numbed bitterness:

Can you appreciate the crushing hopelessness it brought to me? I, who love science, who see in it, or have seen in it, the salvation, the raising of mankind—to see those wondrous machines, of man's triumphant maturity, forgotten and misunderstood. The wondrous, perfect machines that tended, protected, and cared for those gentle, kindly people who had—forgotten.[36]

Laurence Manning's *The Man Who Awoke* (1933), originally a series of stories (book publication did not occur until 1975), may still be the best example of the more critical Wellsian consciousness that had begun to dawn in magazine science fiction. Assimilating a more Stapledonian vision of the future, Manning offers a more challenging series of moral cultural, and spiritual tests to mankind than any that appeared in the standard Wellsian scenario of a progressive world-state emerging from the conflicts of contemporary society and under the tutelage of the New Samurai (in whatever guise). Norman Winters, Manning's protagonist, plays a role Wells himself might envy, as the recurrent savior of mankind in awakenings at five-thousand-year intervals. But Winters' interventions can never bring salvation in the long run. In the year 10,000, for example, he is instrumental in an uprising against the computer Brain that has enslaved mankind, but when he awakens again in the year 15,000, he finds that the human race has taken another false turning: a wholesale retreat into dream machines. Winters is appalled, even when he is reminded of his savior's role:

Yes, and now I awake, after five thousand years, to see the results of that saving! I find what? Great social and scientific strides taken by an enlightened humanity? Pah! I find the most disgusting and vicious custom mankind could imagine set up as convention![37]

Once again, Winter's intervention saves mankind, but only from an immediate danger. At his next awakening, he finds a world dominated by the ultimate Rambos, each riding and living in his own fighting machine (or "city," as he calls it) to defend his imagined prerogatives. Children, born of fleeting sexual encounters, are raised in what we would call Skinner boxes—only Manning thought of them first, and not as a utopian idea. This time, Winters is powerless to swerve the course of history. The Individualists, by nature, have no central control to attack. In the end, the voluntary actions of saner individuals, expressed through a new social contract based on the anarchist principle of mutual aid, bring about a utopian culture. Even then, mankind confronts a spiritual challenge: to find a meaning beyond material and social progress. In a dig at Wells' original growth ethic in *The Food of the Gods* (remember the footstool image), an aged utopian finds even mankind's achievement of the power to "juggle with the very stars in their courses"[38] empty: "Suppose we increase human stature until we stride about using stars for footstools—mere size does not add to our importance."[39] And yet Manning is not an anti-Wellsian in the sense of Huxley; he believes in progress: "Without progress what use can there be in living?"[40] asks Winters at one point. Rather, the path to progress was not as obvious as even Wells himself liked to pretend in his dotage.

If Marxism can have its revisionists, why not Wellsian philosophy? Revisionist versions of the Wellsian vision have played a major part in the evolution of science fiction for more than half a century, and one of the most fascinating aspects of sf is just what different writers have taken from Wells and how they have reinterpreted it. What Wellsian sf writers have in common is, not anything as systematic or confining as an ideology, but a *world view*: a perspective, a way of looking at the universe and man's place in it. The Wellsian world view is virtually what Christian fundamentalists denounce as secular humanism, but it has a concern for mankind's evolutionary experience. Wellsians consider progress, however difficult or perilous, as essential to any truly human existence. But they interpret the meaning of progress differently. Spiritual Wellsians like Arthur C. Clarke consider progress essentially a spiritual adventure. Social Wellsians like Issac Asimov regard the evolutionary quest as the quest for a utopian society. For social Darwinists like Robert A. Heinlein, progress is the sheer survival and expansion of the race. Darwinian existentialists like Algis Budrys, by contrast, see the essential meaning of existence in the struggle of life—all life—against cosmic entropy. In some science fiction, notably that of John Brunner, the Wellsian world view takes on a Marxist admixture; yet in the Soviet Union, where Marxism is the offical ideology, one can see Wells as a liberalizing influence.

Not that the Wellsian world view has gone unchallenged in Western science fiction. Even before Wells, there was a dialectic between the Promethean vision of scientific and technological progress in the early Jules Verne and Vernean school of sf, and the cautionary gothic school that began with *Frankenstein*. The Promethean vision was assimilated by Wells; the gothic attitude has been assimilated by anti-Wellsian literary intellectuals. Although Hillegas does not dwell on it in *The Future as Nightmare*, there is a distinct cleavage among anti-utopians, with at least two distinct world views represented; and one can see a similar cleavage in sf generally. The Christian world view is the more easily defined, or is at least more familiar. Good and evil are absolute values as laid down by God, and it is God's purpose that we live according to His law. But the Fall estranged mankind from God and brought evil into the world. Man is born evil and can be redeemed only by obedience to the law and the grace of God, as embodied in the sacrifice of His only begotten son. Because man is tainted with evil, all his works are also tainted. Scientific progress is suspect, at least, for it magnifies the human capacity for evil, while further alienating man from God. In the works of C. S. Lewis, we see the Christian world view at its purest, but in the writings of Walter M. Miller, Jr., there is an attempted reconciliation with the Wellsian world view.

In the Rousselian world view, nature is the fountainhead of all good. Both nature and the natural man are seen as innocent; it is only civilization that destroys one and corrupts the other. One can see the Rousselian world view manifested in the romantic poetry of the nineteenth century and in the counterculture of the 1960s. In an age of acid rain and toxic waste dumps, its objections to civilization and "progress" are obvious: the march of science and technology threatens to doom the world, let *alone* alienate mankind from natural values. Adherence to the Rousselian world view is very much a matter of degree, and in the works of Clifford D. Simak, Theodore Sturgeon, Brian W. Aldiss, and others, it can find strikingly different expressions. Ironically, the purest form of Rousselian sf may be that of some radical femininsts: only women are innocent by nature, and only women are capable of living in harmony with nature.

Even harder to define is the world view of the New Wave, or Waves (British and American). At its most extreme, it is a sort of godless Calvinism: man is evil, but so is the universe. Or perhaps the universe is absurd and man is condemned to live in it. In either case, a sense of futility is evident: at best, a passionate but doomed sense of social protest and moral outrage; at worst, a smugly self-satisfied world weariness. J. G. Ballard, Thomas M. Disch, Michael Moorcock, Harlan Ellison, and others seemed nihilistic to traditional sf fans at the height of the New Wave. Yet, while they have largely abandoned the genre in their own fiction, they have had a lasting impact on the sensibilities of science fiction, as reflected in such trends as the cyberpunk school of William Gibson, Bruce Sterling, and others. And, as we shall see, there are those who have tried to find a synthesis: Cordwainer Smith and Ursula K. Le Guin.

In the conflict of world views in science fiction, it is possible to discern a further evolution of the essential critical function Wells himself once prescribed for utopian writing. In "The So-called Science of Sociology" (1906), he denied that a true science of sociology can be developed from observation of humanity in its diversity; there must be a synthesis of the scientific and literary methods: "I think, in fact, that the creation of utopias—and their exhaustive criticism—is the proper and distinctive method of sociology."[41] Stanley G. Weinbaum, in an autobiographical sketch (ca. 1935), argued that science fiction can and should take up where science itself, ethically neutral, leaves off:

> For science fiction can do what science cannot. It *can* criticize, because science fiction is not science. It is, or at least ought to be, a branch of the art of literature, and can therefore quite properly argue, reject, present a thesis, proselytize, criticize or perform any other ethical functions.[42]

More than fifty years later, C. J. Cherryh expressed a similar view in *Locus*: "For me, science fiction is not a literary exercise; it's an ethical exercise."[43] In her Alliance-Union future history, Cherryh explores the ethical evolution of the human race: not only the rivalry between Alliance and Union, which seem at first—but only at first—to be Polar libertarian and totalitarian antitheses; but the long-term impact of the experience of space on human values "as mankind begins to revise its ancestral ideas about property and place and territoriality."[44] Despite her disclaimer, however, Cherryh's science fiction is also very much a literary exercises, as all good sf must be. Wells always sought to instruct; what he too often forgot was that literature, even if—perhaps especially if—it is intended to instruct, must first move. It is only as embodied in story and character that ethical arguments, in sf or any other literature, can become humanly meaningful; without that embodiment, they remain empty abstractions, and, as abstractions, we cannot judge them for good or ill, for we can neither see nor feel their consequences. We are discussing the philosophy of science fiction here, but we must never forget that we are discussing literature: The Word must be made flesh.

1

A Tale of Two Wellsians

THE CALL OF THE COSMOS

Man was about to leave his Universe, as long ago he had left his world. And not only Man, but the thousands of other races that had worked with him to make the Empire. They were gathered together, here at the edge of the Galaxy, with its whole thickness between them and the goal they would not reach for ages.[1]

What inspired the Empire to undertake this millenial journey, none of those left on earth a billion years later can guess, but it must have been "very strange and very great," something of "immense urgency, and immense promise."[2] Immensity is the keynote of Arthur C. Clarke's *The City and the Stars* (1956), which draws its basic theme and basic imagery from the work of Clarke's two great mentors: H. G. Wells and Olaf Stapledon. Clarke (1917–) has never concealed his admiration for Wells and Stapledon; his admiration is more than literary: he admires the evolutionary vision of Wells' film *Things to Come* (1936) and the cosmic mythologies of Stapledon's *Last and First Men* (1931) and *Star Maker* (1937). Such eschatological science fiction shaped Clarke's interpretation of the nature and purpose of human existence as fundamentally as the

Creation and the Incarnation shape a Christians's. Nonetheless, interpret his mentors' works he does. Clarke can be characterized as a *spiritual*
Wellsian, inasmuch as he takes little notice of Wells' utopian socialist
ideology. Nor does he seem troubled by Stapledon's spiritual angst;
what he takes from Stapledon is what Wells himself might have taken:
a cosmic vision of human destiny.

Childhood's End (1953), still Clarke's most brilliant novel, is, ironically,
his least characteristic. He admits as much in a warning note to readers:
"The opinions expressed in this book are not those of the author."[3]
Clarke does not really believe in the Overmind as an instrument of
salvation for mankind, any more than he believes in the Galactic Overlords who act on the Overmind's behalf. But Clarke does show his
intimate familiarity with *Star Maker*, for the Overmind, like Stapledon's
Cosmical Mind, is the final goal of evolution, beyond the organic or the
material or the individual. Stapledon always sought to reconcile conflicting ideals of survival and progress, and submission to cosmic fate;
of the spiritual integrity of the individual, and duty toward the collective
and the transcendental. But Clarke sees no such reconciliation in *Childhood's End*; rather, stark alternatives;

> At the end of one path were the Overlords. They had preserved their indi-
> viduality, their independent egos; they possessed self-awareness and the pron-
> oun "I" had a meaning in their language. They had emotions, some at least of
> which were shared by humanity. But they were trapped, Jan realized now, in
> a cul-de-sac from which they could never escape . . .
> And at the end of the other path? There lay the Overmind, whatever it might
> be, bearing the same relation to man as man bore to amoeba. Potentially infinite,
> beyond mortality, how long had it been absorbing race after race as it spread
> across the stars? Did it too have desires, did it have goals it sensed dimly yet
> might never attain? Now it had drawn into its being all that the human race
> had ever achieved. This was not tragedy, but fulfillment.[4]

Only, not for Clarke. He would clearly prefer, like Wells before him,
that mankind conquer "all the deeps of space, and all the mysteries of
time,"[5] yet still remain—somehow—human. Thus, in *The Songs of Distant
Earth* (1986), the Wellsian dream has come to pass, despite the destruction of earth by a nova, through the seeding of colonies on distant worlds
by automated ships. Now the last survivors of earth have fled the holocaust in a quantrum-electric starship that will bear them to a virgin
planet they can make their own. Moses Kaldor, one of the few to be
awakened from hibernation during a stopover at the previously seeded
Thalassa, shares the *Magellan*'s sense of mission. Yet he is still moved
by the ordinary human things, like grief for his beloved wife, long dead
in the holocaust. Rationalizations hardly matter:

> Could grief be an accidental—even a pathological—by-product of love, which
> of course does have an essential biological function? It's a strange and disturbing

thought. Yet it's our emotions that make us human; who would abandon them, even knowing that each new love is yet another hostage to those twin terrorists, time and fate?[6]

For Clarke, then, the essential task of sf is to reconcile the Wellsian vision of science fiction with the ordinary human things. But for him, the Wellsian vision itself is humanistic, expressing deeply *human* needs, as he argues in *Profiles of the Future* (1962):

Civilization cannot exist without new frontiers; it needs them both physically and spiritually. The physical need is obvious—new lands, new resources, new materials. The spiritual need is less apparent, but in the long run it is more important. We do not live by bread alone; we need adventure, variety, novelty, romance. . . . What is true of individuals is also true of societies; they too can become insane without sufficient stimulus.[7]

Clarke's earliest sf reflects the heady optimism and unbounded faith in mankind that was typical of pulp science fiction in its time of innocence. In "Rescue Party" (1946), for example, our sun is about to become a nova, and a Galactic Federation sends a belated mission to try to save a few of the people who have unaccountably given rise to a technological civilization in only 400,000 years. At the risk of their own safety, the aliens search earth for signs of life, even though the very oceans are already boiling. They find the artifacts of a wondrous culture but no trace of its creators, until after they are forced to flee the stellar explosion and make what Rugon, their deputy commander, considers a totally awesome discovery in deep space:

"This is the race," he said softly, "that has known radio for only two centuries—the race we believed had crept to die in the heart of its planet . . . "
"That is the greatest fleet of which there has ever been a record. Each of those points of light represents a ship larger than our own. Of course, they are very primitive—what you see on the screen are the jets of their rockets. Yes, they dared to use rockets to bridge interstellar space!"[8]

Human chauvinism, one might call it. Clarke treats it poetically in "Transience" (1949), a series of vignettes about man and the sea—the sea as seen successively by savage, contemporary and far-future man. The savage is the first to sense "something of the wonder of the sea."[9] A child of the near future watches the last steamship in a world grown used to air transport, but soon he returns to building sand castles. In the far future, another child, called away from similar pursuits, can hardly comprehend that he and his family are leaving the sea behind forever because the solar system is threatened by a Dark Nebula, and the human race must find refuge on distant worlds:

Under the level light of the sagging moon, beneath the myriad stars, the beach lay waiting for the end. It was alone now, as it had been at the beginning. Only the waves would move, and but for a little while, upon its golden sands.

For man had come and gone.[10]

But if Clarke is an optimist, he is not a totally naive optimist. He too knows of mankind's destructive side. In " 'If I Forget Thee, Oh Earth . . .' " (1951), a child raised on the far side of the moon, knowing what stars are but unable to imagine why they should twinkle, is taken by his father to nearside to see earth for the first time. Enchanted by its beauty, he wonders why his people can never return there.

Then Marvin, his eyes no longer blinded by the glare, saw that the portion of the disk that should have been in darkness was gleaming faintly with an evil phosphorescence: and he remembered. He was looking upon the funeral pyre of a world—upon the radioactive aftermath of Armageddon. Across a quarter of a million miles of space, the glow of dying atoms was still visible, a perennial reminder of the ruinous past. It would be centuries yet before that deadly glow died from the rocks and life could return again to fill that silent, empty world.[11]

In much of his best work, Clarke tempers the Wellsian evolutionary dream with common humanity and cautionary revisionism. In *The Deep Range* (1957), for example, the protagonist is Walter Franklin, formerly chief engineer of an interplanetary liner, who must make a new life on earth after an accident in space so traumatizes him that he can never endure free fall again. He is utterly cut off from his wife and children, who are adapted to the lesser gravity of Mars and cannot visit him any more than he can visit them. Progress cannot banish all pain or suffering:

Even in the most perfect of social systems, the most peaceful and contented of worlds, there would still be heartbreak and tragedy. And as man extended his powers over the universe, he would inevitably create new evils and new problems to plague him.[12]

Franklin finds a new career with the Bureau of Whales, where he helps to manage one of earth's most vital food resources. Eventually, he finds a new woman to love; once again, he knows the joys of fatherhood. As his career advances, he can even forget the past—almost— and enjoy a contentment he has never known before. Then comes a challenge to his second career and his second life: an *ethical* challenge. In a secularized world, where other faiths have been discredited, Buddhism has filled a spiritual vacuum, "being a philosophy and not a religion, and relying on no revelations vulnerable to the archaeologist's hammer."[13] Because reverence for life is fundamental to Buddhist thought, the exploitation of whales cannot be condoned. "We believe that all creatures have a right to life," the Mahanayake Thero tells Franklin, "and it therefore follows that what you are doing is wrong. Accordingly, we would like to see it stopped."[14] A transplanted Westerner himself, the Thero knows how best to appeal to Franklin—not by merely reminding him of mankind's long and sorry record of cruelty to animals, but by bringing up an argument that must give even a human chauvinist pause to consider:

Sooner or later we will meet types of intelligent life much higher than our own, yet in forms completely alien. And when that time comes, the treatment man receives from his superiors may well depend on the way he has behaved toward the other creatures of his own world.[15]

In a crisis of conscience, Franklin faces political ruin should he challenge the bureau. An unforeseen role as the hero of an undersea rescue operation restores his moral courage and gives him the chance to speak out freely. At last he can feel whole as he faces the future and its challenge: "Give us another hundred years, and we'll face you with clean hands and hearts—whatever shape you be."[16] In *The Songs of Distant Earth*, the exiles of the *Magellan* have bound themselves by the strict ethic of Metalaw that respects the rights of, not only all other intelligent life, but all other *potential* intelligent life. "The presence of more than a few percent oxygen in a planet's atmosphere is definite proof that life exists there,"[17] and thus is enough to preclude colonization by mankind. In *Rendezvous with Rama* (1973), the passage of a huge alien spacecraft through the solar system offers a chance to study the workings of a nonhuman technology, although the starship's creators remain elusive. But Clarke's heroes disable a missile fired at the alien ship by the xenophobic colonials of Mercury, refusing to credit their fears that the intruder is a threat to mankind.

World government is usually a given in Clarke's near-future works, but he is neither blindly worshipful of the modern state nor insensitive to its dangers. World peace and unity may indeed be noble causes, but not at the price of hypocrisy. Although his sf has long been popular in the Soviet Union and although he counts cosmonaut Alexei Leonov as a friend, Clarke made a point of dedicating *2010: Odyssey Two* (1982) to the then exiled Andrei Sakharov and also of naming a space drive in the novel after him. Seemingly apolitical in most of his sf, Clarke has edged toward a more conscious classical liberalism in his recent works. In *The Songs of Distant Earth*, after millenia of "trial and often hideous error,"[18] a true democracy based on computer nets and universal education has been achieved at last, but the heads of government are chosen at random, with the safeguard "that anyone who *deliberately* aimed at the job should automatically be disqualified."[19] It is this system, more or less, that has been bequeathed to the idyllic colony of Thalassa in the form of "a Jefferson Mark Three Constitution—someone once called it utopia in two megabytes."[20] Perhaps Clarke's ideal of a statesman is seen in *The Fountains of Paradise* (1979): Johan Oliver de Alwis Sri Raja-singhe, an ambassador-at-large who once

moved from one trouble spot to another, massaging egos here, defusing crises there, and manipulating the truth with consummate skill . . . in order that man-kind might live in peace. When he had begun to enjoy the game for its own sake, he knew it was time to quit.[21]

Yet Clarke remains a thoroughgoing secular humanist, who can never accept revealed religion as the foundation of morality. Indeed, it may be just the opposite: more evil has been visited on mankind, he argues, by religious fanaticism than by any other force in history. Those who plan the seeded colonies in *The Songs of Distant Earth* decide to spare them our religious heritage, even at the cost of cultural impoverishment:

With tears in their eyes, the selection panels had thrown away the Veda, the Bible, the Tripitika, the Qur'an, and all the immense body of literature—fiction and nonfiction—that was based upon them. Despite all the wealth of beauty and wisdom these works contained, they could not be allowed to reinfect virgin planets with the ancient poisons of religious hatred, belief in the supernatural, and the pious gibberish with which countless billions of men and women had once comforted themselves at the cost of addling their minds.[22]

Statistical theology discredits faith in the same novel: "Bad things hap-pened just as often as good. . . . Certainly there was no sign of super-natural intervention, either for good or for ill."[23] In what may be Clarke's most controversial story. "The Star" (1955), proof of divine intervention is proof of an *evil* god. A priest's faith is shattered when he realizes why an alien civilization of warmth and beauty was cruelly cut short in its prime by a supernova:

There can be no reasonable doubt: the ancient mystery is solved at last, Yet, oh God, there were so many stars you could have used. What was the need to give these people to the fire, that the symbol of their passing might shine above Bethlehem?[24]

Nor does Clarke have a faith in the essential goodness of nature, common among literary intellectuals. In *Imperial Earth* (1976), Duncan Makenzie has come to the mother planet from Titan to have his own heir cloned. As in *in vitro* fertilization today, several embryos are to be created, only one of which will be brought to term. Makenzie has no sympathy for the traditional moral objection that the procedure is unnatural and murderous:

Old Mother Nature had not the slightest regard for human ethics or feelings. In the course of a lifetime, every man generated enough spermatozoa to populate the entire Solar System, many times over—and all but two or three of that potential multitude were doomed. Had anyone ever gone mad by visualizing each ejaculation as a hundred million murders?[25]

Yet, considering the fact that his estranged friend Helmer, whose clone (unlike Makenzie's, with its damaged genes) could father children, thus bringing genetic diversity into the family, may have more to offer his world than a replicate of himself, Makenzie may well have been moved by the argument of a doctor who has gone out of the cloning business, even if the doctor's actual motives are suspect:

If the Pharoahs had been able to clone themselves, they would certainly have done so. It would have been the perfect answer, avoiding the problem of inbreeding. But it introduces other problems. Because genes are no longer shuffled, it stops the biological clock. It means the end of biological progress.[26]

Makenzie does choose to clone Helmer, motivated by an essentially Wellsian evolutionary ethic. It is the same ethic that motivates the seemingly cynical treason of Robert Molton in *Earthlight* (1955), who uses a lunar observatory to transmit military secrets to the fleet of the Outer Planets Federation which is assailing earth's lunar fortress. Years later, having assured a stalemate in the war and a united humanity, Molton watches children frolicking at a lunar playground:

Professor Molton smiled as he watched them racing toward their bright, untroubled future—the future he had helped to make. He had many compensations, and that was the greatest of them. Never again, as far ahead as imagination could roam, would the human race be divided against itself. Far above him beyond the roof of Central City, the inexhaustible wealth of the Moon was flowing outward across space, to all the planets Man now called his own.[27]

Clarke's Wellsian confidence in the value of progress stands in stark contrast to the gothic sense of dread that has come to permeate much of our culture in face of threatened nuclear annihilation and environmental disaster. Only in *2001: A Space Odyssey* (1968), with the madness of HAL, does he seem to acknowledge the gothic tradition in sf at all, and that could be explained by the influence of Stanley Kubrick on the screenplay and the novel (HAL's madness is explained away, a bit too tidily, by Clarke in *2010*).

The City and the Stars, which Clarke himself has called, "For many years, and for many reasons . . . my best-loved book,"[28] still remains the most vivid realization of his Wellsian philosophy and world view. It is a variation on all the tales of the distant future that began with Wells' own *The Time Machine* (1895). But, in contrast to the gloomy panoramas of decadence and devolution that are common in such tales, the "glowing jewel" of Diaspar seems a beacon of hope. Earth's last great city, it has endured for a billion years, long after the oceans have passed away and the last mountains have been ground to dust. It is the triumph of mankind over entropy—and yet it is actually a surrender to entropy. Mankind is not sufficient unto itself. Although the builders of Diaspar designed into it all manner of artificial novelty and variety, assuring its seeming vitality down through all the eons, none of their devices can compensate in the long run for the lack of frontiers—the lack of any outside challenge or stimulus. Diaspar has turned its back on space and time; even its inhabitants are endless reincarnations, who pursue the same endless round of arts and amusements, never knowing childhood, age or death.

In the story of Alvin, Clarke combines science fiction on a cosmic scale with the romantic quest. For reasons he himself cannot understand at first, Alvin is a misfit in Diaspar. He spoils the fun in interactive adventure sagas like The Cave of the White Worms by trying to shift the action *outside* the Crystal Mountain. In a world of utter sexual freedom, without any complications (people are "born" almost fully grown from the city's memory banks), he can find no really intimate companionship. When his tutor Jeserac reveals that Alvin is "the first child to be born on Earth for at least ten million years,"[29] he finds a sense of mission: "Diaspar might be sufficient for the rest of humanity, but it was not enough for him."[30] He must find a way out, even though none is shown in the memory banks; he must find the truth behind the ancient legends of the Galactic Empire, said to have been destroyed by the Invaders from somewhere beyond, who drove mankind back to its home planet and forbade it ever to leave again. Thus begins the search that leads Alvin to the Tomb of Yarlan Zey, founder of the city, where a directed thought grants him entrance to a long-forgotten transport system and passage to—Lys.

Lys: the antithesis of Diaspar, pastoral rather than urban. While it must be heir to a technology as powerful as that of Diaspar, having preserved a portion of earth's natural splendors—mountains, wildlife, lakes, and rivers—against the encroachment of the global desert, its inhabitants have maintained a simple, seemingly idyllic life. They live in small villages, and they walk from one place to another, instead of being carried on "streets" that flow like water at varying speeds, yet are otherwise solid. They value the powers of mind, rather than machine. Most astounding to Alvin, however, are the children. He finds them a source of amazement and delight and of tender emotions, long forgotten in Diaspar: when they have occasion to cry, over frustrations that are objectively trivial, "their tiny disappointments seemed to him more tragic than Man's long retreat after the loss of his Galactic Empire."[31] Alvin realizes already in his heart what Seranis, one of the elders of Lys, later puts into words:

Long ago, Alvin, men sought immortality and at last achieved it. They forgot that a world which had banished death must also banish life. The power to extend his life indefinitely might bring contentment to the individual, but brought stagnation to the race. Ages ago we sacrificed our immortality, but Diaspar still follows the false dream.[32]

Yet the dream of Lys is as false as that of Diaspar; Lys, too, is afraid of outside challenge or stimulus. Once again, Alvin must escape; an ancient robot, once owned by the Galaxy's last religious zealot, offers a new path for his quest. Raising the Master's starship from the desert, Alvin and Hilvar of Lys set forth for the Seven Suns, once the hub of the Empire, where the Master had found it "lovely to watch the colored shadows on the planets of eternal light."[33] Now the planets themselves are dead or else are devolved to primitive life waging anew the grim Darwinian struggle for existence. Of the fabulous Empire of legend, there remain only enigmatic ruins—and Vanamonde. A pure mentality, he is the crowing achievement of that Empire, before it forsook the Galaxy for an even greater challenge beyond. It is through Vanamonde that Alvin and Hilvar and a reluctant earth learn the truth behind the old legends: how the stars reached mankind before mankind reached the stars; how that challenge to human vanity led mankind to remake itself on a Stapledonian scale, becoming at last worthy to share in a galactic civilization, in a "sweep of great races moving together toward maturity";[34] how the Empire made its goal the creation of a mind without physical limitations, able to reveal for the first time a "true picture of the Universe";[35] how the destruction wreaked by the Mad Mind, disastrous first fruit of that quest, led to the legend of the Invaders. Even in the face of such a setback, the Empire persevered and, eventually, triumphed. Earth, which had shunned the Empire and turned inward, from the sickness of fear and exhaustion, now faces again the challenge of the cosmos, and of evolution:

In this universe, the night was falling; the shadows were lengthening toward an east that would not know another dawn. But elsewhere the stars were still young and the light of morning lingered; and along the path he had once followed, Man would one day go again.[36]

FABIAN OF THE GALAXY

Conditions have been so arranged and so maintained that in a millenium from [the Plan's] beginnings . . . a Second Galactic Empire will have been established in which Mankind will be ready for the leadership of Mental Science. In the same interval, the Second Foundation, in *its* development, will have brought forth a group of Psychologists ready to assume leadership. . . . The First Foundation supplies the physical framework of a single political unit, and the Second Foundation supplies the mental framework of a ready-made ruling class.[37]

That is how a Student of the Second Foundation summarizes the Seldon Plan in Isaac Asimov's *Second Foundation* (1953). Asimov (1920–), like Clarke, is one of the grand old men of science fiction, and his Foundation trilogy is one of its grand old series. More than thirty years later, with *Foundation's Edge* (1982), he began to elaborate on the original series and to alter some of its basic conceptions, but his "science" of psychohistory would still be as famous as his Three Laws of Robotics, even if he had never added another word to the original trilogy. Like the Three Laws, psychohistory grew out of a conference with John W. Campbell, Jr., the editor of *Astounding Science Fiction*. As Campbell was known for his crotchets, particularly elitism, it would be easy to blame the conception of the Second Foundation on him, but, even if it did originate with him, it came naturally to Asimov, for Asimov was and is a social Wellsian.

It is common knowledge that a primary inspiration for the series was Asimov's reading of Edward Gibbon's *Decline and Fall of the Roman Empire* (1766–88).[38] Asimov also admits to having "devoured" H. G. Wells' *The Outline of History* (1920) and *The Science of Life* (1930, with Julian Huxley and G. P. Wells) in his teens.[39] These volumes would surely have introduced him to Wellsian thought, even if Well's sf had not already done so. He was, moreover, brought up in a New Deal liberal household. His brief involvement with the Futurians, a Communist-leaning sf fan group that issued manifestos calling on science fiction to take the lead in saving the world, led to his first argument with the "hidebound conservative" Campbell.[40] One of the distinctive elements of the New Deal was the Brain Trust, which impressed Wells himself. In *The Shape of Things to Come* (1933), Wells' imaginary historian of the future reports that it later "played a significant part in that reconstruction of legal and political method with was America's particular contribution to Modern State ideas."[41] Wells even anticipates psychohistory, for the elitist Modern State Fellowship that remakes the world is guided by a science of Social Nucleation, "the exhaustive study of the psychological laws underlying team play and *esprit de corps*."[42] Psychohistory, a "branch of mathematics which deals with the reactions of human conglomerates to fixed social and economic stimuli,"[43] serves the same function, even if the details are different: a justification and a methodology for the ruling elite. Hari Seldon is the ultimate Fabian, and his disciples are the galactic New Samurai in the tradition of Wells.

Still, Asimov is not Wells, and in some of his science fiction one can perceive an unresolved tension between acceptance and rejection of the Wellsian ideal of a planned world, which is the context of his own Foundation universe becomes a planned galaxy. There is an unresolved conflict, too, over the issue of whether men make history, or history makes men. Psychohistory, which, in theory, is as deterministic as Marxism, sees history as the product of social and economic forces. Yet the success of the Seldon Plan seems to depend on crucial decisions made by the prime movers of the Second Foundation, and even on the initiative and resourcefulness of the more intuitive leaders of the First Foundation. For the most part, however, Asimov's commitment to the Wellsian ideal of a world-state, which reaches its apotheosis in the Galactic Empire, remains unshaken. The universal state is seen as the only guarantor of social justice and the only alternative to war—war which, in our own time, would mean destruction of civilization and probably of the human race itself. A radioactive earth in his Empire novels from the 1950s is a constant reminder of the horrors of war and of the need for a social order strong enough to prevent war. Although Asimov would prefer a benevolent government, benevolence is not required of the universal state for it to command the loyalty of enlightened men, as we learn in *The Currents of Space* (1952).

Set during the emergence of the first Galactic Empire, its devious plot turns on the revelation that the sun of Florina—only source of a luxurious fabric prized throughout the galaxy—is about to become a nova. Florina is a subject planet, whose natives must toil in fields and factories to produce the kyrt that brings wealth and power to the overlords of Sark. Myrln Terens, a Florinan functionary in the Sarkite bureaucracy, mind-wipes a spatio-analyst who has brought the bad news, hoping somehow to turn it to his own advantage and realize vengeance against Sark. Eventually, however, the spatio-analyst (kept hidden away as a field worker on Florina) begins to remember, and his search for the truth sets off multiple intrigues that eventually involve the Squire of Fife and other Sarkite aristocrats, agents of the Spatio-Analytic Bureau, and Trantorian intelligence. The key figure is Ludigan Abel, the Trantorian ambassador to Sark, whose obsession is always: "Will this, or can this, help Trantor?"[44]

Abel is "not the kind of fool who would worship a cluster of stars or the yellow emblem of Spaceship-and-Sun";[45] he does not labor under any illusions about an empire whose "advance had lain through a tangled forest of gutted men, gutted ships and gutted worlds" led by a "nasty, materialistic and aggressive people, careless of the rights of others, imperfectly democratic at home though quick to see the minor slaveries of others, and greedy without end."[46] But Abel longs for peace; "to end the misuse of force, only one solution was left, force itself."[47] A Galactic Empire is the answer: "He was not for Trantor, but for the all-embracing end that Trantor represented."[48] And it is Selim Junz, an agent of the Spatio-Analytic Bureau, who finds a means for Trantor to take advantage of the crisis by buying out Sark's rights and rescuing the endangered people of Florina. The cost will be more than repaid in the good will that will bring Trantor's hegemony a step closer; Junz observes, "The people of the galaxy, they are the victors."[49]

A similar appeal to universal loyalty motivates the denouement of *Pebble in the Sky* (1950), in which an ordinary man of our own century is inexplicably translated to the radioactive and resentful earth of the far future, where he must choose which side to take in a conspiracy by Terran zealots to unleash a plague against the Galactic Empire. By now an established force for universal peace and social justice, that empire must claim precedence over the parochial loyalty to a homeworld. In *The Stars Like Dust* (1951), the United States Constitution turns out to be a secret weapon against tyranny in the Nebular Kingdoms of a pre-Empire future. This idea, however, was imposed by Horace L. Gold, the editor of *Galaxy*, in which the novel was serialized.[50] Shorn of such a misleading element, the war of liberation against the Tyranni is clearly fought in a more Wellsian cause: "the right of twenty million human beings to take part in the development of the race."[51] Rhodia and other planets on the verge of industrialization have been kept at the agricultural level. It may take *centuries* for the Tyranni hegemony to decay:

And when those centuries have passed, we will still all be agricultural worlds with no industrial or scientific heritage to speak of, while our neighbors on all sides, those not under Tyrannian control, will be strong and urbanized. The Kingdoms will be semicolonial areas forever. They will *never* catch up, and we will be merely observers in the great drama of human advance.[52]

For Asimov, history itself is the real hero; the only individual heroes are those who can senses the process of history and help guide it in the right direction. They are the Richlieus of the Galaxy—shrewd, cunning, and often amoral—like Salvor Hardin, the mayor of Seldon's colony of exiles on Terminus in "Foundation" (1942). Terminus is threatened by the breakaway kingdoms of the galactic periphery, and Hardin seems to be the only one who appreciates the threat or who even realizes that the Foundation must have a purpose other than compiling an encyclopedia. It is up to him to find the "obvious" solution to the crisis, foreseen by Seldon. Thirty years later, in "Bridle and Saddle" (1942), the answer turns out to have been a religion, which makes something supernatural of atomic power, knowledge of which has been lost by the Four Kingdoms, and establishes Foundation atomic scientists and engineers as priests. Technicians from the barbarian realms are taught plant engineering by rote, and they carry the faith home. The superstitious populations come to hold the Foundation in awe. When Wienis, the rebellious lord of one of the kingdoms, dares to launch an attack on Terminus, his troops mutiny in face of such a sacrilege. A witty exchange between Wienis, "the man of action," and Hardin is occasioned by the latter's announcement that Anacreon has been placed under interdict:

"Give me none of that, Hardin. Save it for the mob."
"My dear Wienis, whoever do you think I *am* saving it for?"[53]

Economic warfare, in "The Big and the Little" (1944), succeeds in the war against Korell, which has held out against the religious Trojan horse while accepting military aid from the Empire. Hober Mallow, one of a growing class of merchant princes, has succeeded Hardin. Knowing the "religion game" is played out, he plies Korell with technological innovations like miniature atomic generators and personal force fields. Reindustrialization and a flow of consumer goods into the Korellian economy soon follow, and the ruling Commodor who still wants to play the Empire's game finds a greater game being played against him. The whole planet has become dependent on trade with the Foundation; without it, it faces an economic depression so severe that the people will rise up against the government. Mallow sums up the situation pithily:

The whole war is a battle between those two systems, between the Empire and the Foundation, between the big and the little. To seize control of a world, they bribe with immense ships that can make war, but lack all economic significance. We, on the other hand, bribe with little things, useless in war, but vital to prosperity and profits.[54]

But when the Empire itself, under the brilliant generalship of Bel Riose, moves to reclaim the periphery in "Dead Hand" (1945), none of the Foundation's cunning seems to avail. The blind force of history is all that can stop Riose, whose very name reveals Asimov's intended parallel with Belisarius, the sixth-century Byzantine general recalled by Emperor Justinian for succeeding too well in the Italian campaign. Ducem Barr, a Siwennian who holds the Foundation in awe, warns Riose at the outset that his campaign is doomed, "Because of the dead hand of the mathematics of human behavior that can neither be stopped, swerved, no delayed."[55] Lathan Devers, a Foundation merchant trader, who believes a secular equivalent of the proverb about God helping those who help themselves, snatches Barr from the clutches of the imperial forces and sets out for Trantor itself to stir up suspicions in the court of Cleon II. The mission is a disaster and they barely escape, only to learn that Riose has been recalled in disgrace and charged with treason—not, of course, because of anything they did, but because of the historical logic of the situation. In a declining empire, a successful general *must* be seen as a threat to the throne: "the greater the success, the surer the failure."[56]

So far, the Seldon Plan appears to be moving like clockwork: each crisis facing the Foundation is not only resolved in the only possible way, but right on time for Seldon's holographic image to appear in the Time Vault on Terminus and explain all. But psychohistory can not predict everything. In "The Mule" (1945), a mutant who can control individual minds and manipulate mass emotions upsets all calculations. Foundation commanders go over to the enemy; panic and depression spread among the civilian population. Relying blindly on the Seldon Plan to save them, hereditary Mayor Indbur III and his retainers gather at the Vault to hear Seldon's next prerecorded message, but that message has nothing to do with the Mule, whose forces are already bombarding Terminus. As all resistance collapses before him, the Mule seems to be a man of destiny: a second Galactic Empire can be realized seven hundred years in advance of the Seldon Plan's schedule. Only, it can not be. Like the personal empires of Attila or Tamerlane, the Mule's hegemony lacks the social or political infrastructure to make it last beyond his lifetime. At most, by spreading the advanced technology of the Foundation through much of the galaxy, he can play the role of an Alexander the Great. Like Alexander, he is obsessed by the need to conquer all before him including the Second Foundation.

In the contest of wits and wills that develops between the Mule and the Second Foundation in "Now You See It . . ."(1948), it becomes clear that the Seldon Plan could never have been as automatic as it seemed. Behind the scenes, agents of the Second Foundation have been working all the time, doubtless even stage-managing the timing of crises to nurture the confidence of the First Foundation in its own manifest destiny. Nor is that all. As Bail Channis, the agent chosen to confront the Mule at the decisive moment, explains, Hari Seldon never claimed godlike omniscience:

So he created his Foundations according to the laws of psychohistory, but who knew better than he that even those laws were relative. *He* never created a finished product. Finished products are for decadent minds. His was an evolving mechanism and the Second Foundation was the instrument of that evolution.[57]

In order to guide that evolution, the Second Foundation must protect itself at all costs, even at the cost of the slaughter of millions on Tazenda, which the First Speaker has tricked the Mule into believing its supreme headquarters: "The alternative would have been a much greater destruction generally throughout the galaxy over a period of centuries."[58] It is the same cosmic utilitarianism that guides the Second Foundation in its intervention against the First Foundation, which has become aware of the Second's powers, in " . . . And Now You Don't" (1949–50). Success of the Seldon Plan depends on the *unconscious* reactions of conglomerates, and that condition has been violated. Jealous of its rival, the First Foundation develops a Mental Static device to expose the agents of the Second. But those "exposed" are self-chosen martyrs who have set up a false headquarters on Terminus itself to convince the captors that the Second Foundation has been destroyed, and may be disregarded.

The guardians have saved themselves and, thereby, have saved mankind. "They brought the plan through, because they loved the greater Plan,"[59] says First Speaker Preem Palver of the fifty martyrs. Who need watch over the guardians? Asimov assigns a similar position of incorruptible guardians to the Machines in "The Evitable Conflict" (1950). Like the positronic robots before them, the Machines are bound by the First Law of Robotics, but they now interpret it socially: "No Machine may harm humanity; or, through inaction, allow humanity to come to harm."[60] All mankind, even seeming opponents of the Machines, is being manipulated. But robospychologist Susan Calvin scoffs at the idea that mankind has lost any "say" in its own destiny:

It never had any, really. It was always at the mercy of economic and sociological forces it did not understand—at the whims of climate, and the fortunes of war. Now the Machines understand them; and no one can stop them.[61]

Yet in *The End of Eternity* (1955), Asimov plays Devil's advocate against his own premise. The Eternals' mission is to watch over mankind, not just through all space, but through all *Time*. By introducing their Reality Changes in various centuries, they solve pressing economic and social problems, but only at the price of smothering any real advance by mankind. In the Hidden Centuries, closed to the Eternals, men have become aware that their past, and therefore their present and future, is being manipulated. And they know the outcome: "there was a loss of purpose, a sense of futility, a feeling of helplessness that could not be overcome. Eventually there was one last decline of the birth rate and finally, extinction."[62] Noÿs Lambent is sent by them to seduce an Eternal Technician, Andrew Harlan, into destroying Eternity and all it has wrought, although that means all its manipulated realities, even her own, will be blotted out of existence. And her argument seems to be just the opposite of Susan Calvin's, or Preem Palver's:

In ironing out the disasters of Reality, Eternity rules out the triumphs as well. It is in meeting the great tests that mankind can most successfully rise to great heights. Out of danger and restless insecurity comes the force that pushes mankind to newer and loftier conquests. Can you understand that? Can you understand that in averting the pitfalls and miseries that beset man, Eternity prevents men from finding their own bitter and better solutions, the real solutions that come from conquering difficulty, not avoiding it?[63]

In *Foundation's Edge*, however, Asimov's social thought has taken still another turn, one which seems to come out of left field but actually comes from "Green Patches" (1950, as "Misbegotten Missionary"). On Saybrook's Planet, a scientific expedition encounters a native life that is multiorganismic in the same sense that ours is multicellular. Each organism shares in a collective consciousness and purpose. One of them stows away aboard the expedition's ship hoping to bring all the blessings of biological communism to mankind, but it is killed by accident, thus saving the "anarchic world of life that was Earth."[64] Sura Novi, in *Foundation's Edge*, is the spokesman for Asimov's new version of the same concept—Gaia, the living galaxy—which she contrasts to the ideals and goals of the First and Second Foundations:

> The Second Galactic Empire—worked out after the fashion of Terminus—will be a military Empire, established by strife, maintained by strife, and eventually destroyed by strife. It will be nothing but the first Empire reborn.
> The Second Galactic Empire—worked out after the fashion of Trantor—will be a paternalistic Empire, established by calculation, maintained by calculation, and in perpetual living death by calculation. It will be a dead end . . .
> Greater Gaia! Galaxia! Every inhabited planet as alive as Gaia. Every living planet combined into a still greater hyperspatial life. Every uninhabited planet participating. Every star. Every scrap of interstellar gas.[65]

Golan Trevize, a man of the First Foundation with an unexplained intuitive sense of what is right for mankind, is given the power and the opportunity to choose for all, but he is troubled about why his choice is for Gaia. In *Foundation and Earth* (1986), he sets out for the lost mother planet in hopes of learning the reason. Asimov, meanwhile, backtracks in time to reveal the robots as the real prime movers of human history in *The Robots of Dawn* (1983) and *Robots and Empire* (1985), sequels to *The Caves of Steel* (1953) and *The Naked Sun* (1956). It seems an awkward marriage of two series, for the apparent absence of robots in the Foundation trilogy and the disappearance of the long-lived Spacers prominent in the original robot novels must both be explained. Even the radioactive earth of *Pebble in the Sky* gets a new explanation: not atomic war, but sabotage on the part of Spacer fanatics—condoned by the telepathic robot Giskard because it will free earth's own settlers on other planets from their apron strings: "without Earth to set up as a god of the past—they will establish a Galactic Empire."[66]

R. Daneel Olivaw, the robot partner to detective Elijah Baley in *The Caves of Steel* and *The Naked Sun*, reprises the role of the Machines in *Robots and Empire* by coming up with a "Zeroth Law of Robotics:" it is again *humanity* that must not be harmed or allowed to come to harm. At first, Giskard is skeptical:

You know that I have read widely in human history. In it, I have found great crimes committed by some human beings against each other and the excuse has always been that the crimes were justified by the needs of the tribe, or of the state, or even of humanity. It is precisely because it is an abstraction that it can be called on so freely to justify anything at all.[67]

Nevertheless, it is the dying Giskard who implements the Zeroth Law by preventing Daneel from intervening to forestall the sabotage of earth. And the collective interests of humanity, as embodied in the swarming settlers of Baleyworld, are contrasted with the alienated individualism of the Spacers, especially the Solarians, who, in *The Naked Sun*, show a pathological aversion to any sort of community and live alone on huge estates tended by thousands of robots: "Without the interplay of human against human, the chief interest in life is gone, most of the intellectual values are gone; most of the reason for living is gone."[68]

But in *Foundation and Earth*, Asimov seems to have painted himself into a philosophical corner. As they search for earth, Trevise and his companions, Janov Pelorat and the Gaian woman Bliss, keep up a running argument about the problem of the individual and society. Trevise, even though he has chosen for Gaia, finds its submersion of the individual repugnant. But Gaia is simply a perfect shelter, like any well-designed home or spaceship, argues Pelorat; what's wrong with that?

"What's wrong with that," said Trevize, "is that my house or my ship is engineered to suit *me*. I am not engineered to suit *it*. If I were part of Gaia, then no matter how ideally the planet was devised to suit me, I would be greatly disturbed over the fact that I was also being devised to suit it."[69]

A harrowing experience on Solaria, which has hidden itself from the rest of the galaxy to pursue its cultural perversion to the ultimate—a race of hermaphroditic hermits living underground—gives Pelorat an argument against Trevize and against individualism:

Why, on Solaria, we see what Isolates—or individuals, if you prefer—can become. The Solarians can hardly bear to divide a whole world among themselves. They consider a life of complete isolation to be perfect liberty. They have no yearning for even their own offspring, but kill them if there are too many.[70]

It is Daneel Olivaw who has the final word. Gaia is the fruit, after nearly 20,000 years, of his labors to create a superorganism that will make "humanity" more than an abstraction—a concrete, to which the Zeroth Law can be applied; psychohistory was only a stopgap. What he leads Trevize to understand is that Gaia is absolutely essential to the survival of mankind: our species may be alone in the galaxy, but what of other galaxies that might present a challenge only a truly *united* race could meet? And, with that peculiar appeal to military necessity, the social Wellsian argument in Asimov's science fiction has come full circle: there can be, there *must* be, no other way.

2

Among the Anti-Wellsians

DEFENDER OF THE *TAO*

Conversation with Mr. Jules was always difficult because he insisted on re-garding himself not as a figurehead but as the real director of the Institute, and even as the source of most of its ideas. And since, in fact, any science he knew was that taught him at the University of London over fifty years ago, and any philosophy he knew had been acquired from writers like Haeckel and Joseph McCabe and Winwood Reade, it was not, in fact, possible to talk to him about most of the things the Institute was really doing.[1]

Horace Jules plays a dramatically minor, but thematically central role in *That Hideous Strength* (1945), the final volume of a trilogy (often called the Ransom trilogy, after its protagonist, Elwin Ransom) by C. S. Lewis (1898–1963), one of the seminal Christian intellectual figures of this cen-tury. Jules, despite a disclaimer by Lewis' biographers, Roger Lancelyn Green and Walter Hooper,[2] is obviously a satirical caricature of H. G. Wells. Indeed, the entire Ransom trilogy is a rebuttal of that world view we have characterized as Wellsian, and *That Hideous Strength* is Lewis' dark vision of its practical consequences for mankind. Jules, of course, has no idea of the monstrousness of the National Institute for Co-or-dinated Experiments (N.I.C.E.); and yet its aims, Lewis argues, are the logical outcome of the ideas expressed by Wells and other thinkers such as Olaf Stapledon and J. B. S. Haldane whose governing philosophy he characterized as "scientism" or

the belief that the supreme end is the perpetuation of our own species, and this is to be pursued even if, in the process of being fitted for survival, our species has to be stripped of all those things for which we value it—of pity, of happiness, and of freedom.[3]

Lewis certainly bore no personal animosity toward Wells; he even admired Wells' early science fiction, especially *The First Men in the Moon* (1900–01).[4] But he made a clear distinction between *that* Wells and Wells the prophet of an anthropocentric evolutionary mythology. In his atheistic youth, Lewis found a certain romantic appeal in what he called, for want of a better term, "Wellsianity."[5] "I grew up believing this Myth and I have felt—I still feel—its almost perfect grandeur," he freely admits in "The Funeral of a Great Myth". "Let no one say we are an unimaginative age: neither the Greeks nor the Norsemen ever invented a better story."[6] From his later Christian perspective, he came to see that myth, not only as false, but also as blasphemous—placing a vain belief in the destiny of mankind above obedience to God, the pursuit of purely materialistic ends about all considerations of morality, and the mere survival of the species above the salvation of the individual. He would have nothing to do with attempts to reconcile Christianity and evolutionary philosophy, such as the teachings of Teilhard de Chardin. In a 1960 letter to Father Peter Milward, he approved the suppression of Teilhard's work by the Jesuits on the grounds that Teilhard was promoting the cause of *man* against *men* at a time when it was the rights and dignity of *men* that really needed defending.[7]

In *The Abolition of Man* (1943), Lewis argued at length against the modern rejection of absolute standards of truth, beauty, and morality. His immediate targets were educators who treated all value judgments as subjective and trivial, but his greater purpose was to defend the *Tao*— the common moral tradition of mankind—against attempts to substitute a supposedly "objective" set of values based on human "instincts." What this must inevitably lead to, he declared, is the imposition of wholly arbitrary values by a self-appointed intellectual elite:

Either we are rational spirit obliged for ever to obey the absolute values of the *Tao*, or else we are mere nature to be kneaded and cut into new shapes for the pleasure of masters who must, by hypothesis, have no motive other than their own "natural" impulses.[8]

That Hideous Strength raises the same argument; it is, as has been recognized by both Mark Hillegas[9] and Green and Hooper,[10] a realization in fiction of the nightmare imagined in *The Abolition of Man*. Even in *Out of the Silent Planet* (1938), written before Lewis had any notion of a trilogy, the thematic purpose was anti-Wellsian. As Lewis explained in a letter to an unidentified "lady" in 1939, what had set him to writing the book was the discovery that one of his students took the science fiction dream of man's colonization of the planets quite seriously, and that there must be thousands of others who interpreted the whole meaning of the universe in terms of the survival of the species: what he would elsewhere call "Wellsianity" was thus a serious rival to Christianity.[11]

No doubt the student had read much of Wells, perhaps of Stapledon, even of Haldane. Whatever the sources, he had absorbed a Wellsian world view. In *Out of the Silent Planet*, that world view is personified by an amoral physicist, Edward Weston. Weston, who seeks the Greater Glory of Man, sets out for Mars with his henchman Richard Devine, who cares only for gold. Believing the Martians to be savages, they shanghai the philologist Ransom for possible use as a human sacrifice. When they make their landing, Ransom, having overheard their plans, does not stick around to find out what the Martians really want with him: he has read enough sf to imagine only terrifying creatures with "twitching feelers, rasping wings, slimy coils, curling tentacles."[12] His panic-stricken flight is the beginning of a spiritual odyssey which at last awakens him to the truth Weston and Devine cannot or will not understand.

For Malacandra, as it is known in the Old Solar language that dates back to the Creation, is a world still in a state of grace. Three races of intelligent natives live in harmony with one another and with their world under the guidance of the Oyarsa, an angel of the Lord. They can accept their own mortality, and even that of their planet, for they know that in death they "go to Maledil [God]."[13] Evil is unknown to them, as are all irrational passions: Ransom is surprised to learn that the *hrossa*, first of the peoples he meets, not only mate for life but can not imagine having sex more often than necessary to keep the population in equilibrium with the environment. What seems an idyllic sojourn among the *hrossa* is interrupted when Weston and Devine come looking for Ransom, and they kill his new-found friend Hyoi without even knowing what they do. Ransom has unwittingly brought this tragedy upon the *hrossa* by ignoring a summons from the Oyarsa; now he can delay no longer, and he undertakes the journey to Melidorn, seat of divine government for the planet. In taking the shortest route, across the Martian highlands, he almost succumbs to the cold and thin air, but he is succored by one of the sorns: the very people he had fled when they sought him out at the landing site.

In a hilarious scene at Melidorn, Weston and Devine themselves are later brought before the Oyarsa. Weston makes a buffoon of himself, at first assuming that he is being interrogated by an aged *hross* who is actually asleep and therefore responding with a string of boasts and threats—in pidgin Martian. That does not go over very well, so he enlists Ransom as his interpreter. Ransom's plain-talk interpretations of all of Weston's high-flown phrases get to the heart of Lewis' message:

"Life, of course," snapped Weston. "She has ruthlessly broken down all obstacles and liquidated all failures and to-day in her highest form—civilized man—and in me as his representative, she presses forward to that interplanetary leap which will, perhaps, place her forever beyond the reach of death."

"He says," resumed Ransom, "that these animals learned to do many difficult things, except those who could not, and those ones died and the other animals did not pity them. And he says the best kind of animal now is the kind of man who makes the big huts and carries the heavy weights and does all the other things I told you about; and he is one of these and he says that if the others all knew what he was doing they would be pleased. He says that if he could kill you all and bring our people to live on Malacandra, then they might be able to go on living here after something had gone wrong with our world. And then if something went wrong with Malacandra they might go and kill all the *hnau* in another world. And then another—and so they would never die out."[14]

Even as he condemns Wells' world view, Lewis takes advantage of what he has learned from Wells' world creation in *The First Men in the Moon*. *Out of the Silent Planet* has a richness of both invention and description that was uncommon for its time in science fiction. Not only do the Martians—the playful *hrossa*, the austere *seroni*, and the little-seen but industrious *pfifltriggi*—come alive in Lewis' prose, but also the very environment and landscapes. Even science fiction's literary tradition of Mars is successfully fused with the mythology of the Bible: we learn that the *handramits*, or canals, became necessary to provide a livable habitat for the *hrossa* and the *pfifltriggi* after the Bent One (Satan) nearly destroyed the planet's biosphere in his revolt against Maleldil; in the highlands, one can still see the dead forests of old Malacandra, "stone cauliflowers the size of cathedrals and the colour of pale rose."[15] Like all good created-world fiction, *Out of the Silent Planet* has not been dated by current knowledge of other worlds.

Perelandra (1943), the second volume of the trilogy, is not nearly as successful, although the invention remains strong. Venus, a sensually vivid world of floating islands on a nearly shoreless sea, is the setting for a new Garden of Eden, complete with a new Adam and Eve. Ransom is sent by Maleldil to oppose the efforts of the Bent One, in the person of Weston, to tempt the new Eve and bring about a new Fall. Weston has, by this time, abandoned his Wellsian anthropocentrism for a new philosophy of "emergent evolution" that is closer to Stapledon's conception:

Man in himself is nothing. The forward movement of Life—the growing spirituality—is everything. I say to you quite freely, Ransom, that I should have been wrong in liquidating the Malacandrians. It was a mere prejudice that made me prefer our race to theirs. To spread spirituality, not to spread the human race, is henceforth my mission.[16]

But the "spirit" Weston claims to serve is Satan himself, and with a truly Satanic endurance he sets about his work. Going without sleep, he can assail Eve almost constantly with the most seductive arguments, for the Devil, as we all know, is very resourceful. What can Ransom do with his merely human powers? Even Lewis seems to be at a loss; in the end, he has Maleldil intervene by putting Weston to sleep. The next morning, Ransom defeats Satan's instrument by beating him to a pulp. In such a manner, according to Lewis' vision, can myth become fact. But it is hard to understand—for a skeptic, at least—what this achieves that Maleldil could not have achieved simply by unmaking Weston. There are other problems with the novel from an sf standpoint. Although they have green skins, the unfallen Adam and Eve are otherwise human in every detail, and we are given to understand that they are God's final model for the incarnation of intelligence—never again will there be creatures like the *hrossa* or *seroni*. Such needless anthropocentrism is inconsistent with Lewis' prior condemnation of Weston's fixation on loyalty to kindred as a perversion of part of the *Tao*. Moreover, while Weston's born-again Stapledonian philosophy may indeed be evil, too, it is not as obviously evil as his old genocidal interplanetary Darwinism, and *Perelandra's* moral argument is thus not fully developed.

That Hideous Strength, although Ransom still figures in it, takes a distinctly different turn from the first two novels of the trilogy. Its setting is contemporary earth, or Thulcandra as it is called in Old Solar, the "silent planet," which is ruled by the Bent One and is cut off from all intercourse with other worlds. Its motifs are more those of the supernatural novels of Charles Williams, a contemporary and close friend of Lewis, than of science fiction. But its anti-Wellsian theme provides a connecting link with *Out of the Silent Planet* and *Perelandra*. Here, the theme becomes an all-out assault on the amoral and totalitarian manipulation of ordinary humans and human nature in the name of progress. Mark Studdock, who has applied for a job with N.I.C.E., gets an inkling of this early on:

"What sort of thing have you in mind?" [Studdock asks.]
"Quite simple and obvious things, at first—sterilization of the unfit, liquidation of backward races (we don't want any dead weights), selective breeding. Then real education, including pre-natal education. By real education, I mean one that has no 'take-it-or-leave-it' nonsense. A real education makes the patient what it wants infallibly: whatever he or his parents try to do about it. Of course,

it'll have to be mainly psychological at first. But we'll get on to biochemical conditioning in the end and direct manipulation of the brain. . . . "

"But this is stupendous, Feverstone."

"It's the real thing at last. A new type of man: and it's people like you who've got to begin to make him."[17]

Lord Feverstone is the one-time Richard Devine, now an influential public figure. But Feverstone's shocking revelations are far from the worst; even he does not know the worst: N.I.C.E. is an intricate web of deceit and betrayal. Once the *Tao* is rejected, Lewis is warning, there are no longer any moral restraints. The masses must be deceived, of course; ordinary men and women would not choose to be reshaped into the Institute's image of Man. Among the first experimental subjects are convicts who are "released" from the finite punishment of prison to the unlimited "tortures and assaults on personal identity"[18] of Remedial Treatment. But even the supposed initiates . . . "Elasticity" is the word John Wither, deputy director under the ceremonial Jules, invokes every time Studdock tries to find out precisely what his job is, or anything about the duties he is supposed to perform. Ends as well as means are never quite defined.

Since this novel was written by the author of *The Screwtape Letters* (1942), it comes as no surprise that the true aims of N.I.C.E. are, not simply diabolical, but Diabolical. Satan, whom Wither believes to be an emissary of a higher order of life, the Macrobes, gives policy directives through the severed head of Alcasan, a French radiologist guillotined for the murder of his wife. Studdock is at last shocked out of his complacency, and complicity, by the revelation of the true nature of the Head and its ultimate plans to "improve" on Nature by turning the earth into a world as barren and sterile as the moon. Although there is an obviously apocalyptic air to the goings-on, Lewis is not so presumptuous as to end *That Hideous Strength* with the Second Coming; rather, divine intervention takes the form of a resurrected Merlin and angelic powers who destroy N.I.C.E. as God once destroyed Babel, through the confusion of tongues. Studdock is saved, but there is no escape—in this life, or the next—for Wither, or Feverstone, or Jules.

Lewis' almost medieval cosmology, let alone his orthodox faith, is so foreign to the dominant traditions of science fiction that it is likely to blind some readers to his moral arguments. Yet, not only in his fiction, but also in his essays, one finds again and again an honest conviction that sets his conservative religious and moral values apart from the shabby excuses for racism, militarism, and anti-intellectualism so often preached. Christianity for Lewis was a demanding faith—but what it demanded of him was humility before God and submission to moral law. Never did he take the smug satisfaction in religious belief that is characteristic of such earlier works of Christian science fiction as Victor Rousseau's *The Messiah of the Cylinder* (1917), an anti-utopian novel that shows surprising insight into the dangers of totalitarianism but under-cuts its own argument through sheer vituperation and such idées fixes as divorce being a fundamental moral and social evil.

In contemporary sf, even the witty and inventive R. A. Lafferty (1914–) illustrates the limitations of a strict Christian world view. A devout Catholic, he is uncomfortable with the idea of even biological evolution, and in *Past Master* (1968) his critique of secular humanist utopia seems as forced as Rousseau's but with less grounds. Astrobe suffers from too much perfection, but the only alternative seems to be the masochism of those who abandon utopian comforts for the festering slums of Cathead and Barrio. World leaders summon Thomas More from out of the past to advise them. Naturally, we learn that More intended his *Utopia* (1516) to be a bitter warning against "that sickest of all possible worlds, that into which my own world seems to be turning."[19] Naturally, too, we learn that Astrobe is the creation of robots, who seek to destroy life in the name of Holy Nothingness. In "Ishmael into the Barrens" (1971), Lafferty assails one of his bêtes noires—birth control. A secular humanist society that has grown out of the counterculture is depicted as evil primarily because of its harsh population curbs. Meanwhile, in an off-stage Catholic utopia, people breed like rabbits: God will provide, never mind how.

Walter M. Miller, Jr. (1912–), by contrast, has tried to integrate Christian values into the secular milieu of science fiction. Although he is best known for his classic post-holocaust novel, *A Canticle for Leibowitz* (1959), Miller's short fiction is often of equal interest. As a Catholic, Miller shares a moral and theological vision in common with Lafferty and the Anglican Lewis. But his background in genre sf, with its ideological roots in Wells, leads him into a treatment of the Christian and Wellsian world views that is more balanced and mutually sympathetic. Miller's acceptance of space travel, the embodiment of a Satanic evil in the Ransom trilogy, is only his most obvious departure from Lewis, for wherever his sf deals with the Wellsian evolutionary mythology, it seems to see value in that mythology, fraught though it may be with moral pitfalls because of mankind's Fallen state.

In "Crucifixus Etiam" (1953), for example, Miller even suggests a par-allel between the Wellsian cause of the advancement of mankind and the Path of the Cross. Manue Nanti is a common laborer on a project to terraform Mars: "a grim, womanless, frigid, disinterestedly evil world."[20] Like others of his kind, he came simply to make money, but he'll be lucky to make it out alive. Mars takes a ruinous toll of the health of those who work there, even though most of them are, like Nanti,

Andean Indians chosen for their earthly adaptation to a thin atmosphere and a harsh climate. If accidents don't get them, progressive deterioration of their lungs will. And for what? It will take hundreds of years for their labors to bear fruit; neither Nanti nor any of his comrades will ever reap the rewards they have toiled for. As a project supervisor watches Nanti's "desperate Gethsemane,"[21] he knows exactly which words can bring solace:

> "Some sow, others reap," he said.
> "Why?" the Peruvian choked.
> The supervisor shrugged. "What's the difference? But if you can't be both, which would you rather be?"
> Nanti looked up into the wind. He imagined a city to the south, a city to be built on tear-soaked ground, filled with people who had no ends beyond their culture, no goal but within their own society. It was a good sensible question: Which would he rather be—sower or reaper?[22]

Yet, while Nanti has found meaning to his life in sacrifice to an "eight-century passion of human faith in the destiny of the race of Man,"[23] one is left with a lingering sense of futility as to the worth of that sacrifice if it is no better served by the reapers. A similar sense of futility seems to find expression in "The Big Hunger" (1952), an almost Stapledonian epic of Man's conquest of the universe compressed into a few thousand words. Told from the viewpoint of an old starship, it is the tale of mankind's hunger, "the song of his endless thirst."[24] Again and again men go forth, "in cylinders of steel and wandering, riding starward on a heart-tempest that had once sung them down from the trees to stalk the plain with club and torch."[25] Yet never do they seem to find the goal they are seeking. Colonies are planted, but they often lapse into savagery before they give rise to new civilizations that are inspired anew by cosmic wanderlust. On some worlds, already inhabited, Man adds genocide to the list of his crimes. And after each wave of intersellar migration, there are those left behind, whose cultures become peaceful, prosperous—and decadent. At last, Man has extended his dominion unto the farthest reaches of the galaxy, but there is no fulfillment, no inner peace, and, worst of all, no place to *go*—save back to old, previously settled worlds, on which they look "with bitter, lonely eyes."[26] Earth itself, by now a legendary Eden, is rediscovered and conquered by nomads from space, whose only gift to the world, which they refuse at first to believe to be Man's birthplace, is atomic war. The dream of space is ended, and any who would revive it are hanged for treason. "The Big Hunger," so summarized, would seem a bitter lament for human vanity, but there is also an utter sincerity in Miller's poetry, and the last words of the starship, as it recalls those who understood the Big Hunger, are "I have seen the pride in their faces. They walk like kings."[27]

What can be the purport of all this? Perhaps Miller, like Lewis, is suggesting that all Man's worldly aspirations, however lofty, are only imperfect reflections of the longing for God. Perhaps he is arguing, as Lewis did of sexual love in *The Allegory of Love* (1936), that a Wellsian longing for evolutionary progress must find Christian sanctification in some manner, as courtly love was sanctified in a romantic intepretation of Christian marriage. But what form that sanctification might take is never revealed in Miller's sf. Nor can he, despite his evident sympathy for the Wellsian world view, find any terms for a reconciliation between the religious and secular conceptions of moral and social order in *A Canticle for Leibowitz*. We know, of course, from the overall context, that the Church is right about the Fall of Man and all that means for the hopes of a better civilization arising from the ashes of our own. Yet we wait in vain for some sign of what might have been done to make the Christian moral vision more effective in the secular world. For if advanced knowledge inevitably leads to destruction, was it then wrong for the Church to have so carefully preserved it through the ages, and even to have nurtured a technological renaissance? Father Paulo seems to suggest otherwise in his confrontation with the secular scholar Thon Taddeo, who yearns to restore Man's lost dominion over nature and who has accepted a local despot's patronage to that end, with the excuse that he has no other choice.

But who will govern the use of the power to control natural forces? Who will use it? To what end? How will you hold him in check? Such decisions can still be made. But if you and your group don't make them now, others will soon make them for you.[28]

Yet how can Taddeo, even supposing him to be moved by the abbot's plea, oppose Prince Hannegan? How can he and other scientists prevent the use of knowledge for evil, save by suppressing it? All through the new Dark Age, the Church has never sought the temporal power. Are the scientists to do so now, as in some Wellsian technocracy? Miller makes no such suggestion; indeed, he seems to see the Second Holocaust as an inevitable consequence of the same secular humanist ethos that permits a relief organization called the Green Star to urge euthanasia for the burn victims of the first atomic blast. "Dearest God, how did those two heresies get back into the world after all this time?"[29] cries Abbot Zerchi after hearing a medic declare pain the only evil and "society" the only judge of right and wrong. Yet Zerchi cannot see in the medic a simple villainy like that of Lewis' Weston or Devine:

He'd probably been living on benzedrine and doughnuts since the shot that killed the city. Seeing misery everywhere and detesting it, and sincere in wanting to do something about it. . . . From a distance, one's adversaries seemed fiends, but with a closer look, one saw the sincerity and it was as great as one's own. Perhaps Satan was the sincerest of the lot.[30]

No matter sincerity, or anything else: mankind puts its homeworld to the fire again, without even the excuse of not knowing what it does. Yet this time, the Church can carry its mission to the stars; has the Second Renaissance, however doomed, thus served a divine end? Michael Bishop, in two sequels to Miller's novel, sees no such hope. Mankind's mutant descendants on earth, in "The White Otters of Childhood" (1973), and the genetically engineered peoples of a distant colony, in *Beneath the Shattered Moons* (1976), both contend in vain against the dark legacy of Original Sin, without the solace or guidance of Christian faith.

THE WAGES OF HUBRIS

Bruce Fox and Gregory Rolles are much exercised about the Fourth Dimension, Charles Darwin, and stars full of socialists. Both are young men in their twenties, rather unremarkable inhabitants of a hardly more remarkable East Anglian town. But then, they have "sworn to Think Large, thus distinguishing themselves, at least in their own minds, from all the rest of the occupants of Cottersall in these last years of the nineteenth century."[31]

It comes as no surprise that among their acquaintances is a young writer named H. G. Wells; but in "The Saliva Tree" (1965), written near the centenary of Wells' birth, Brian W. Aldiss (1925–) exploits the conventions of the Wellsian short story for an indictment of Wellsian philosophy no less damning than that of C. S. Lewis. No less than Lewis, Aldiss admires Wells as a storyteller; no less than Lewis does he abhor Wells the prophet and the world view Wells bequeathed to sf in such proselytizing works as *The Food of the Gods* (1903–4) and *Things to Come* (1936, film). A speech at Nagoya, Japan, apparently on the occasion of a screening of *Things to Come* in 1970, criticizes Wells' faith in a super-scientific utopia: "The World State [is] now abhorrent to us because we have learned sadly that we foster within us tyrannies undreamed of by the rational Fabian Mr. Wells."[32] But even beyond that, the Wellsian dream that a "sane and happy" existence would come of science has proved a delusion:

Here is the future, and our palaces are built on rubbish dumps. Behind every beautiful new building lie seamy backwaters where human derelicts hide their wounds away. Even worse, we see that every scientific advance advances us merely a shade nearer some ultimate confusion.[33]

Aldiss occupies what seems at first an odd position in literature. On one hand, he is a literary radical, author of controversial sf works like *Barefoot in the Head* (1969, from a 1967–68 series), with its avant garde techniques reminiscent of James Joyce, and *Report on Probability A* (1967), which incorporates the methodology of the French anti-novel. Yet he remains seemingly conservative in his moral and social values, as witness his lampoon of Communism in *Enemies of the System* (1978) and the attitudes of his protagonist in *Life in the West* (1980), a contemporary novel set at an international cultural conference dominated by Marxists. In the context of twentieth-century cultural history, however, Aldiss' position is not at all odd: it is that of the estranged literary humanist, appalled at the evils of a society that proclaims its belief in science and material progress, but is unable to accept the comforting certainties of traditional religion or the millenial promises of Communism. He thus stands in the company of E. M. Forster, Aldous Huxley, and other critics of the values associated with the Wellsian world view in sf.

Not that Aldiss considers himself estranged from science fiction; rather, he sees himself as the defender of its essential values, which are set forth in his own history of sf, *Billion-Year Spree* (1973). In his own definition of science fiction, he reveals an understanding of the central importance of world views to sf, as well as an implicit prescription for what the genre's world view should be:

> Science fiction is the search for a definition of man and his status in the universe which will stand in our advanced but confused state of knowledge (science), and is characteristically cast on the Gothic or post-Gothic mode.[34]

All sf thus begins with Mary Shelley's *Frankenstein* (1818), which was a synthesis of the gothic novel, with its horrid revelations about human depravity, its brooding theme of sin and retribution, and the traditional Faustian drama of the pursuit of forbidden knowledge. For Aldiss, "Frankenstein's is *the* modern theme, touching not only on science but man's dual nature, whose inherited ape curiosity has brought him both success and misery."[35] From *Frankenstein*, the line of descent is clear through the gothic sf works of Edgar Allan Poe and Nathaniel Hawthorne, Robert Louis Stevenson's *Dr. Jekyll and Mr. Hyde* (1886) and the early Wells, i.e., *The Time Machine* (1895), *The War of the Worlds* and *The Invisible Man* (1897) and, in particular, *The Island of Dr. Moreau* (1896). Nor does Aldiss exhaust the catalogue of post-Wellsian gothic sf. Curt Siodmak's *Donovan's Brain* (1943), filmed several times (like *Frankenstein*, *Dr. Jekyll and Mr. Hyde*, and *The Invisible Man*), is just one example of the continuing popularity of the original gothic mode. Fred M. Wilcox's film *Forbidden Planet* (1956) is pure Faustian gothic; indeed, gothic attitudes seem to have been typical of cinematic sf, at least before George Lucas' *Star Wars* (1977). A post-gothic mode, which might be called the social gothic, involving a collective retribution against the collective hubris of mankind, has long been popular in both Britain and continental Europe. One can trace it back to Shelley's *The Last Man* (1826), in which a plague wipes out mankind. Examples from our own time include visions of a prideful civilization brought down by a disease that attacks iron in S. S. Held's *The Death of Iron* (1931), the sudden loss of electricity in René Barjavel's *Ashes, Ashes* (1943), and an alien spore that infects concrete in D. G. Compton's *The Silent Multitude* (1967). Against the gothic tradition in sf, Aldiss contrasts the naive optimism of too much popular science fiction:

> Most sf takes for granted that technology is unqualifiedly good, that the Western way of life is unqualifiedly good, that both can sustain themselves forever, out into galaxy beyond galaxy. This is mere power fantasy. As I have often argued, we are at the end of the Renaissance period. New and darker ages are coming. We have used up most of our resources and most of our time. Now nemesis must overtake hubris, for this is the last act of our particular play.[36]

Although Aldiss never associates power fantasy with Wells, it is clear from "The Saliva Tree" that he realizes where its ultimate roots lie. Young Fox and Rolles, rivals for the affections of Farmer Grendon's daughter, discover that an alien spacecraft has landed in a pond at the farm. At first, both are excited about the wondrous promise of contact with an alien species, advanced far beyond mankind. Has not Rolles been preaching the wonders of the coming Electric Age, when all men will be brothers? But a close encounter with an invisible alien, which kills the farmer's dog and nearly drowns Rolles himself, leaves Rolles with a sense of dread. Fox, almost like the stock fuzzy-minded scientist of Howard Hawks' *The Thing* (1950), refuses to believe anything ill of the visitors. "Try thinking of these chaps as invisible socialists and see if that doesn't make them any easier to deal with,"[37] Fox quips. But in the ensuing days and weeks, the evil of the aliens becomes ever more apparent. A strange dew causes farm animals to multiply like rabbits and crops to grow to enormous size; however, this is no food of the gods as in Wells' optimistic allegory of evolution. A foul taste infects all of Grendon's milk, eggs, and produce, and the townspeople refuse to buy them. Then comes a frightening harvest: seemingly healthy piglets are found sucked of their contents, collapsed like balloons. The same terrifying fate overtakes Mrs. Grendon, before Rolles' very eyes. Eventually, he manages to rescue the daughter from her increasingly demented father, but the experience has altered his entire outlook. Whatever he may have to say to Wells, who has just arrived in town at the end of the story, it will not be about men like gods or stars full of socialists. Once, he had believed that only a greater and wiser civilization could cross space; now he fears the precise opposite is true:

As soon as he thought it, his mind was overpowered with a vast diseased vision of the universe, where such races as dealt in love and kindness and intellect cowered forever on their little globes, while all about them went the slayers of the universe, sailing where they would to satisfy their cruelties and their endless appetites.[38]

"The Saliva Tree" reiterates the message of *Starship* (1958, a.k.a. *Non-Stop*), Aldiss' first sf novel. Here the tragedy of hubris bringing forth its nemesis is played out aboard a generation ship, like that in Robert A. Heinlein's "Universe" (1941) and so many works since. In Aldiss' story, it is not the ship that is lost, but rather *humanity*. The ship itself has long since returned to earth, but a plague picked up from an alien world, combined with a lack of nutrients, has reduced the descendants of the original crew to pitifully small creatures with accelerated lifespans, condemned to live forever as ignorant savages in an artificial environment that the last captain, in his log, compares to Belsen in its moral depravity:

Nothing but the full flowering of a technological age, such as the Twenty-fourth Century, could have launched this miraculous ship; yet the miracle was sterile, cruel. Only a technological age could condemn unborn generations to exist in it, as if man were mere protoplasm, without emotion or aspiration.[39]

"We have passed the technological phase of our civilization," declares a representative of earth near the end of *Starship*, but nothing is shown of what has succeeded it.

In his heart, Aldiss is a Rousselian; but such is his pessimism that he cannot seem to realize a Rousselian utopia save in the most ironic terms. In *The Dark Light-Years* (1964), mankind encounters the Utods, which show none of the outward signs of advanced civilization that men take for granted, apparently spending their time wallowing in shit. Yet the Utods have a highly sophisticated culture and even their own interstellar travel (although their ships, like their wallows, are full of shit). They have never known either evil or alienation, except for the brief ascendancy of a puritanically technocratic civilization three million years before, but they are entirely too innocent to survive the onslaught of mankind's imperialism, even if our aggressions are destroying our kind as well as theirs. Few men realize that the Utods may have taken the better path: "Oughtn't we to have stayed in the mud?" one asks. "Mightn't it be more healthy and sane down there?"[40]

Aldiss can be of two minds about progress. *Frankenstein Unbound* (1973) in his most formally gothic sf novel, in which Joseph Bodenland finds himself in the role of mankind's savior after he is carried by a timeslip (the result of wanton nuclear weapons testing) into the nineteenth century of Mary Shelley, where Frankenstein is a real man, his monster a harbinger of the Age of Science:

Was that not the whole weight of his argument, that Nature needed in some way to be put to rights, and that it was man's job to see it was put to rights? And had not that song passed like a plague virus to every one of his fellowmen in succeeding generations? . . . The Conquest of Nature—the loss of man's inner self![41]

But when Bodenland gets a taste of early nineteenth-century "justice," during his imprisonment for the alleged murder of Frankenstein, he comes to see a value in the modern civilization he has so piously condemned. The poor are no longer hanged for stealing to feed their families, nor are debtors thrown in prison, nor are women and children forced to work in factories. Only "the growth of social conscience in the general mass of people"[42] has fostered social progress, but only Frankenstein's science made it *possible*:

One of the direct results of science and technology has been an increase in production, and a "spin-off" or yield of such things as anesthetics, principles of bacteriology and immunology and hygiene, better understanding of health and illness, the provision of machines to do what women and children were earlier forced to do, cheaper paper, vast presses to permit the masses to read, followed by other mass media, much better conditions in homes and factories and cities—and so on and on in a never-ending list.[43]

A complementary ambivalence is evident in *Barefoot in the Head*, in which Colin Charteris becomes a religious messiah in Europe after most of the population has gone on a permanent drug trip from the effects of the PCA (psycho-chemical aerosol) bombs launched by the Arabs. Charteris' gospel is inspired mostly by P. D. Ouspensky and G. I. Gurdjieff, but it also seems to owe a lot to the multivalued logic of Alfred Korzybski, which inspired A. E. Van Vogt's *The World of Null-A* (1945) and which seems to be parodied as Charteris is assaulted by a rival prophet: "Even in this extreme situation, Charteris thought, multivalue logic is the Way. I am choosing something between being hit and not being hit; I am not being hit very hard."[44] Charteris is so spaced out that, even when he kills Phil Brasher a few moments later by throwing him into the path of a speeding truck, none of the reality of mangled flesh registers on him; all he can see is his own inner vision: "So many alternatives."[45] Such irony continues through the rest of the novel, in which Charteris appropriates Brasher's wife as well as his followers to preach in Belgium and Germany. When he fails to save a boy from drowning, he is acclaimed as if he *had* for a "miracle." When a follower is killed in a road accident while driving Charteris' car, the rest of his followers and Charteris himself account this the fulfilled prophecy of his own death and resurrection. Nicholas Boreas, who shows up to film a gushingly sympathetic documentary on the crusade, becomes disgusted when the crusaders later praise the film just as gushingly, when, in fact, the film never arrived for the screening they all think they have just seen. Perhaps he should have listened to Angeline Brasher, who, despite her liaison with Charteris, comes to the defense of Western civilization:

Okay, I agree as everyone must that there were many greedy faults but put at its lowest wesciv maintained in reasonable comfort a high population which must now die badly by plague and starve to its last wither.[46]

As she appeals to Boreas, so she later appeals to Charteris to "show us how to keep a grip until the bomfact wears thin."[47] After he settles down in (apparently) his native Serbia, Charteris does seem to play a positive role, becoming a wise old man who thinks much but speaks little. It seems to matter little what he actually preaches—"My ultimate wisdom my nonsense."[48] What does matter is the harmony in which his disciples have learned to live, with one another and nature. Has Western civilization, as Boreas predicted, actually passed without leaving any pain? Has Aldiss embraced, at last, the philosophy he seems to have satirized?

In *The Malacia Tapestry* (1976), he seems unable to find any solace in the medievalism some literary intellectuals have exalted over the values of modern civilization. Malacia, an alternate world Renaissance kingdom, seems utopian by medievalist standards: it knows nothing of the real and threatened evils of our time—industrial pollution, regimentation of life, nuclear holocaust. Yet the apparent miracle that protects the city-state from change is called the Original Curse, and we begin to realize why as we follow the rather picaresque escapades of Perian de Chirolo, an impoverished actor who longs to marry into an aristocratic family. For Malacia is also a city where heretics are burned at the stake, where rapacious nobles live in idle luxury but the masses are condemned to hopeless poverty and squalor, and where plague is a constant threat (although *that* can at least be turned against the invading Ottomans). Otto Bengtsohn, who waxes wroth at the injustices de Chirolo takes for granted, hopes to build a revolutionary climate by exploiting *mercurization*, a form of photography he has invented:

If your mind is ordinary, your station in life is sufficient, you are then safe, enchanted, when at least youthfulness is with your side. But if you are poor, if you have a mind beyond ordinary—if you think!—then you need to change things, then the world with its powerful men roll against you like a spiked wheel.[49]

De Chirolo takes a part in Bengtsohn's magic-lantern adaptation of a traditional play, but only to advance his career so that the Malacian authorities will permit him to marry Armida Hoytola, who is hopelessly above his station as things stand. He also wins brief notoriety as the city's first balloonist; balloons, another of Bengtsohn's inventions, are tolerated (temporarily, as it turns out) for their military value. Bengtsohn's own motives, however, are ignoble; in the end, he is betrayed, in any case, by an aristocracy that has no further need for him. Malacia, like Aldiss, seems caught between the evils of stasis and the perils of progress.

Although the invention is often fanciful, with men descended from reptiles and a polytheistic orthodoxy dominant, in a world in which the broad outlines of history are otherwise unchanged, *The Malacia Tapestry* reveals a genius for world creation on a scale Aldiss had never before attempted. That genius finds its fruition in the Helliconia trilogy, an epic work which seems destined to become one of the true landmarks of a genre for which Aldiss, whatever his doubts, has shown an abiding love. Helliconia is a world much like earth, save for its Great Year. Its sun is the G–4 class Batalix, around which it revolves in a Small Year of 480 days, but Batalix itself follows an eccentric orbit around the fierce A class Freyr. During the Great Year of 1,825 Small Years (or 2,592 earth years), the Helliconian climate follows a cycle from tropical in Great Summer to arctic in Great Winter. As the climate follows a cycle, so do the fortunes of humanity, which contends for dominance with another sentient species, the phagors. During Great Winter, the phagors rule, and men even worship the phagor gods; during Great Spring and Great Summer, men reassert their supremacy, and phagors are hunted down and killed or enslaved. Yet the two species are partners in symbiosis, for the phagors carry ticks that are vectors for the hellico virus essential to the seasonal metabolic changes that enable humanity to survive. During Great Spring, the Bone Fever kills much of the human population, but the survivors—and, through mutation, their offspring—are transformed from endomorphs to ectomorphs. During Great Autumn, the Fat Death reverses the process.

In *Helliconia Spring* (1982), we follow the reawakening of humanity, as Great Winter ebbs. Yuli, a tribesman of the snowy wastes, is left to fend for himself after a phagor attack, and he makes his way to Pannoval, a city of natural caverns and tunneled warrens, which is ruled by a priesthood. In time, he becomes a priest himself; but Pannoval is wracked by heresies, and eventually, Yuli finds he can accept none of the priestly teachings: "I don't believe. I believe nothing."[50] After fleeing Pannoval through a series of unexplored tunnels with the woman Iskador and other companions, he at last founds a new community. Several generations later, their descendants conquer Embruddock, once a mighty city during the previous cycle but now a small village. Spring is coming, however, and Embruddock—Oldorando, as it is renamed by its conquerors—seems to be destined for great things. As the climate warms, there is a revival of agriculture, and with it there comes a revival of trade and general prosperity. Yet there is an ominous sign of the duality of human nature in the estrangement between Aoz Roon, ruler of the city, and Shay Tal, sorceress turned scholar. The hubris of power and the hubris of knowledge are manifested, as Roon seeks imperial glory for Oldorando while Tal founds an academy to encourage learning and promote scientific progress. But the two also represent the polar values of the secular and the religious, for Tal would bring back the priests of Wutra, expelled by Great Yuli; Roon considers Oldorando well rid of them. Their conflict, moreover, embodies the clashing ideals of collectivism and individualism:

"What I hate is division, constant division," Aoz Roon roared. "We survive by collective effort, and always have done."
"But we can grow only through individuality," Shay Tal said. Her face grew paler as the blood mounted in his cheeks.[51]

Although her academy has contributed such practical knowledge as a technology for bridge construction to the city, Roon considers her only an idling dilettante, a pernicious influence on the community. In a fit of pique, Tal resolves to leave Oldorando, and her departure is followed (coincidentally) by disaster: first the Bone Fever then a mass invasion by the phagors that ends in the burning of the city. These are mere temporary setbacks; centuries later, in *Helliconia Summer* (1983), human supremacy is at its height. Oldorando, Pannoval, and Borlien, now great kingdoms, are united by the common worship of Akhanaba, "the Two-in-One, man and god, child and beast, temporal and eternal, spirit and stone."[52] Once again, however, there is division in the human soul. For reasons of state, King JandolAnganol of Borlien is divorcing his beloved Queen MyrdemInggala to marry Princess Simoda Tal of Oldorando, SartoriIvrash, meanwhile, discovers that men and phagors alike are descended from lower forms, but that the phagors were first and that their mythology is still the foundation of the Church of Akhanaba. As an atheist, he fails to understand the true importance of or need for religion: "His love of knowledge for its own sake, his hatred of his fellow men, had betrayed him."[53] His heresy brings bloody religious conflict, on top of the wars that are already sapping the strength of the three kingdoms.

Sibornal, an autocratic power to the north, has developed firearms and embarks on a campaign of imperial conquest in the South. More centuries pass, and in *Helliconia Winter* (1985), the struggle continues between Sibornal and the Pannovalan hegemony, now a Country of a Thousand Cults. Victorious Sibornalese forces are betrayed by their own government's venal intrigue, however, and Luterin Shokerandit, a youthful noble, is caught up in that intrigue as his homeland prepares for the Great Winter. Ever alienated from themselves as well as nature, men find the wrong answers again. Sibornal becomes a rationalistic oligarchy, imposing a puritanical discipline in the name of collective survival, even though it knows that some of its edicts—such as that combatting the Fat Death—are contrasurvival. Phagors are ordered destroyed; the Church of God the Azoiaxic is hounded. Shorekandit, discovering that his father is the Supreme Oligarch behind the growing oppression, commits patricide, and the must take refuge in the Great Wheel of Kharnabhar, a revolving religious shrine that makes a full turn in ten years. Yet even he is alienated from nature at the end, by hardness of heart:

> An act of defiance . . . that's mankind's nature. It's no good just sitting back and smoking occhara. Otherwise we should never progress. The key to the future must lie with the future, not the past.[54]

Aldiss intends a parallel with the experience of earth, which has gone through a long (nuclear) winter of its own. Helliconia is observed by men on the artificial satellite Avernus, which transmits a running television broadcast back to earth. Avernus, like its counterpart in *Starship*, is an expression of technological hubris, and eventually its overly artificial society self-destructs. Mankind on earth, meanwhile, has advanced toward a new, but unconvincing, harmony with nature and can even play a role in Earth Mother–to–Earth Mother contact between the planets. But the vision is more powerful than the intended message: on Helliconia, nature is as cruel as mankind; they exist in tragic symbiosis and estrangement.

3

The Men of Feeling

KEEPER OF THE TALISMAN

For after all, there is no friendliness or goodness in the universe. We have no proof that the Cosmos is benevolent. Long ago our ancestors believed in love. This was a fallacy. Evil is greater than good.[1]

From the very beginning of his career, with "The World of the Red Sun" (1931), Clifford D. Simak (1904–88) was obsessed with the question of teleology: whether the universe itself has some meaning or purpose. "I think that basically I am religious," he stated. "I cannot believe that the universe came into being by pure chance. Nor can I believe that by pure chance we have the precision and orderliness that we see in the universe."[2]

Simak can easily, and misleadingly, be typed as a conservative. A lifelong resident of the Midwest, he is best known for the rural settings and rustic characters that recur in much of his science fiction, settings and characters that would seem out of place in the writings of any other sf writer. Yet his world view is actually far more subtle and complex than a casual reader might suspect. None of his works reflect any orthodox faith, and he thought it "provincial that we must insist God is for man alone and for this planet alone."[3] For Simak, faith was a matter of feeling—a fragile feeling, perhaps no more than a hope—that there is something in the universe, somewhere, which cares. His sf nearly always stands or falls on how convincingly it can embody that feeling.

At times, he openly confronted the doubt that there is, indeed, any purpose in the universe. A bleak Wellsian vision of the dying earth is the controlling image in "The World of the Red Sun," in which a man of the year 700,000 confesses his despair over the absence of "friendliness or goodness" in the cosmos. A giant brain—the disturbing emblem of advanced evolution in H. G. Wells' "The Man of the Year Million" (1893) and a symbol for futility of the intellect in pulp science fiction—rules over what is left of the human race. Two time travellers from the twentieth century vow to end its tyranny, but their work of liberation proves futile. Eons later in their journey through time, they encounter a crumbling monument erected in their honor—but no people. Unable to manufacture the synthetic food the giant brain had provided, mankind died out. The time travellers themselves, betrayed by a machine that cannot take them home, are marooned—"Alone at the end of the world."[4] In "The Answers" (1954), Simak is again overwhelmed by doubt. Pilgrims from a galactic empire discover a remote, long-lost world, where legend has it that the ultimate truth about the universe has been found, but the natives have abandoned their city and live humbly without ambition of any kind. Once, they had built a great computer to find the Answers, and it gave them the Answers: *The universe has no purpose. The universe just happened. . . . Life has no significance. Life is an accident.*[5] That is why the seekers of wisdom have become a simple people.

It is not only the universe that tested Simak's fragile faith, but human nature. He may not, like C. S. Lewis, have actually believed in the historical reality of the Fall; but Man's long record of hatred, violence, and lust for power often appeared to him powerful evidence of some ineradicable evil that makes our species unworthy of whatever salvation the universe may have to offer. *City* (1952), widely regarded as Simak's finest work—it won the International Fantasy Award—becomes an expression of despair for humanity toward the end. Not a novel, but a collection of stories that are hardly linked at all in a conventional sense, *City* begins as an exercise in futuristic sociology, but it takes on an increasingly mystical and philosophical tone in later episodes. With the mass migration of most of the human race to Jupiter, in "Paradise" (1946), earth is inherited by a new culture of intelligent dogs, under the benevolent guidance of robots like Jenkins, once a servant to the Webster family. "*Mystic, perhaps, and visionary,*" he muses in "Hobbies" (1946); "*Probing into mysteries that man had brushed by as unworthy of his time, as mere superstition that could have no scientific basis.*"[6] Although mankind had reached a seemingly utopian state by the time of "Paradise," its influence is regarded as malignant thereafter. Even Jon Webster, the last of his family on earth, fears that influence and tries to isolate himself and the other remaining humans behind a force field at Geneva.

Jenkins, meanwhile, works to eliminate the very memory of man. In "Aesop" (1947), the dogs have created a new Eden, a peaceable kingdom in which the lion lies down with the lamb—or, at least, the wolf and the bear lie down with the rabbit and the raccoon. All things great and small have learned to live in harmony with nature and one another, except the websters, the descendants of a few wild humans who escaped the sealing off of Geneva. Although they are no longer known as "men," their nature can not be changed. Like the serpent in the original Eden, they can bring only evil. Young Peter casually reinvents the bow and arrow and kills a bird. "It is the first faint stirring of an atom bomb,"[7] fears Jenkins, who removes the threat by exiling the websters to a "cobbly world." It is a bitter lesson for him in the meaning of humanity:

Once I thought that Man might have got started on the wrong road, that somewhere in the dim, dark savagery that was his cradle and his toddling place, he might have got off on the wrong foot, might have taken the wrong turning. But I see that I was wrong. There's one road and one road alone that Man may travel—the bow and arrow road.[8]

Although he related his attitude in "Hobbies" and "Aesop" to the mass killing of World War II in general, it is clearly the spectre of Hiroshima that had most moved Simak to a distrust of mankind and modern civilization in particular. In other works, his moral condemnation was reserved for that civilization—with hope still held out for Man, if he can find an alternative. In *A Choice of Gods* (1972), for example, a new culture that is spiritually close to the land has been created by American Indians, after the mysterious removal of most of mankind by an unseen power. Members of the one remaining white family have developed strange powers, such as making astral journeys into the cosmos, and all men are blessed with millenial life spans, but their idyllic utopia is threatened by an imperialist-technocratic civilization, recreated from scratch by the billions exiled to three distant worlds a thousand years before. Simak must invoke *deus ex galaxia*, in the form of an enigmatic Principle contacted by religiously obsessed robots, to save earth from that civilization, which has apparently learned nothing from the sins of its past.

Wish fulfillment is a strong element in several other Simak novels. Mutants in *Ring Around the Sun* (1952) open up a whole series of parallel worlds to mankind, encouraging those enervated by our present "lopsided mechanical culture of clanking machines"[9] to rediscover the pleasures of rural life there. Inventions like "forever cars" that throw millions out of work provide an added inducement to emigration, as does the promise of near immortality. Out of all this will come:

The pastoral-feudal stage for resting and thinking, getting thoughts in order, for establishing once again the common touch between Man and the soil, the stage in which was prepared the way for the development of a culture that would be better than the one they had left.[10]

All Flesh Is Grass (1965) is even more Rousselian in its evocation of an alternate world in which intelligent flowers hold the answer to mankind's salvation. Tupper Tyler, a gentle idiot in the tradition of Harper Lee's Boo Radley in *To Kill A Mockingbird* (1961), is the first to contact the flowers, which can (among other things) alter their forms to supply all mankind's wants—rather like the shmoos in Al Capp's *L'il Abner*.

Yet for all his distrust of technological civilization, Simak was too much a science fiction writer to reject in utterly. What could be more mechanical than the robots that recur in so much of his sf, even in the pastoral utopia of *A Choice of Gods?* In *Project Pope* (1981), it is the robots themselves who pursue Simak's quest for the true faith, for a true principle that will illuminate the meaning of the universe. Enoch Cardinal Theodosium, one of the robot hierarchs of a new Vatican on a distant planet, tries to reconcile that quest with the material origins of his own kind. Are they not tainted by Original Sin, and was that sin not materialism?

But it could not have been, for if our brother humans had not attempted to better their condition, they never would have reached the mental capacity to conceive that great religion we admire so much. They would still be worshiping, if they worshiped at all, some nonsense spirit represented by an awkward structure of mud and sticks and bones, gibbering in their caves against an unreasoned fear of dark, gibbering of omens.[11]

In the same novel, His Holiness, the cybernetic Pope created by robots, even argues for a naturalistic approach to the problem of religion:

It is not a matter of faith alone, not a matter of finding the right deity . . . but a matter of untangling the many survival and evolutionary systems that have been developed by the people that our Listeners are discovering. It is only by the study of such systems and the thinking of the beings residing in these patterns, I am now convinced, that we can find the answers that will lead us to what you call a true religion.[12]

Even in *Cosmic Engineers* (1939), Simak was attempting to reconcile the Wellsian and the Rousselian in his own thought. As seemingly crude and melodramatic as any space opera, it offers the apocalyptic drama no space opera can do without: our universe is about to be annihilated by a collision with another. And, of course, there is a monstrous evil: the Hellhounds, who hope to take advantage of the cataclysm to fashion a new universe in their own image. But *Cosmic Engineers* is otherwise a departure from the usual conventions of its time. For starters, it has a *female* protagonist—Caroline Martin, a scientist imprisoned for a thousand years on a derelict ship for having refused to lend her knowledge to military use during an interplanetary war. Awakened from her suspended animation by newsman Gary Nelson, she reveals that her mind never slept during all those years and that she has learned to tune in on the thoughts of aliens, "talking over many light-years with one another."[13] She has thus heard the summons of the Cosmic Engineers for volunteers to save the universe.

Only she can master the mathematics of "space-time contortion" to answer that call, but when she and her comrades reach the world of the Engineers, they find that the ancient and seemingly all-powerful robots are assailed by doubt. "Life is so seldom found throughout the universe," one laments. "I sometimes think that life is merely a strange disease that should not be here at all . . ."[14] When Martin and the ostensible male heroes seek elsewhere for a means to defeat the Hellhounds, even travelling in time to consult a wise man on a far-future earth, their quest is not merely for the "fifth-dimensional energy" to obliterate the Hellhound fleet and to create a pocket universe to bleed off the forces of cosmic cataclysm. It is a quest for *meaning*, for universal values to share with the inhuman aliens also summoned by the Engineers. Nelson is at first a skeptic: "There was no such thing as parallel physical evolution, why should there be parallel mental evolution?"[15] Yet the Engineers are not even protoplasm, and they care for all life that exists, or ever will exist. Suddenly, Nelson, too, can believe:

An ideal. Something to fight for. A spur that kept Man going on, striving, fighting his way ahead.
Save the universe for that monstrosity in the glass sphere with its shifting vapors, for the little, wriggling, slug-like things, for the mottled terror with the droopy mouth and the glint of humor in his eyes.[16]

Again, in the moment of final triumph, Nelson is torn between doubt and belief. The universe has been saved, yet that universe is still only an "ordered mechanism . . . hostile to life."[17] But then he reflects on the improbable series of events that brought Martin and himself and the others together in time of need:

And in that chain of happenings he seemed to see the hand of something greater than just happenstance. What was it the old man back on Old Earth had said? Something about a great dreamer creating stages and peopling them with actors.[18]

Simak also introduces a cautionary note: as they celebrate the victory they have won, Martin and the rest learn that a vast, untenanted city on the Engineers' world has been prepared for mankind; but mankind may not enter its New Jerusalem until it has overcome "the old dead weight of primal savagery and hate."[19] Nor should mankind forsake the humbler virtues in its pursuit of a cosmic destiny. Even in the far future, the old man of Old Earth reveals, our kind has avoided such false turnings as evolution into "specialized monstrosities—great, massive brains that had lost the power of locomotion"; rather, "We kept our balance. We kept our feet on the ground when dreams filled our heads."[20]

In *Time and Again* (1950), Simak dispensed with the conventions of space opera, but again he sought to bring together the various threads of his philosophy. Asher Sutton is at the center of a web of intrigue that reaches across space and time because of a book he has never written and may never write. For in *This Is Destiny*, if it ever does appear, he reveals what he learned when he died and was born again on a world of 61 Cygni that no other man has ever been allowed to reach:

> *We are not alone.*
> *No one is ever alone.*
> *Not since the first faint stirring of the first flicker of life on the first planet of the galaxy that knew the quickening of life has there been a single entity that walked or crawled or slithered down the path of life alone.*[21]

Every living thing carries with it a symbiote that is not exactly a soul, but rather a *guide*. Sutton's revelation is not welcomed by mankind, for mankind seeks its own manifest destiny in the galaxy—driven "by his colossal conceit, by his ferocious conviction that Man was the greatest living thing the galaxy had spawned."[22] Thus Sutton is hunted from world to world, and even into other times, by those who would have him revise his book to support their anthropocentrism. At one point, he is marooned for ten years in twentieth-century Wisconsin, where he earns his keep as a laborer on his own remote ancestor's farm but finds renewal of his spiritual resources in an environment "kindlier and closer to Earth and life,"[23] where even the doings of birds and mice offer fresh insight into the brotherhood of life. In his own time, however, although he does not realize it, his only allies are androids and robots. Eva Armour, who loves him, is herself an android, and she cannot follow him to the exile in which he will finally write his book, lest he learn the truth. "He had to keep on thinking there were some humans he had helped, that there were still some humans who believed in him"[24] for the Revisionists have threatened him with a fate worse than death:

> Your name will go down as the blackest blot in all human history. The syllables of your name will be a sound that the last human will gag upon if he tries to

speak it. Sutton will become a common noun with which one man will insult another . . .[25]

Yet for all the moral courage he displays in accepting the obloquy of treason to mankind, Sutton is a pawn and a victim to the end, failing to provide *Time and Again* with the strong central focus it needs. Moreover, Simak's convoluted plot, and the artificiality of the symbiotes and the powers (such as direct access to cosmic energy) they can bestow, strain credibility. It is with *Way Station* (1963) that Simak succeeded most in bringing the disparate elements of his world view into harmony.

Enoch Wallace, the Union Civil War veteran recruited to tend a way station on one of the interstellar transmission routes of a community of worlds, is not only Simak's most fully realized hero, but also one of the most memorable protagonists in the annals of science fiction. In making him mankind's only contact with a galactic civilization of truly Stapledonian grandeur, Simak was at last able to bring together the homely values that have always been represented by his rustic heroes, and the transcendent values of the brotherhood of intelligent life in a purposeful universe that he had always dreamed of.

A century has passed since Wallace was appointed Keeper of Station 18327. In all that time, he has hardly aged, but his near immortality is the only reward for his service. He has been given no miraculous powers like Asher Sutton's; his only strengths lie in his moral character and a willingness to learn from experience. Earth is lurching toward what may well be its last war. Earth is also closing in on Wallace himself; the clannish natives of southwestern Wisconsin are willing to leave him alone, but not the government—not when it learns of his inexplicable youth. Wallace knows all this; what he does not know is that he is about to become the center of a galactic crisis as well.

The community of worlds that embraces thousands of alien cultures is bound together, not by an elusive faith, but by a spiritual force as real as "time and space and gravitation."[26] Unlike the Force of George Lucas' *Star Wars* (1977), however, it is no source of power—only of an "assurance that life had a special place in the scheme of existence, that one, no matter how small, how feeble, how insignificant, still did count for something in the vast sweep of space and time."[27] Contact with the force is maintained through the Talisman, a device which is based on both mechanical and psychic concepts. Only the rare Sensitives are able to operate the Talisman. The most devoted among them, its custodian, carries it "from star to star in a sort of eternal progression,"[28] thus renewing in turn the communion of each world with the force. Only now, the Talisman has mysteriously disappeared. Galactic Central has concealed the loss. "And yet, even with no one knowing, the galaxy is beginning to show wear," says Wallace's closest friend, the being he calls Ulysses. "In time to come, it may fall apart."[29]

Simak's narrative is complex, full of flashbacks and digressions that at first seem to have little or nothing to do with the main plot. Yet each part has its place, and each contributes to the whole. One example, an idea Simak had once thrown away in "Shadow Show" (1953), involves an alien device Wallace only half understands, by which he can summon up lifelike figures out of his fantasies: an idealized version of himself as a dashing soldier, of a woman he might have loved a century earlier. But the fantasy figures take on a life and consciousness of their own, testing Wallace's growing sense of moral responsibility; in the end, he must learn to put aside childish things. The fantasy entertainment device is only one of the gifts from the aliens who have passed through his station. Wallace's study is filled with artifacts from many worlds: some functional, others only to look at, still others of unknown purpose. For years, he has collected wood samples from across the galaxy, for his local mailman to use in carvings. His journals are filled with entries on species like the Thubans, "perhaps the greatest mathematicians in the galaxy,"[30] according to Ulysses.

Way Station itself is filled with epiphanies which illuminate Wallace's growing involvement with the community of worlds. His initial encounter with Ulysses is all unknowing; the alien just seems to be a passing tramp, who engages him in idle conversation about the possibility of life on other worlds. In the flash of lightning from a coming thunderstorm, the stranger reveals it is not so idle, after all: "For the stranger's face had split and began to fall away, and beneath it he caught the glimpse of another face that was not a human face."[31] Again, many years later, one of the Hazers, wondrous beings with golden auras, dies suddenly at the station in mid-conversation and becomes an "angular and bony and obscene, a terribly alien thing there upon the floor."[32] Hazer custom dictates he must be buried here; as Wallace reads the service, the old words take on new meaning: *"In my Father's house are many mansions; if it were not so, I would have told you . . ."*[33]

On a broken-down farm not far away lives Lucy Fisher, "a creature of the woods and hills, of springtime flower and autumn flight of birds."[34] A deaf-mute with the gift of healing, she is branded a witch and is savagely abused by her own father. Wallace befriends her, although she seems of no cosmic importance and although he faces such serious challenges as the robbery of the Hazer's grave by government agents. Instantly aware of the desecration, the Hazers hold earth responsible. Wallace feels a terrible sense of isolation: "One man alone could not stand against both earth and galaxy."[35] Yet somehow, he *does*. He intimidates the CIA into returning the alien's body. One night, without any warning, a vile, ratlike thing materializes in his station, bearing what turns out to be the stolen Talisman. The fate of the universe depends on Wallace as he pursues the creature into the dusk and finally spots it, struggling with Lucy on a lonely ridge. Years of practice with his rifle stand him in good stead; his aim is as true as his heart. Having accomplished his purpose, he can cast aside violence as he casts aside the gun itself. He has saved more than the Talisman itself; Lucy is the new custodian, "The one we've hunted through the years,"[36] Ulysses reveals. But, most important of all, a sense of *meaning* has been affirmed:

A million years ago there had been no river here and in a million years to come there might be no river—but in a million years from now there would be, if not Man, at least a caring thing. And that was the secret of the universe, Enoch told himself—a thing that went on caring.[37]

THE MAN WHO LEARNED LOVING

His name was Mensch; it was once a small joke between them, and then it became a bitterness. "I wish to God I could have you now the way you were," she said, "moaning at night and jumping up and walking around in the dark and never saying why, and letting us go hungry and not caring how we lived or how we looked. I used to bitch at you for it, but I never minded, not really. I held still for it, I would've, just for always, because with it all you did your own thing, you were a free soul."

"I've always done my own thing," said Mensch. "And I did so tell you why."[38]

His name was Theodore Sturgeon, and he likewise always did his own thing, and he told us why. His message was a simple one, as Robert A. Heinlein reminds us in an introduction to the posthumous *Godbody* (1986): "Love one another."[39] But Sturgeon (1918–85) knew it was not simple, not at all. Who else, during the decade of the flower children, would have written a story like "Brownshoes" (1969), in which Mensch is a man who so loves—*loves*—mankind that he sacrifices—*sacrifices*—himself to a life of wealth and power to save the world? Sturgeon's world view is one which can seem incredibly naive, or incredibly brave: it assumes a fundamental goodness in mankind, against all evidence to the contrary. Where Clifford D. Simak seeks salvation from without, in the assurance of a meaningful universe, Sturgeon seeks it from within, in an assurance that love can conquer all. There is a sense of innocence in much of his science fiction, and yet it is not the foolish innocence of one who has never seen evil, but the much harder innocence of one who has seen past it: Sturgeon's innocence is innocence regained.

Nowhere is that recovery of innocence expressed with greater intensity than in "Thunder and Roses" (1947). It is a tale of nuclear holocaust, a subject hardly extraordinary for its time, or for any time since. There have been many such stories: some angry, others depressing, still others moralistic; but none as ethical as Sturgeon's. It seems at first a typical right-wing scenario: America has been devastated by the Soviets in a first strike, without having managed to launch a missile of its own in retaliation. On the day after, none are left but the dead and dying. For the latter, who grow fewer every day, there can no longer be any hope—save, perhaps, vengeance. And they can have it: at various secret command centers, there are still undamaged launch controls. Pete Mawser could be an avenger; he is a typical soldier, stationed at one of the bases which (unknown to him) houses one of those command centers. It is through Starr Anthim, a beautiful singer who touched the heart of a nation before and can still touch it now, that he learns that he can decide the fate of the world. She has appeared on television, singing "Thunder and Roses," a song that "comes from the part of men and women that is mankind—the part that has in it no greed, no hate, no fear."[40] With the song comes a message: *"It doesn't matter."*[41] It doesn't matter who started the war. What does matter is that there is still a chance for mankind, albeit only a slim one, if Americans can do "the one noble thing left to us"[42] by foregoing retaliation. Even without retaliation, the enemy will suffer for untold generations from mutations and worse; but if a nuclear strike is launched against them, there will be no hope at all for the eventual recovery of mankind—perhaps not for any life on our planet.

Even when he meets her face to face, for she has broadcast from his own base this time, Mawser feels torn between love and hatred—not hatred for the enemy, but for mankind: "What creatures were these, these corrupted, violent, murderous humans? What right had they to another chance? What was in them that was good?"[43] Yet Starr is good, and she is human. And he himself is responsible for good or evil, like all men:

> He looked down through the darkness for his hands. . . . These hands were the hands of all history, and like the hands of all men, they could by their small acts make human history or end it. Whether this power of hands was that of a billion hands, or whether it came to a focus in these two—this was suddenly unimportant to the eternities which now infolded him.
>
> He put humanity's hands deep in his pockets and walked slowly back to the bleachers.
>
> "Starr."
>
> She responded with a sleepy-child, interrogative whimper.
>
> "They'll get their chance, Starr. I won't touch the key."[44]

Even when he must slay another who would touch that key, there is no more hatred in him. After destroying the controls, he even pauses to stroke the dead man's hair, before sitting down to die himself and cry out his last message to posterity: " 'You'll have your chance,' he said into the far future. 'And by heaven, you'd better make good!' "[45]

But how mankind can make good here and now, as well as in the long run, recurs as Sturgeon's obsession in subsequent works. Love may be the key, but how can it find practical expression? In some of his works, it is a rather mechanical means. "Unite and Conquer" (1948) is an example; it may well have introduced the device, later exploited by television's *The Outer Limits*, of uniting mankind by concocting a bogus alien menace. Sturgeon recognizes the problem at the outset, when he has Leroy Simmons point out H. G. Wells' penchant for gimmicks:

In each case there's a miracle—a Martian invasion in "War of the Worlds," a biochemical in "Food of the Gods," and a new gaseous isotope in "In the Days of the Comet." And it ultimately makes all of mankind work together.[46]

That observation, and a cat fight at a restaurant, interrupted when the two bimbos see the object of their affections walk in with a third woman, give Leroy's brother Rod the idea. Yet it is hard to believe that, even granting his extraordinary mind, Rod Simmons can single-handedly bring off the hoax that makes it appear a fleet of Outsider ships is attacking our planet. In Meyer Dolinsky's "The Architects of Fear" (1963), for *The Outer Limits*, it is a group of scientists, and their approach is to make over a sacrificial volunteer into an alien horror by plastic surgery.

In "The Skills of Xanadu" (1956), which Sturgeon frankly admitted was "wishful thinking,"[47] an investigator from an authoritarian planet meets more than his match on the seemingly idyllic world of Xanadu. His mission is to determine the best means of conquest, for Kit Carson (his homeworld) has a book to cover every contingency—except a world with, not only no central government, but an advanced technology without any centralized industrial base. The people of Xanadu kill him with kindness, even indulging his ridiculous privacy taboos. Building a house to his specifications, each shows the skills of specialists—not in mere handicrafts, but in sophisticated technology. They insist they just do what comes naturally; if there is a shortage of strontium, for example, those with nothing much else to do feel a need to produce it, by breeding shellfish that grow strontium carbonate shells. It isn't natural, of course; the secret is in the mysterious black belts they wear: devices that communicate skills among them at need. Bril of Kit Carson dashes home with one and has it mass produced; within a year, his planet seems organically united under the Leader. Only then do the belts begin to reveal the rest of their function:

A billion and a half human souls, who had been given the techniques of music and the graphic arts, and the theory of technology, now had the others: philosophy and logic and love; sympathy, empathy, forbearance, unity in the idea of their species rather than in their obedience; membership in harmony with all life everywhere.[48]

Wishful thinking, but not without its relevance to the real world. Years after its publication, Sturgeon related, Dr. Toni Morrison (quite fortuitously, apparently having not read it) summed up the theme of "The Skills of Xanadu" (paraphrased) "your freedom is worthless unless you use it to free someone else, and that happiness is not happiness unless it makes others happy."[49] Sharing is always the most important thing; in "The Man Who Lost the Sea" (1959), it even enables the protagonist to face a lonely death without regret. In his state of shock, the spaceman imagines himself back on earth, having just escaped from near death at sea as once he had, many years ago. But that satellite he times: its orbital period is seven and a half hours; it can not be one of those men placed around earth. That sunrise: too abrupt. That sea: not a sea, but the sands of Mars after the night frost has evaporated. His tracks: they lead back, not to the water but to the wreckage of his ship. Yet he can still identify with mankind, however distant:

> Then he speaks, cries out; then with joy he takes his triumph at the other side of death, as one takes a great fish, as one completes a skilled and mighty task, rebalances at the end of some great daring leap; and as he used to say "we shot a fish" he uses no "I."
>
> "God," he cries, dying on Mars, "God, we made it!"[50]

That same sense of identification is the theme of *More Than Human* (1953), but on an evolutionary scale. Sturgeon's greatest novel, it has remained in print even when his other works have been neglected. It is a superman story, but not like other superman stories, for its superman is a gestalt—a fusion of several individuals into something greater than the sum of their parts. Like any organism, it is motivated by the drive for survival, as its "head," Gerard Thompson, realizes when he goes to a psychiatrist to find out why he killed a kindly lady who took in the group. The security she offered was a threat to the gestalt; its components could no longer *blesh.*

> I figured she had to be killed or it—*I*—would be. Oh, the parts would live on: two little colored girls with a speech impediment, one introspective girl with an artistic bent, one mongoloid idiot, and me—ninety per cent short-circuited potentials and ten per cent juvenile delinquent." I laughed. "Sure she had to be killed. It was self-preservation for the gestalt.[51]

It is Janie, the artistically inclined "body" of the gestalt, who enlists the aid of Hip Barrows, already once the victim of Thompson's persecution, to teach him the beginnings of morality: "He's got to learn to be ashamed."[52] But what can a mere *man* teach the gestalt?

Define:
Morals. Society's code for individual survival. (That takes care of our righteous cannibal and the correctness of a naked man in a nudist group.)
Ethics: An individual's code for society's survival. (And that's your ethical reformer; he frees his slaves, he won't eat humans, he "turns the rascals out.")[53]

But neither concept seems to apply to the gestalt—an "individual" without a species to guide or be guided by. What it needs is neither a code of morality nor a code of ethics, but something greater still—an *ethos*. It too will provide a code for survival, but "a greater survival than your own, or my species, or yours."[54] It must recognize mankind as the parents of the gestalt and reverence them as such; by helping mankind, the gestalt will help itself by making it possible for others of its kind to be "born," so that it will no longer be alone, and it can have a "posterity" of its own to reverence and to guide:

And when there are enough of your kind, your ethics will be their morals. And when their morals no longer suit their species, you or another ethical being will create new ones that vault still farther up the main stream, reverencing you, reverencing those who bore you and the ones who bore them, back and back to the first wild creature who was different because his heart leapt when he saw a star.[55]

Only when he has accepted this ethos, and Barrows as the conscience of the gestalt, is Thompson himself accepted by other gestalts who have been there all along, serving as

the Guardian of Whom all humans knew—not an exterior force, nor an awesome Watcher in the sky, but a laughing thing with a human heart and a reverence for its human origins, smelling of sweat and new-turned earth rather than suffused with the pale odor of sanctity.[56]

Thompson and the gestalt, however, have an advantage over the rest of us: whatever morality, ethics, or ethos they follow, they can make it *matter* in the real world. So can the people of Xanadu with those magical black belts. It is as if the dead weight of social inertia could be just wished away, given paranormal powers or an amulet to simulate them; yet we have none. What we do have are laws, customs, and institutions, which often seem as rigid as natural laws, even though they are all in our heads. Sturgeon was one with Rousseau in feeling that man is born free, yet is everywhere in chains: chains, moreover, that men either deny, or—more incredibly—cling to with a fervor greater than the longing for love, or life itself. Like other Rousselians, Sturgeon inveighed against every form of puritanical repression that denies the natural and beautiful in mankind; he was still preaching the same gospel in *Godbody*, in which the Christ-like figure is a messenger of sexual and spiritual love combined. "If All Men Were Brothers, Would You Let One Marry Your Sister?" (1967) takes that gospel to its extreme. Vexvelt is the only utopian world in the galaxy, but the rest of the galaxy doesn't even want to recognize its existence. Although it has natural resources that would otherwise attract exploiters like flies and has a cure for every cancer and although it carries on a small foreign trade through intermediaries, it is almost impossible to get there, or even to find out anything about the planet. Charli Bux perseveres and learns the answer when, after having spent some time sampling the delights (sexual and otherwise) of Vexvelt, he comes across his new-found lady friend, Tyng, making love with her father. Shocked beyond belief, he manages to overcome his shock and listen to the patient explanations of Vorhidin: incest is not a natural taboo; it does not lead to defective offspring—"Any livestock breeder will tell you that."[57] Most important of all, it does no psychological damage when it is accepted as normal; it is actually beneficial in that it eliminates sibling rivalry, the Oedipus complex, and other syndromes originating in thwarted and therefore inverted love feelings. Rejected by his fellow men for having accepted Vexvelt on its on terms, Bux opts to return there for good, but still he wonders: "Why? Why? How did human beings come to hate this one thing so much that they would rather die insane and in agony than accept it? How did it happen, Vorhidin?"[58]

Even Vorhidin doesn't know, but Sturgeon had an idea how the seed of evil could be planted in the human heart. In *The Synthetic Man* (1950, as *The Dreaming Jewels*), Pierre Monetre is a brilliant surgeon accused unjustly of causing a death in a simple appendectomy. Rather than deal with his problem constructively, he takes the path of self-pity: first in alcoholism, then in a perverse despite for those who have wronged him and for the rest of humanity as kin to them:

He enjoyed his disgust. He built himself a pinnacle of hatred and stood on it to sneer at the world. This gave him all the altitude he needed at the time. He starved while he did it; but since riches were of value to the world at which he sneered, he enjoyed his poverty too. For a while.[59]

Such passive sneering is not enough, after awhile—Monetre needs active outlets for his misanthropy. He dabbles in causes ranging from radical politics to avant-garde art, never out of a sense of conviction, but only out of contempt for humanity. Eventually, he finds another outlet: crystalline alien life-forms which have the strange power to create duplicates of plants, animals—and humans. Indulging both his intellectual curiosity and a growing sadism, he forces the crystals to create human freaks for a travelling carnival that is both an expression of his need to humiliate others and a cover for spreading crystal-mutated plagues and pestilences around the country. By turning his back on humanity, he has turned his back on any hope of salvation for himself, and the futility of his evil is manifested in his defeat at the hands of Horty Bluett: an innocent, himself a creation of the crystals, allowed to fulfill the promise of *their* plan rather than being twisted to fit Monetre's.

"Slow Sculpture" (1970) and "Brownshoes," by contrast, are stories of redemption. In both, the protagonists face the same temptations as Monetre, yet they manage to overcome them. In the manner of their personal redemption, moreover, Sturgeon suggests how the world itself might be redeemed by love, as indeed it is in the latter story. Although "Slow Sculpture" was published after "Brownshoes," it may well have been written first, as part of a series of stories that poured from his typewriter under the inspiration of a real-life love.[60] In any case, it comes first thematically, for its nameless genius has turned his back on the world. His solitude is interrupted by a panic-stricken woman, whose cancerous breast tumor he proceeds to cure almost as casually as one might treat an ordinary headache with aspirin. He could as easily offer his medical miracle, and breakthroughs in any number of fields, to the world, but he refuses. He anticipates the woman's argument:

The one about my duty to humanity. It comes in two phases and many textures. Phase one has to do with my duty to humanity and really means we could make a classic buck with it. Phase two deals solely with my duty to humanity, and I don't hear that one very often. Phase two utterly overlooks the reluctance humanity has to accept good things unless they arrive from accepted and respectable sources. Phase one is fully aware of this but gets very rat-shrewd in figuring ways around it.[61]

Years ago, he had made a lot of money selling an exhaust system that would have virtually eliminated pollution. *Would* have because the automobile company that bought the device suppressed it fearing it was too disruptive. Mankind is stupid as well as evil; there is no salvation for it. But the woman urges him to think of humanity as he thinks of the bonsai tree he has so lovingly nurtured for half his life:

People are living growing things too. I don't know a hundredth part of what you do about bonsai. But I do know this: when you start one, it isn't often the strong straight healthy ones you take. It's the twisted sick ones that can be made the most beautiful. When you get to shaping humanity, you might remember that.[62]

In "Brownshoes," first published as "The Man Who Learned Loving," Mensch has already learned that and more. When he invents a new energy system that could revolutionize the world, he is driven to tears and sleepness nights, for he knows that in the world as it is, some people would kill to possess his invention, and others would kill to suppress it. It could feed the world's hungry or be turned to mass destruction. But he loves mankind, and that leaves him only one possible decision. He gives up his life as a flower child. He gets his hair cut, takes a regular job at an electronics plant, joins the church, and hangs out at the Legion post. He gets degrees in law and engineering, buys a small plant, introduces his invention in disguised form, and he makes a mint. Slowly, but surely, he nurtures the technological revolution that saves the world. Only his woman rejects him, accusing him of having rejected love.

He thought of fat Biafran children and clean air and unpolluted beaches, cheaper food, cheaper transportation, cheaper manufacturing and maintenance, more land to lessen the pressures and hysteria during the long process of population control. What had moved him to deny himself so much, to rebel, to move and shake the status quo the way he had, rather than conforming— conforming!—to long hair and a lute? *You could have had love.*

"But I did," he said; and then, knowing she would never, could never understand, he got in his silent fuelless car and left.[63]

4

Darwinians—Social and Otherwise

SURVIVAL OF THE FITTEST

Either we spread and wipe out the Bugs, or they spread and wipe us out—
because both races are tough and smart and want the same real estate.[1]

"Social Darwinism" has come to be used so often as an epithet that
it has almost ceased to have any actual meaning. Associated with Herbert
Spencer's defense of laissez-faire capitalism, it has the connotation of
equating material wealth with "fitness"; but, as Spencer himself was
well aware, the only Darwinian tests of fitness are survival and reproduction: a welfare mother is thus more "fit" than a childless billionaire.
While that example is admittedly facetious, it should be sufficient warning to armchair theorists who use Darwinian, or for that matter any
scientific arguments, merely to buttress theories they already believe in
for other reasons. Robert A. Heinlein (1907–88), however, took his Darwinism straight; in *Starship Troopers* (1959), all moral, social, and philosophical issues are seen from a single perspective: survival of the
species.

Mankind is engaged in a war with the Bugs. Heinlein never pretends
that war has anything to do with any lofty ideals; it is purely a matter

of evolutionary competition. Evolution, his protagonist argues, proves "that any breed which stops its own increase gets crowded out by breeds which expand."[2] If mankind were to limit its population and live peaceably on its own planet, the Bugs—or some other, more competitive species—would inevitably move in for the kill. That is the ultimate, cosmic meaning of the survival of the fittest. Without a recognition of that fundamental reality of the universe, there can be no basis for any moral arguments whatever. Does mankind have the right to conquer the universe? Johnnie Rico, mobile infantryman, knows the answer:

> Man is what he is, a wild animal with the will to survive, and (so far) the ability, against all competition. Unless one accepts that, anything one says about morals, war, politics—you name it—is nonsense. Correct morals arise from knowing that man *is*—not what do-gooders and well-meaning old Aunt Nellies would like him to be.
> The universe will let us know—later—whether or not Man has any "right" to expand through it.[3]

Starship Troopers is more relentless in communicating Heinlein's Darwinian world view than anything else he ever wrote, yet the essentials of that world view are explicit or implicit in most of his science fiction, and those essentials changed hardly at all through the nearly five decades of his career. Heinlein is frequently denounced as a reactionary, and one of the most curious pieces of literary criticism in the genre is a monograph on his works by H. Bruce Franklin, a radical Marxist. Yet the conservative Christian C. S. Lewis could surely find no more to admire in Heinlein's views than Franklin. Heinlein has recently been praised as a libertarian, particularly for his vision of a future, anarcho-capitalist (after a fashion) revolution on the moon in *The Moon Is a Harsh Mistress* (1965–6). Yet even though the novel has contributed a slogan ("TANSTAAFL," or "There ain't no such thing as a free lunch") to the libertarian movement, it is not quite *of* the movement. Individual freedom is valued in Heinlein's world view but as a means to an end—free men are better survivors and are therefore fitter in the evolutionary struggle. In *Beyond This Horizon* (1942), his utopian society is a blend of universal welfare state (free food and a monetary policy that would make John Maynard Keynes seem a disciple of Adam Smith) and individualism at its ruggedest (an armed citizenry and every man for himself when it comes to settling disputes by code duello). Although the genetic engineers practice selective breeding to eliminate obvious defects and conserve such obvious qualities as intelligence and physical vigor, they do not try to make radical changes in the nature of Man. During the Genetic Wars, we learn, the Empire of the Great Khans tailored specialized forms of men through artificial mutations and endocrinology, from hyperbrains (thirteen varieties) to almost brainless matrons, pseudo-feminine free-martins, and neuter mules. The Khans thought the mules would make perfect soldiers—they combined intelligence, endurance, and obedience—but they miscalculated:

The mules fought us—yet the true men won. Won because they fought and continued to fight, as individuals and guerrilla groups. The Empire had one vulnerable point, its co-ordinators, the Khan, his satraps and administrators. Biologically the Empire was a single organism and could be killed at the top, like a hive with a single queen bee. At the end, a few score assassinations accomplished a collapse which could not be achieved in battle.[4]

It is the same basic argument for the advantages of individuals as unspecialized animals that recurs in *The Puppet Masters* (1951), in which an invasion of earth by slug-like parasites from Titan is defeated in the end by the greater adaptability and resourcefulness of free men. In *Starship Troopers*, mankind again enjoys those advantages in its conflict with the totally specialized and collectivized Bugs. Yet fitness can be proved only in the conflict; reality is the only judge. In *Beyond This Horizon*, a cabal of totalitarian genetic engineers attempts a coup. For a time, the conspirators seem to have a good chance of success, for the utopian world-state has only a limited police force. Even if they fail to win, they may get amnesty for themselves by holding the world plasm bank hostage. As he prepares to defend the bank against a rebel attack, while waiting for volunteer reinforcements, Hamilton Felix wonders what it would mean if the rebels won. Wouldn't it be the Policy Board's fault for not sanctioning a larger police force? Not at all, according to the District Moderator of Genetics, Mordan Claude: "If the rebellion is successful, notwithstanding an armed citizenry, then it has justified itself—biologically."[5] Logic would require that the slugs and Bugs could justify themselves in the same manner.

Heinlein's world view seems almost inevitably materialistic as well as amoral. Even the psychology in *Starship Troopers* and other works has an aura of behaviorism. In History and Moral Philosophy, a high school course everyone is required to take (although not to pass), Lt. Col. Jean V. Dubois, the instructor for Rico's class, compares educating children to housebreaking dogs: the moral and social breakdown of the twentieth century is blamed on the failure to impose the negative reinforcement of physical discipline on children. Just as it would be absurd to scold a puppy for making a mess on the floor, while never actually punishing it, and then shoot the adult dog for still being unhousebroken, so was it absurd to be lenient with so-called juvenile delinquents until they grew up to be incorrigible criminals. Man has no *moral* instinct, only an instinct for survival, Dubois stresses:

But the instinct to survive can be cultivated into motivations more subtle and much more complex than the blind, brute urge of the individual to stay alive. . . . Survival of the family, for example. Of your children, when you have them. Of your nation, if you struggle that high up the scale. And so on up. A scientifically verifiable theory of morals must be rooted in the individual's instinct to survive—*and nowhere else!*—and must correctly describe the hierarchy of survival, note the motivations at each level, and resolve all conflicts.[6]

In 1950, Heinlein predicted the downfall of Freudian analysis and its replacement by "a growing, changing 'operational psychology' based on measurement and prediction," and in 1980 he believed his prediction was "beginning to come true."[7] In *Double Star* (1956), Lorenzo Smythe, a ham actor, is required to impersonate John Joseph Bonforte, a Terran statesman who has disappeared on the eve of crucial negotiations with the Martian nests. Smythe has a problem: he can't stand Martians. But a quick indoctrination under deep hypnosis solves the problem, and the negotiations are a triumph; Smythe is adopted into a nest and a potential interplanetary crisis or even a war is averted. (The Terran and Martian environments are sufficiently different that evolutionary competition does not mandate species conflict.) Hypnotic conditioning is also part of Rico's training in *Starship Troopers*, and when he complains of the shakes before a jump, the ship's psychiatrist checks his brain waves. Psychotherapy, like education, is a matter of Pavlovian conditioning and or hypnotic indoctrination. No doubt much of this is exaggeration for effect, but the rigorously materialist approach to moral education and psychology seems essential to Heinlein the social Darwinist.

But then, there was the *other* Heinlein, Heinlein the mystic, who believed in the soul as distinct from the body and in some form of life after death—perhaps reincarnation, perhaps another dimension. It is one thing for an author to embrace a world view based on acceptance of the supernatural—whether it be the orthodox Christianity of C. S. Lewis, some other established faith, or even the mystical revelations and prophecies of the New Age movement—it is quite another to embrace a supernatural world view and a materialistic one simultaneously, without even attempting to reconcile or integrate them. If the end of life is, indeed, an afterlife or reincarnation, then it is absurd to construct a morality or philosophy around our common experience in this life, this universe. In *Beyond This Horizon*, Hamilton Felix, although he bears Star Class genes, refuses to have children because he cannot see any point to human existence. During the rebel attack on the plasm bank, he tells Mordan what *would* give it a point: "The one thing that could give us some real basis for our living is to know *for sure* whether or not anything happens after we die. When we die, do we die all over—or don't we?"[8]

In return for his agreement to propagate, the Policy Board agrees to undertake a Great Research into that question and into such others as the origin and destination of the universe. Hamilton's son, Theobald, turns out to be telepathically sensitive, and that sets up the denouement. Theobald can sense the thoughts of his unborn sister Justina, and they are clearly not the thoughts of a fetus without experience of the world. They are the memories of one who has lived before, specifically Madame Espartero Carvala, the late grand old lady of the Policy Board—"the main question: *'Do we get another chance?'* had been answered—by the back door."[9] During the previous debate over funding the Great Research, one Policy Board member has suggested that the only rational philosophy based on the assumption that death is final would be complete hedonism, but the opposite assumption seems equally problematical. What need have souls for selective breeding? The entire basis of Heinlein's utopia must be, assuming the reality of reincarnation, not merely insufficient, but *irrelevant.* For that matter, so is the drive for individual, or racial, survival. The essential contradiction between his two world views is apparent even in *Stranger in a Strange Land* (1961), widely regarded as his greatest novel, in which the survival of mankind is at stake in its confrontation with the Martians—but everyone gets to be god in the life beyond. Without that life beyond, it seems, all is futile—ashes to ashes, dust to dust, zygote to zygote. Yet there is much in Heinlein's other science fiction that is of enduring value, for it expresses values that are truly enduring.

In keeping with his strict Darwinian world view, these are survival values, but that does not mean mere combativeness, as one might gather from *Starship Troopers.* Rather, Heinlein's values are all those values essential for the survival of civilization: a respect for knowledge and the skill to use it, for learning from experience as well as from textbooks, for hard work and long-term commitment, for both individual freedom and cooperation with others for the common survival and the common good. In the contemporary world, it often seems that the real survival values are neglected, or even denigrated. How often have we read about how schools are raising generations of cultural illiterates, who know practically nothing about history, science, literature, or anything else: "Occupational therapy for morons!"[10] a typical Heinlein father calls it in *Have Space Suit—Will Travel* (1958). Most people's knowledge of civilization seems limited to what they can glean from television; "roughing it" would mean nothing more to them than taking the Winnebago to Yellowstone Park. Mindless togetherness competes with mindless self-indulgence as an ethical ideal, and fashions in mores (sexual and otherwise) oscillate from one extreme to another in equally mindless pendulum swings. It is socially acceptable to believe in television evangelists; orthodox conservative and liberal pundits; gurus of the counterculture; even conventional radicals (Marxist or otherwise))—but never in plain reason or common sense. In such a cultural environment, Heinlein at his best can be like a life preserver to a drowning man. That best can often be seen in his juvenile sf, written for an age group that needs guidance most, yet never written down to it.

Take *Tunnel in the Sky* (1955), a robinsonade in which teenagers on a survival exercise are marooned on an untamed planet when the space-time distortion of a supernova makes it impossible to reestablish a star-gate connection with earth on time. Rod Walker, like his classmates, is taking Advanced Survival because it is a prerequisite to the college de-grees required for men and women to qualify for emigration to the Outland worlds opened to an overcrowded earth by stargate technology. Among the skills any professional must have mastered for a degree in Outland Arts are "hunting, scouting, jackleg mechanics, gunsmithing, farming, first aid, group psychology, survival group tactics, law, and a dozen other things the race has found indispensable when stripped for action."[11] Walker's teacher warns him against taking a romantic attitude toward the coming exercise; what he needs are practical care and caution. Walker gets his best practical advice from his older sister Helen, an assault captain in the Amazon Corps: *don't* take a gun, for example; it can be a temptation to fatal overconfidence—better to pack just a knife, and enough rations to last until he can learn to live off the land.

During his first day on Tangaroa, he learns the wisdom of his sister's advice, when he comes across the body of a classmate who thought it was a great idea to go through the gate armed Rambo-style with a high-powered energy rifle and an attack dog to boot. Walker himself is ne-glectful of caution, and he considers himself lucky that whoever robbed him of everything but one knife had only knocked him out instead of killing him. When he runs across another student finishing off and appropriating a deerlike animal he himself has wounded and tracked, what begins as a quarrel is resolved into an agreement to become a team: both realize that there is safety in numbers. Something, they know, has gone dreadfully wrong; the deadline for recall has passed—they could be stranded for years, perhaps even for the rest of their lives. When they find yet another student in trouble, they save him, and they decide to keep a signal fire burning to alert other survivors, who straggle in a few at a time.

But forging a community takes more than just numbers. It takes more than individual survival skills. It takes cooperation based on trust and a willingness to compromise on practical details without betraying basic principles. Any differences that might have mattered on earth do not matter here: when a bunch of toughs gets the drop on the men and tries to take over the camp, it is the women—including Caroline Mshiyeni, a Zulu who becomes Walker's most trusted confidante—who save the day by getting the drop on the toughs. Walker emerges as the informal leader, but when the camp finally organizes a government, Grant Cow-per, who has more theoretical knowledge, sweeps the election for mayor. Although Cowper proves to be arrogant and inept and although there is no love lost between him and Walker, it is Walker himself who squelches a motion to dump Cowper at a later town meeting; a struggling community cannot afford a factional feud. But Cowper gets the message that there is widespread discontent, and he works out his differences with Walker and his backers. Government, he later remarks, is "the art of getting along with people you don't like."[12] Walker still argues with Cowper about such issues as building a protective wall for the com-munity, and he is proved right when the dopy joes, seemingly harmless animals, turn vicious and dangerous during a mass seasonal migration. Cowper dies heroically helping to defend the camp; Walker once again takes the reins. By now, he has learned patience, as must they all. Art Nielsen is frustrated, for example, because until coal can be found, the best he can do in metallurgy is spongy wrought iron. True, Walker points out, but what about Cliff Pawley, who is trying to develop cereal grains from native grasses? Only their great-grandchildren will reap the re-wards of Pawley's work.

But you yourself will live to build precision machinery—you know it can be done, which, as Bob Baxter says, is two thirds of the battle. Cliff *can't* live long enough to eat a slice of light, tasty bread. It doesn't stop him.[13]

That's taking the long view, so essential to sf, and the long view is still what counts, even when the Tangaroan Robinsons are rescued. It is what matters in *Farmer in the Sky* (1950), in which pioneers on Gany-mede must labor to *create* a living world from primordial ice and rock for their own sake and the sake of their families, their descendants, and even mankind itself. Heinlein still takes the long view here, but is is not a utopian long view. In his youth, he once admitted, he became a lapsed Christian.[14] At some point in his career, he also seems to have become a lapsed Wellsian. Where he once looked forward to a progressive social order evolving from eugenics (*Beyond This Horizon*) or General Semantics (The History of the Future), he came to be stoically reconciled to an eternal recurrence in human affairs. In *Starship Troopers*, where only veterans are allowed to vote and the affairs of mankind are thus in the hands of those who have proven their willingness to give their lives for the same of the species, there is a utopian vision of sorts: "personal freedom for all is the greatest in history, laws are few, taxes are low, living standards are as high as production permits, crime is at its lowest ebb."[15] But even if he believed such a system would be the best of all possible political worlds, he apparently never saw much chance of its coming to pass.

In *The Moon Is a Harsh Mistress*, which has become one of the icons of the libertarian movement, even as *Stranger in a Strange Land* became a bible to many hippies, the revolution Manuel O'Kelly and his comrades fought for in 2076 is coming to pieces a generation later, as the Luna City Council busies itself with regulations and taxes against all public food vendors operating under municipal pressure. It is a failure of the long view, but the very organization and strategy of the revolution was necessitated by a similar failure. Luna is a penal colony, like early Australia, only primarily for political offenders. Since the warden and his administration have never done anything for the Loonies other than policing them, the Loonies have had to learn to do for themselves. Some of their solutions to social problems are ingenious. Line families, in which new husbands and wives are brought in over the years, offer both emotional and economic security in a world where there is no such thing as welfare, social security, or medicare. Want insurance? Place a bet on your life with a bookie. Education is anybody who knows something teaching those who do not, for all the traffic will bear. What necessitates the revolution, however, is not authoritarian interference with any of these laissez-faire arrangements; it is an ecological disaster in the making. Luna exports wheat to earth, but farming depends on water, of which our satellite has precious little: it has to be mined from primordial ice, which is being exhausted. Many Loonies see the issue solely in economic terms and demand a better price for their wheat. Professor Bernardo de la Paz, theoretician of the revolution to come, knows better; each grain of what, no matter how vacuum-processed, takes some water with it: "Every load you ship to Terra condemns your grandchildren to slow death. The miracle of photosynthesis, the plant-and-animal cycle, is a *closed* cycle. You have opened it—and your life-blood runs downhill to Terra."[16]

Most of *The Moon Is a Harsh Mistress* is a dramatized textbook on the theory and practice of revolution, from the organization of cells to the stage-managing of incidents: "Like a perfect dinner, a revolution has to be 'cooked' so that everything comes out even,"[17] O'Kelly points out early in the game. That remark, and others like it, reflect a basic elitism in Heinlein's philosophy. At heart, Heinlein was as thorough an elitist as H. G. Wells or Isaac Asimov, and the lunar revolution, with the sentient computer Mycroft in a key role, is just as manipulative as the Second Foundation. Yet, without that manipulation, disaster is a virtual certainty—the lunar farmers, en masse, may never realize the gravity of the ecological crisis until it is too late. The are not taking the long view. And, after the revolution succeeds, the libertarian ideals of de la Paz are forgotten: "They never adopt *any* of his ideas," laments O'Kelly. "Seems to be a keep instinct in human beings for making everything compulsory that isn't forbidden."[18]

Heinlein's stoicism is shown best in *Citizen of the Galaxy* (1957). Col. Richard Baslim of the Hegemonic Guard has consecrated his life to the struggle against slavery, sacrificing his own freedom to live as a beggar in Jubbulpore, capital city of the capital planet of a squalid autarchy called the Nine Worlds, in order to gather intelligence on the slave trade. One day, he buys a slave boy named Thorby, whom he raises as his own, teaching him languages, mathematics, galactography, and a host of other subjects. And then, something goes wrong: Baslim is found out, and his head ends up decorating a pole. But he has arranged for one of the Free Trader Ships to rescue Thorby and to deliver him to the Guard. Thorby's adoption by the *Sisu* is only the beginning of an odyssey that leads him to two startling revelations: that the slave trade survives in large measure through the covert assistance of the Hegemony's leading starship construction concern and that he is Thor Bradley Rudbek, the long missing heir to an interstellar conglomerate that controls that very firm. Already he has learned how persistent slavery is:

It starts up in every new land and it's terribly hard to root out. After a culture falls ill of it, it gets rooted in the economic system and laws, in men's habits and attitudes. You abolish it; you drive it underground—there it lurks, ready to spring up again . . . [19]

Now he must make the most difficult moral choice of his life. His heart's desire is to return to the Guard and to fight against slavery as Baslim did. Yet the Guard itself advises him that he can make a greater contribution to the struggle by asserting his authority over the family business empire. To do that, he must first fight a lengthy court battle to get control of that empire from a distant in-law who has run it for years under power of attorney. Then he must learn all the subtleties of running the business so that he can root out its slave trade connections without harming its legitimate operations and the innocent people who work for them. It will be the work of a lifetime; even as slavery is eradicated on one world, it will break out on another. The struggle against evil is like the labor of Sisyphus; yet Thorby, knowing that struggle can never end, refuses to shirk it: "A person *can't* run out on responsibility."[20] It's almost an existentialist attitude.

THE DEATH MACHINE

Death is in the nature of the universe, Barker. Death is only the operation of a mechanism. . . . Did you expect a *machine* to care what it acted upon? Death is like sunlight or a falling star; they don't care where they fall. Death cannot see the pennants on a lance or the wreath of glory in a dying man's hand. Flags and flowers are the inventions of life. When a man dies, he falls into enemy hands—an ignorant enemy, who doesn't merely spit on banners but who doesn't even know what banners are.[21]

Edward Hawks, Doctor of Science, is explaining to Al Barker, hero, what it is that has just killed him—and will kill him again and again until it can be charted and tamed. It is an artifact on the moon: nature and purpose (if any) unknown. It has been there for millions of years, and in all that time it has never bothered anyone. But when men attempt to explore it, they are killed horribly without even knowing how or why. Dead men tell no tales, but Hawks has a way around that; he uses a matter transmitter to create exact duplicates of volunteers here on earth, and on the moon. As long as the earth duplicate is kept in a state of sensory deprivation, he shares the consciousness of his double on the moon, who tries to make his way through the maze of the artifact. The lunar double invariably dies, but that's not Hawks' problem. His problem is that the earth double is invariably driven insane by the shock of experiencing "his" own death and can provide little if any useful information. What makes Barker different is that he has exactly the mindset Hawks needs: "a man who's attracted by what drives other men to madness."[22]

That is the situation in Algis Budrys' *Rogue Moon* (1960), but the theme is suggested by Budrys' original title, *The Death Machine*. That lunar artifact is a death machine itself, but it is also a metaphor for a greater one. For as Hawks tells Barker, what he has seen there is, "as clearly as anyone could ever see it, the undisguised face of the unknown universe."[23] Budrys (1931–) is the exemplar of a world view that does not have a commonly accepted name, but which can be called Darwinian existentialism. For Budrys and those who share his world view, the central fact of existence is the confrontation between caring life and an uncaring universe. Being and Nothingness, save that, in science fiction, the universe is not mere nothingness. It is a place of order, not chaos; of strict Law, but a Law made neither by men nor for them. To the extent that the Law allows, men can create an existence in which love and compassion, justice and mercy, have meaning. But these are the things of life; the universe remains ever indifferent to them. Out of a blind cosmic process, out of the coldly Darwinian natural selection of evolution, purpose may have come into being. But that purpose is only in life itself, never in the indifferent cosmos from which it sprang. The ultimate Law of the cosmos is entropy, the tendency towards maximum disorganization, and, as Hawks tells his woman friend Elizabeth Cummings, life is in eternal conflict with entropy:

The thing is, the universe is *dying!* The stars are burning their substance. The planets are moving more slowly on their axes. They're falling inward toward their suns. It's all running down. Some day, it'll stop. Only one thing in the entire universe grows fuller, and richer, and *forces* its way uphill. Intelligence— human lives—we're the only things that don't obey the universal law.[24]

The tragic struggle against entropy was already implicit in H. G. Wells' *The Time Machine* (1895), and Olaf Stapledon made it the stuff of cosmic tragedy in *Star Maker* (1937). The more immediate struggle with the unrelenting laws of the physical universe is the subject of a more immediate tragedy in Tom Godwin's "The Cold Equations" (1954), in which a stowaway aboard an interstellar ship on a vital emergency mission to bring serum to a plague-stricken colony must be jettisoned because there simply is not enough fuel to carry her as well as the pilot and cargo. The pilot is not a cruel man; if he could have saved her, he would have, even at the cost of his own life. She is the victim, not of man's inhumanity to man, but of "forces that killed with neither hatred nor malice."[25] Godwin's story is unsettling to many readers; in the Soviet Union, Aleksandr Kazantsev even attempted a rebuttal in *The Road to the Moon* (1960). In Kazantsev's story, heroic sacrifice by a pilot does save a stowaway, but the circumstances are different, of course, and Godwin's thesis remains unanswered.

Raymond Z. Gallun (1911–) seems to have been the first to adopt a consistent Darwinian existentialist world view and to distinguish it from the social Darwinism with which some might confuse it. Social Darwinism makes each species an enemy, or at least a potential enemy, to every other. But for Gallun, the cold equations of the universe are the enemy and all species share in a common struggle that makes them, at least potentially, all brothers. In "Old Faithful" (1934), an alien creature who makes a hazardous journey from Mars to Earth is greeted as a brother despite his inhuman appearance:

He has brains; he can feel pain like any human being. Besides, he has courage of the same kind that we all worship. Think of the pluck it took to make the first plunge across fifty million miles of cold, airless void! That's something to bow down to, isn't it?[26]

In "Godson of Almarlu" (1936), the same sense of brotherhood motivates the inhabitants of the ancient fifth planet, doomed by a neutron star that destroys their world, to save mankind from the same fate millions of years later. Jefferson Scanlon, a young inventor and entrepreneur, is their instrument, although he does not know it. Inspired he knows not how, he produces one revolutionary invention after another, from the first practical rocket motor to a process to produce power from coal right at the mine and transmit it over ionized beams instead of wires. In revolutionizing the world's economy, Scanlon becomes one of the most powerful and influential men on earth. Only in recurrent dreams does he have an inkling of the true source of his ideas, including what he regards as his crowning achievement: a colossal power installation that will tap the kinetic energy of the earth's rotation. His reputation sells the world on the project, but it turns into disaster, touching off tidal waves, earthquakes, and volcanic eruptions around the world. Only at the last moment is its true purpose revealed, from the knowledge planted in his brain in infancy by an alien device: to funnel as much air and water as possible to the moon, which, lacking a neutronium core, survives the passage of the neutron star. Although billions must perish, Scanlon and a few hundred thousand others who have escaped to the moon by rocket plane will have another chance:

Jeff looked at the fernlike lunar sprouts in the damp soil; he thought of food and of sleep and of work. Already the godson of Almarlu was turning over in his mind plans for the future. Adventure was at an end. Tomorrow toil would begin in earnest. Jeff was pleased . . .

And the long-dead people of another sphere might have been pleased also, had they seen the successful termination of the thing they had planned—the survival of the folk who were, in a sense, their children.[27]

Gallun was among the first to consider human values in the context of man's existential confrontation with the universe. In "The Restless Tide" (1951), his favorite among his own stories, a couple who helped pioneer Mars now lives in comfortable retirement in New York. But, just as they once had their fill of danger and hardship, so now they feel the frustration of too much comfort and security. After much soul-searching, they embark for Titan, taking rejuvenation treatments along the way to prepare them for the rigors of life on a world only partly terraformed. Even with an orbiting artificial sun, and eons-old ice newly melted into streams and lakes, it seems a dreary place to live, and Benjamin finds himself resorting to what seems a rationalization for their coming: "Life is movement, Brenda. It is restless and primitive. It is never crystalized perfection. The shifts and changes and surprises are what we are designed to enjoy. . . . It's the contrasts that count."[28] Yet the rationalization is true—for now. There is no sanction by the universe for either the values they have sought or for those they have left behind. Men yearn, by turns, for freedom and adventure, and for comfort and security, because that is their nature. Gallun ends by comparing Man to "a rough, sturdy plant, growing, thrusting; crude but magnificent, and caught between rot and fire."[29]

Rot and fire are the keynotes of several stories by Henry Kuttner (1914–58), who takes a Darwinian existentialist approach to ethical issues. In "Clash by Night" (1943), there has already been too much fire: earth itself has been destroyed in nuclear armageddon. Mankind still survives on Venus, in undersea Keeps, for the continents are savage jungles. War survives, too, in highly ritualized conflicts fought on behalf of rival Keeps by the Free Companies: bands of mercenaries bound by a strict code of honor. The Keeps themselves are never attacked, and should any warrior band break the taboo on atomic weapons, the others will turn on it and destroy it without mercy. Scott commands one unit in a typical war for economic advantage between the Montana and Virginia Keeps. But his loyalty to the Doones comes to seem a foolish one; the romantic ideals of the Free Companies are delusions: "Blind, stupid folly!"[30] He longs for the hedonistic comforts of the Keeps. In the end, however, he cannot abandon his company, for it helps serve an objectively necessary end: preserving the Keeps from the danger of war, until the Keeps themselves tire of war and make the mercenaries objectively unnecessary:

> The Doones meant nothing. Their ideal was a false one. Yet, because men were faithful to that ideal, civilization would rise again from the guarded Keeps. A civilization that would forget its doomed guardians, the waters of the seas of Venus, the Free Companions yelling their mad, futile battle cry as they drove on—as this ship was driving—into a night that would have no dawn.[31]

In *Fury* (1947), the season has changed: rot is now the objectively greatest threat to mankind. The Keeps have turned inward, refusing the challenge of conquering the land; in their decadent hedonism, they have surrendered to a cultural entropy that can lead only to extinction—"it wasn't the individual who paid. It was the race that was paying."[32] Most decadent of all are the immortals of the ruling class, one of whom, Blaze Harker, turns to decadent cruelty when his wife dies giving birth: he strikes out at his newborn son by having his endocrine glands altered so that the infant will grow into a short, squat, ugly creature looking nothing like a Harker and knowing nothing of his heritage. Sam Reed grows up embittered, not only by his ugliness but also by his obsession with the injustice of being (as he believes) a mere mortal in a society ruled by immortals. Motivated only by envy and rage, he turns to crime, at which he succeeds so well that the immortals themselves seek him out for a murder contract against Robin Hale, a veteran of the Doones whose crusade for colonization of the land is upsetting the decadent social equilibrium. Their mistake was that Reed almost instinctively sides with Hale and therefore with Hale's cause. The cunning and ruthlessness that once served Reed in the underworld now serve him in the struggle to defeat a savage environment and thus win the survival of mankind. Only, that is never his motivation; he never thinks of anything but his own survival and vengeance against the immortals. His crimes range from blackmail to murder; when his false promise of immortality for colonists is exposed, he sabotages the Keeps, forcing millions to abandon them or die. He has saved mankind, but now the oracular visionary called the Logician must put him to sleep, lest he endanger mankind:

Men like you are mighty rare, Sam. When they get to the right position, at the right time, they're the salvation of the race of man. But it's got to be the right time—a time of disaster. The drive never stops, in a man like you. . . . If you can't conquer an enemy, you'll conquer your friends. Up to now, the enemy was Venus, and you licked it. But what have you got to fight now?[33]

Is morality, then, irrelevant to the salvation of mankind? Not in "Two-Handed Engine" (1955). Here again, decadence is the threat, but it is moral decadence. In a luxuriously utopian world, where men depend on machines but never on one another, moral sensibilities have withered. Words like "sin" and "guilt" no longer evoke any response. There are no internalized controls, nor even any internalized goals. The birth rate is dropping, as emotional attachments dwindle, and the end is in sight. One man of clear vision sees the danger and sets a new program for the cybernetic machines that manage the affairs of the world: "Mankind must be made self-responsible again. You will make this your only goal until you achieve the end."[34] Gone are the days of free luxuries, but that is not enough. The machines create the Furies, tireless robots whose task is to haunt, and end, the lives of any and all who commit murder:

For the rest of his days, the man would hear those footsteps behind him. A moving jail with invisible bars that shut him off from the world. Never in life would he be alone again. And one day—he never knew when—the jailer would turn executioner.[35]

Yet the fear the Furies can evoke is only external; conscience has yet to be reborn. Danner has none; when Hartz promises him a life of luxury in return for murder, his only concern is how he can get away with it. Hartz wants to be Controller of the Calculators; only O'Reilly stands in his way. But he doesn't have to worry; under the iron law of the Furies, retribution falls only on him that slays, not on him that pays. All he has to do is convince Danner he can call off a Fury. Once the deed is done, Danner finds to his horror that he has been betrayed: his Fury appears, like fate itself and shadows him relentlessly. He forces his way into Hartz's office, gun in hand. Even as the Fury deflects his aim, Hartz shoots in self-defense. Self-defense, however, is no excuse—not to the machines. Hartz must do for himself what he would not do for Danner: the Fury is dismissed and is told to forget. But Hartz cannot forget; now it is he who feels a creeping horror: he is the supreme guardian of the machines, but he has corrupted them. "Mankind's survival still depended on the computers, and the computers could not be trusted."[36] As he leaves his office, he hears footsteps behind him, but there is no Fury—no *visible* Fury:

It was as if sin had come anew into the world, and the first man felt again the first inward guilt. So the computers had not failed, after all.

Hartz went slowly down the steps and out into the street, still hearing as he would always hear the relentless, incorruptible footsteps behind him that no longer rang like metal.[37]

Kuttner evidently assumes the same godless universe as Gallun and Budrys—a universe that Clifford D. Simak and other men of feeling, even Heinlein in his longing for a life beyond life, find unendurable. Lester del Rey (1915–) is not sure a universe *with* a god would be comforting. In one of the most memorably blasphemous sf stories of all time, "For I Am a Jealous People" (1954), earth is being invaded by an alien race. The Rev. Amos Strong, his own son just killed in the battle of the moon, tries to succor his flock with the familiar reassurances of the Old Testament: "Wait on the Lord: be of good courage, and he shall strengthen thine heart."[38] Strong is then faced with the shattering revelation that God himself has betrayed mankind and has entered into a new covenant with the invaders, who can call down miraculous calamities even as the Jews did of old to aid their cause. Yet mankind is not wholly defeated; in Denver, kamikaze pilots fly divinely sabotaged missiles to their targets: "It was as if God could control weather and machines, but not the will of determined men."[39] So it is that a minister finds a new creed to rally his people: " 'God has ended the ancient covenants and declared Himself an enemy of all mankind,' Amos said, and the chapel seemed to roll with his voice. 'I say to you: He has found a worthy opponent.' "[40]

If mankind can triumph over the enmity of God, the mere absence of God seems a trivial matter. If we are cast back on our own resources, in a godless universe, we can still find some meaning in existence. But what about a *lifeless* universe? In "The Years Draw Nigh" (1951), mankind seeks not mere conquest of the universe but *communion*. Pursuing the Wellsian dream, it has "come boiling out from Earth, bent for the stars."[41] Only on Mars, however, have traces of alien life been found, and the ancient Martians have been dust for ten million years. When the last starship returns from exploring the galaxy, with proof that the abandoned ruins on a distant world were only Martian ruins, an Earthman understands the fate that overtook their kind, and is now overtaking ours:

It must have been a hardy race, since it had dared to set up a colony across all those innumerable parsecs of space, without even the inspiration of other life.

Then, when that colony had failed, the race had returned to the loneliness of its own little world, where the stars looked down grimly, no longer promising anything.[42]

In "Recessional" (1952), del Rey offers a more optimistic variant of the same scenario. For generation upon generation, ships from earth have searched the galaxy, seeking new worlds for mankind. Never has the longed-for new Eden been found; yet in their wanderings and "spawnings," the men of earth have created a series of new shipboard cultures. Now one branch has come upon an ideal planet, "a world that might have been made for them."[43] Indeed it might, for the planet is lost earth itself. But rather than the advanced utopia they have dreamed of, the wanderers find a degenerate world of warring petty states, of chattel slavery, and of other ancient evils reborn. Lissa, one of the fleet captains, calls for the outright conquest of earth and an end to their long quest. Another captain, Bran, is more compassionate: "The future of man belongs to the universe, not to mythical Cruise-endings."[44] His son Fane contrives to make it appear that the primitive earthlings have repulsed an attack by Lissa's ship, so that their morale is restored in face of a challenge that will "cure their little fights, and get them moving toward some real progress."[45] Fane elects to remain behind and aid that progress:

It was, after all, only another world, another place for a branching. Someday a grandson or a great-grandson of his would be on another great ship, headed outwards to the unlimited frontiers of space. Earth could produce one more spawning, at least. He and Bran would see to that.[46]

Like Kuttner, del Rey holds to a Darwinian existentialist version of situational ethics, and the situation is grim indeed in *The Eleventh Commandment* (1962). In a post-holocaust America, a schismatic Catholic Church has fostered a nightmare of overpopulation through its fanatical ban on birth control. People live in a state of constant hunger, squalor, and disease, made even worse by the tragic incidence of mutations caused by lingering radiation. When Boyd Jensen arrives from Mars to pursue research in biology (only later does he learn he has been exiled because of the tainted genes of his earth ancestors), what astounds him most is the universal acceptance of the Eleventh Commandment: church festivals turn into orgies; a seeming appeal for black market birth-control pills is actually an appeal for fertility pills. It is as if earthmen have an intuition denied to Jensen. After a series of arrests for breaking church law, he learns the truth from the Archbishop of New York himself: mankind has created such a hell of genetic pollution that the Eleventh Commandment is the only hope for the ultimate survival of the species:

During many more generations, the weaknesses and faults already present are going to spread and become more and more dangerous to us. Only a maximum population with a maximum variety of types can assure us of finding enough who are viable to carry on the race. . . . And if there are horrors now, we must bear them . . . [47]

In Budrys' sf, too, the social or ecological environment wrought by mankind can be as remorseless as the iron law of the cosmos. "Between the Dark and the Daylight" (1958) is perhaps the most chilling example; it is as close as pure science fiction gets to pure horror. Trapped on a world so hellish that no man could survive unprotected on it for more than a few minutes, Brendan's folk have labored for ten generations to breed and bioengineer a race that can survive there. For ten generations, they have lived under a concrete dome twenty feet thick, their daily lives punctuated by the constant *chip, chip, chip* of the world's native life trying to break in. Now at last, the final generation is ready to leave the dome; but only Brendan—like the others of his generation, he is a monstrous creature with massive bones and muscles and canine teeth—knows what that will mean. When his son Donel and the others are sent forth, the attack from outside ceases—for a while. But in defeating the native life, they realize Brendan and his generation do not belong: "There was a new sound echoing through the dome. 'Now they don't need us to let them out, anymore.' There was a quick, sharp, deep hammering from outside—mechanical, purposeful, tireless. 'That . . . that may be Donel now.' "[48]

A libertarian revolution has swept away the ancient tyrannies of Europe—but not the ancient human passions—in Budrys' "The Burning World" (1957). A new source of power has freed men from centralized government and even from the need for a centralized economy. But Josef Kimmensen, the patriarch of the revolution, is losing the younger generation, even his own daughter, to the firebrand Anse Messerschmidt, who campaigns for a return to tighter social organization to meet an alleged threat of invasion. Ironically, it turns out that Messerschmidt is right, but he can take little comfort in having had to unleash the ultimate weapon of the Freemen's League against friend as well as foe. Budrys' theme, however, is basically Gallun's: the restless tide of human existence:

That seemed to be the way of it. And Messerschmidt would someday die, and other revolutions would come, as surely as the Earth turned on its axis and drifted around the sun. But no Messerschmidt—and no Kimmensen—ever quite shook free of the past, and no revolution could help but borrow from the one before. [49]

In *Rogue Moon*, the challenge of the lunar artifact is a challenge to Hawks' conscience as well as his ingenuity. It is *he* who has sent volunteers to the moon again and again, knowing they will be driven to madness. If the daredevil Barker is a willing victim, he is still a victim, in ways he cannot even grasp. In their relationship, one can see two contrasting—yet each valid, in its own way—reactions to the same blindly indifferent cosmos. Indifferent, *not* malevolent, Hawks explains to Barker; the artifact may be the alien equivalent of a discarded tomato can in the path of a beetle. Of course, says Barker, a smart beetle can just walk around the can, but no more than Hawks is he willing to ignore it: it is a chance to validate himself as a hero—in his own eyes and in those of others. For Hawks, however, it is a test of human intelligence in conquering the unknown. He knows that he lacks the courage to face the kind of death Barker faces repeatedly, and yet only he can grasp the truth of that experience: that each death is a *real* one, however much it seems to Barker only a nightmare from which he has awakened safe and sound. Hawks knows, therefore, that he is a murderer. In using Barker and others to help conquer the unknown universe, he is as pitiless as that universe: "I haven't played fair with any of you. I've never once shown any of you mercy, except now and then by coincidence."[50] Yet he is not an unfeeling monster, as his tender relationship with Cummings shows; he even feels a need to pay his dues.

For the final journey through the artifact, its deadly traps charted at last, Hawks has himself scanned, destroyed, and duplicated to accompany Barker. As they have interpreted its challenge differently, so they even see it differently, although its laws are the same for all. But Hawks must explain afterward, when they have lost telepathic contact with their earth doubles, why they cannot return: the doubles have a right to "their" lives, and, in any case, it is almost impossible to transmit a human pattern *to* earth as opposed to *from* it. Hawks M wanders off to die; Barker M chooses a life of exile on the moon. Back on earth, Barker L, knowing nothing of all this, still cannot understand why Hawks L insists he is *not* Hawks; but Hawks L knows, as he opens a message from the Hawks he knows is dead and gone, yet who could love in the face of death: "Remember me to her."[51]

5

The Literary Reformation

IT CAME FROM INNER SPACE

"I've always thought of the whole of life as a kind of disaster area,"[1] remarks Charles Ransom, protagonist of *The Burning World* (1964), one of the highly stylized disaster novels that put J. G. Ballard on the literary map. Ballard (1930–) became one of the heroes of the New Wave in science fiction, or one of the New Waves, for critics still disagree about whether there was one New Wave, or two, or many. At the time, roughly from 1964 to 1971, most of the alleged adherents of the New Wave, or Waves, denied its (or their) existence, even while they endorsed most of each other's works, denounced the same alleged reactionaries and their works, and otherwise behaved like partisans in a common cause.

Colin Greenland's *The Entropy Exhibition: Michael Moorcock and the British 'New Wave' in Science Fiction* (1983) offers a sympathetic view, but all the same a revealing one, of the British New Wave that was the center of much, if not most, of the controversy. Entropy—the tendency toward universal disorganization—is what academic critics might call the "controlling metaphor" of the New Wave; it is what sets New Wave sf apart from traditional science fiction. In traditional sf, the tendency of life in general and the mission of intelligent life in particular is to either bring order and even purpose into existence, or, in sf influenced by the Christian or Rousselian world views, to realize the *natural* order and purpose of the universe and to live in accordance with it.

Even traditional anti-Wellsians have recognized the importance of order in reality and in literature. Brian W. Aldiss, who felt a natural sympathy for the New Wave's rejection of evolutionary optimism, still felt it had gone too far. In a letter to Judith Merril, chief spokesman for the movement in the United States, he explained why: "I'm strongly against the abolition of structure in fiction, or at least in long fiction. . . . I'm for structure in fiction because I believe fiction must mirror and/or shape reality and because I believe the external world has a structure."[2] Aldiss could thus mimic the form of the French anti-novel in *Report on Probability A* (1967), yet go on to write more structured sf in defiance of the literary doctrine of the anti-novel, which holds that traditional plot, characterization, and insight are absurd impossibilities. In *The Entropy Exhibition*, Greenland contrasts Aldiss' *Greybeard* (1964), a disaster novel in which the focus is "on the causes of the disruption, its effects, and the parties responsible,"[3] with M. John Harrison's "The Ash Circus" (1969), in which there is no real explanation of the scenes of disaster, nor even any connection between them: "This is merely 'the process of dislocation,' the unnamed catastrophe that features in so much New Wave fiction."[4]

"The Ash Circus" is a Jerry Cornelius story, part of a series begun by Moorcock himself, who farmed out the character to other writers of the *New Worlds* circle. Moorcock (1939–), who assumed the editorship of the magazine in 1964, promising "a new kind of sf which is unconventional in every sense,"[5] is in some ways uncharacteristic of his own movement. His fiction is prolific, often commercial. There may be more readers who know him for his sword-and-sorcery novels like *Stormbringer* (1965) than for his sf. Some of his sf novels, notably *The Ice Schooner* (1969), are surprisingly traditional in form and content. Still, none could doubt his commitment to the New Wave in other works, such as *The Black Corridor* (1969), which introduces what Greenland characterizes as a "new fictional stock type . . . the Mad Astronaut."[6] In Moorcock's case, it is Ryan, who somehow commandeers a starship to carry himself and his immediate family and friends away from an earth swept by the insanity of xenophobia, but who finds he is only carrying mankind's madness with him. As the heroic astronaut was an archetype of traditional sf, so did his antithesis become an archetype of the New Wave; the New Wave itself was the antithesis of traditional sf.

"I think science fiction should turn its back on space,"[7] declared Ballard in 1962, anticipating one of the fundamentals of the New Wave two years before the movement had emerged. Readers were bored with interstellar travel, alien worlds, and all the familiar themes of sf, he argued: "The only truly alien planet is Earth."[8] And so came the shift, from aliens to alienation. As Greenland put it, the radicals of the New Wave "wrote of estrangement not from parents, political regimes, or nations, but from reality itself."[9] While they shared the antipathy of Aldiss and others toward the Wellsian celebration of technological progress ("they seemed to fear the technology that is shaping that future"[10]), New Wave sf writers clearly felt a far deeper estrangement. Thomas M. Disch, most gifted of the American sf writers associated with the British New Wave, was perhaps the most explicit in *The Genocides* (1965). Disch creates a grimly pessimistic scenario of a doomed humanity under the onslaught of unseen alien invaders who have transformed the very ecology of earth into something menacing and incomprehensible. As the last pitiful survivors make their way through the tangle of alien vegetation, we read:

Just as a worm passing through an apple may suppose that the apple, its substance and quality, consists merely of those few elements which have passed through his own meager body, while in fact his whole being is enveloped in the fruit and his passage has scarcely dimished it, so Buddy and Maryann and their child, Blossom and Orville, emerging from the earth after a long passage through the labyrinthine windings of their own, purely human evils, were aware of the all-pervading presence of the larger evil that lies without, which we call reality. There is evil everywhere, but we can only see what is in front of our noses, only remember what has passed through our bellies.[11]

Disch (1940–) obviously is not happy with the world; neither are a number of the more traditional sf writers. The difference between them, though, is that it is impossible to imagine a world in which Disch *would* be happy. He cannot imagine one himself in *The New Improved Sun* (1975), billed as an anthology of utopian sf. Disch's own contribution to his anthology, "Pyramids for Minnesota" (1974), is facetious; most of the others range from facetious to sardonic. Disch's own sardonicism comes out in "Thesis on Social Forms and Social Controls in the U.S.A." (1964). Each "freeman" of an "atopic" state is subjected to slavery every fifth year to keep the economy going, but he never remembers about it afterward. In a similar manner, other Orwellian concepts, such as War is Peace, and Ignorance is Strength, are put into practice. Like that of Jonathan Swift, the sardonicism of Disch is acidly misanthropic, and, of course, he shares the intelligentsia's traditional disdain for the middle class.

"Hatred of the bourgeois is the beginning of wisdom,"[12] declared Gustave Flaubert. By that standard, Disch is wise indeed. Yet the context has changed: all Flaubert had to contend with was philistinism; whereas today, bourgeois values can be seen as a threat to the survival of earth itself. Disch makes the point forcefully in his introduction to *The Ruins of Earth* (1971), an anthology of disaster fiction, recalling a surburban childhood in an America dedicated to "an almost fanatic faith in the growth of the GNP," in "larger and lovelier supermarkets," and in "wider highways . . . with longer cars."[13] All that has led instead to a nightmare of environmental and social disaster, and it can only get worse as long as we cling to our bourgeois technocratic materialism. Bourgeois values are savaged in stories like "Casablanca" (1968), in which the outbreak of World War III strands a boorish American tourist couple in Morocco. They cannot seem to understand why a hotel manager wants them to pay their bill immediately, why nobody will take their travelers' checks, or why there are anti-American riots. To the very end, the irate husband curses the dirty Reds, abuses the native beggars, and generally throws his weight around as if it still *meant* something to be a U.S. citizen. In "Descending" (1964), a typical victim of consumer society, unemployed and down to the end of his cash and credit, finds himself trapped on a department store escalator that has no exit and descends endlessly into the abyss, like the consumer treadmill itself.

Had Disch been born a generation earlier, he might well have become a Marxist, but belief in anything comes harder to modern intellectuals, whether from experience of the world, from immersion in the grim despair of contemporary literature and philosophy, or from both. So in "Moondust, the Smell of Hay, and Dialectical Materialism" (1967), Disch rips away the illusions of a Soviet astronaut dying a lonely death on the moon (the Soviet Union never publicizes its failures). Mikhail Karkhov tries to believe that he is dying for Science, for Love, finally for the State, for the glorious future of Communism; however, "in the face of death, nothing is glorious, nothing is proud, nothing is of worth but a little more life, a few seconds, another breath."[14] Karkhov cannot make an identification with mankind, like Theodore Sturgeon's astronaut in "The Man Who Lost the Sea" (1959); "there is never a good reason for dying."[15] Nor is there a reason for living; only in a few works, such as *On Wings of Song* (1979), does Disch seem to offer any vision of an alternative to the alienation of our times. Here it is a fanciful one: escape from the repression of a puritanical near-future society through psychic "flight" inspired by music. But it is a short escape for Daniel Weinreb, who is shot dead by his old social studies teacher when he finally achieves Flight.

Disch's most highly regarded sf novels are still *Camp Concentration* (1967) and *334* (1972). *Camp Concentration* is typical in its contempt for bourgeois society: President (Robert) McNamara has led the United States into another Vietnam War (or maybe the *same* Vietnam War), and the military-industrial complex is using imprisoned dissidents as guinea pigs for Nazi-like medical experimentation. Sheeplike middle-class Americans, who know nothing of what is going on deep underground in Camp Archimedes, seem to support the war wholeheartedly; if they *did* know what was being done to poet Louis Sacchetti and the rest, they probably would not care. What is atypical of the novel is a "happy" ending—one which is almost dictated by the circumstances. The object of Camp Archimedes is to create genius: prisoners of ordinary intelligence are injected with a mutated variety of syphilis that quickly works its way to the brain; the victims are doomed to painful death, of course, but before they die, they can serve the state with their enhanced intelligence. At first, the subterranean prison seems to be another metaphor for a malevolent universe, which is how Mordecai Washington, a long-forgotten classmate of Sacchetti and the instigator of Sacchetti's transfer to the camp from a federal prison for conscientious objectors, puts it: " 'It isn't just Germany,' he said. 'And it isn't just Camp Archimedes. It's the whole universe. The whole god-damned universe is a fucking concentrtion camp.' "[16]

Washington and the other victims already seem to be succumbing to the insanity of advanced syphilis, for they have ordered arcane books on alchemy, and they have built a Rube Goldberg device that they insist can confer eternal life. Humphrey Haast, the camp commandant, is naturally eager to volunteer for *that*—only the demonstration, carried out amid suitably arcane chants and rituals, seems a spectacular failure. Shortly afterward, Sacchetti learns that he too has been injected with the deadly syphilis. We follow him through fits of near madness and despair, even as "Auschwitz," a play he has written in prison, is freely published for the edification of a nation using tactical nuclear weapons against poor Southeast Asians. The first batch of guinea pigs has died; another arrives: volunteers from the Gates of Hell, which are, of course, located at M.I.T. Skilliman, their leader and mentor, wants to develop a "geologic bomb" to blow up the world. One of the students, Schipansky, reveals a redeeming love for music, and he befriends Sacchetti; but he is only one man in a loathsome society. Just when all seems blackest, however, Disch pulls a rabbit out a hat: that Rube Goldberg setup was actually a mind-transfer device and the arcane ritual a subterfuge. "Haast" is now Washington, and most of the other original guinea pigs now inhabit the bodies of guards. Rather than give away the game, they have continued to play the roles of their former tormentors.

Of course, there's still a plague of mutated syphilis in the outside world, spread by a straightlaced biddy of a psychiatrist who managed to get raped or seduced and subsequently left the camp. Even in their new, politically well-connected bodies, Washington and the rest have their work cut out for them putting the world to rights. Sacchetti, meanwhile, is not at ease in the new, much better, flesh he has inherited, with Washington's miracle of rare device, from one of the guards. Still

he feels an existential sense of vastation; his mind is "destitute and bare
. . . a force without an object" in a meaningless cosmos: "I exist without
instincts, almost without images, and I no longer have an aim. I resemble
nothing. The poison has not had two effects—genius and death—but
one. Call it by which name you will".[17]

It would take a miracle to save the world, Disch seems to suggest,
but even a miracle cannot save the individual. Miracles are hard to come
by in the real world, in any case (Washington's mind-transfer device is
far out even for many sf writers), and none comes by New York in 334,
which may be the most depressing vision of the urban future that exists
in science fiction. Its pessimism goes beyond the bleak projection of
social breakdown—James Tiptree, Jr., once wrote a story called "All the
Kinds of Yes" (1972); 334 could be characterized as All the Kinds of No.

The social breakdown can be seen in the federal bureaucracy MOD-
ICUM and its decaying housing projects like the one at 334 East 11th
Street, New York, where much of the action takes place: "one of twenty
units, none identical and all alike, built in the pre-Squeeze affluent '80's
under the first federal MODICUM program."[18] By 2021 it is the home
of 3,000 (the optimum was 2,250) people, not counting the temps. The
elevator does not work, of course, and the paramedics will not climb
the stairs to rescue anyone in an emergency. When Shirley Ann (Shrimp)
Hanson, an otherwise apathetic resident, starts a petition to get the
elevator fixed, she is praised for her "*wonderful* sense of responsibility"[19]
by a "toadstool" at the MODICUM office; however, the only result is
that her mother, Mrs. Nora Hanson, is evicted on a technicality. Thrown
out on the street, she sets fire to the furniture in a futile protest of her
own. Sent to Bellevue, Mrs. Hanson begs for euthanasia to end her
wretched existence. Shrimp, meanwhile, has been going through both
medical and psychiatric complications of repeated surrogate mother-
hood; she has been in and out of the hospital and the asylum. Her sister
Lottie tries prostitution for a while, which gives Disch a chance to indulge
in a small but telling bit of invective: her worst johns are members of
what her pimp calls "our technologically *ee*—leete clientele,"[20] engineers
and programmers who get their jollies by pissing on her.

At a slightly higher stratum, MODICUM functionaries and others of
the managerial class indulge in drug-induced interactive fantasy lives,
playing the roles of Roman nobles and the like. Disch uses the occasion
to meditate on the parallels between the later Roman Empire and our
own time, with references to Oswald Spengler, the *Meditations* of Marcus
Aurelius, and a fifth-century account by the priest Salvian of how free
citizens of Rome suffered themselves to become serfs in face of the
insecurities of poverty brought about by the ruinous taxes imposed by
a corrupt regime to support an army of homemade vandals. To the social
and historical sources of evil, Disch adds the Calvinistic doctrine of total

depravity. Ab Holt, a hospital orderly who sells corpses to necrophiliacs, doesn't feel any qualms until the night he sells the wrong body: the deceased had an insurance policy for cryogenic freezing in hopes of later revival. For good measure, Holt is always talking about "science," using his supposed expertise to intimidate an accomplice: "Science battered everyone into submission if it was given its way."[21] He is also brutal in sex; anger is his only aphrodisiac. Other denizens and victims of *334* include the teenagers who dream of committing a justified murder to give meaning to their lives, like Raskalnikov in Fyodor Dostoyevsky's *Crime and Punishment;* and Birdie Ludd, who cannot score high enough on a standardized test or in a creative essay to qualify for fatherhood rights, and whose last resort is to join the Marines and take his chances in the war in Burma. Milly, Birdie's sweetheart, marries Boz Hanson, widow Nora's son by a posthumous artifical insemination with her husband's sperm; Boz shares in nursing his and Milly's child, thanks to breast implants. Toward the end, Lottie Hanson voices what may be a hope, but (given what seems to be the total pervasiveness of evil) may instead be a lament: "And anyhow the world *doesn't* end. Even though it may try to, even though you wish to hell it would—it can't."[22]

Compared to *334*, a lot of New Wave sf seems almost routine in both its pessimism and its reverse clichés. In "The Poets of Milgrove, Iowa" (1966), for example, John T. Sladek takes on the space program by having a disillusioned astronaut enlighten the folks back home: "All the pigshit you hear about astronauts is so much fucking—uh—shit. What the fuck, a guy goes up inside this little metal room, see, it don't mean a fuck of a lot."[23] Barry N. Malzberg (1939–) has practically made a career of insane astronauts in works like *Universe Day* (1971, as K. M. O'Donnell), *Beyond Apollo* (1972), and *The Falling Astronauts* (1975). In *Beyond Apollo*, Harry M. Evans has returned from a failed expedition to Venus, during which the captain disappeared. Evans is so far around the bend he cannot even remember whether the captain's name was Joe Jackson or Jack Josephson. But we do learn a lot about his repressed homosexual tendencies, disassociation reactions, and so on. No doubt he killed the captain himself, as he tells psychiatrists in one of several contradictory stories. Whatever happened, it was part of a random, purposeless process: "events control our lives, although we have no understanding of them nor do they have any motivation."[24] Malzberg merits admiration for, if nothing else, his sheer persistence in keeping one of the major New Wave themes alive long after everyone else had lost interest in it.

It is J. G. Ballard who remains the archetypical figure of the British New Wave, and Ballard is a true original. One can imagine other writers being trained to write like Malzberg, or even Disch—but only Ballard could have written *The Burning World* or "The Terminal Beach" (1964). There are obvious influences in his work, from Joseph Conrad to the

surrealists, but the foundations of his sf are autobiographical, as we
have learned in *Empire of the Sun* (1984), the novel of the part of his
childhood spent in a Japanese internment camp in China, which was
brought vividly to the screen by Steven Spielberg (1987). For Ballard,
World War II was a traumatically personal education in the Decline of
the West. As an eleven-year-old in the international settlement in Shanghai at the end of 1941, he belonged to a privileged class, who seemed
to be the lords of the earth; yet their lordship was a surreal fantasy swept
away overnight by Japanese forces. Young and impressionable, Ballard
came to identify with the Japanese, to find a paradoxical sense of comfort
and security in the disaster that had overwhelmed him. Toward the end
of the war, he even felt a certain resentment against the Americans,
whose air raids disrupted supplies of food and other necessaries to the
camp: "sometimes he wished that the Americans would return to Ha-
waii. . . . Then Lunghua Camp would once again be the happy place that
he had known in 1943."[25]

Today we call that feeling the Stockholm syndrome, after a famous
incident in which hostages came to identify with the terrorists who held
them—even against their rescuers. In Ballard's science fiction, we see a
cosmic Stockholm syndrome, in which his protagonists embrace, even
find spiritual fulfillment in, the incomprehensible disasters that over-
whelm Western civilization. *New Worlds* critic James Cawthorn dubbed
Ballard's new archetype the Dissolving Hero: "Faced with the breakup
of the Universe, he does not fight, but instead seeks, literally, to be
absorbed."[26] Even the concrete images of his childhood internment, such
as the clouds of dust raised by captured Chinese who were forced to
build the Lunghua airfield, find their way into his sf. But more important
is Ballard's attitude of calm acceptance and resignation in face of what
may well be the end of the world. Even in his most conventional novel,
The Wind from Nowhere (1961), he identifies with the *wind*, against a villain
who will not let go of his hubris: in this case, Hardoon, a business
magnate who puts up a huge pyramid-shaped redoubt in which he
fondly believes that he and his followers can safely ride out the cataclysmic storm:

Only I, in the face of the greatest holocaust ever to strike the earth, have had
the moral courage to attempt to outstare nature. That is my sole reason for
building this tower. Here on the surface of the globe I meet nature on her own
terms, in the arena of her choice. If I fail, Man has no right to assert his innate
superiority over the unreason of the natural world.[27]

Indeed Man has no right, for Hardoon has not reckoned on nemesis,
or at least he has not reckoned on what the wind will do to the gravel
substrate on which the Hardoon Tower is set. Having disposed of Har-

doon, however, the Wind from Nowhere begins to die down as inexplicably as it arose—a scenario of last minute reprieve for mankind that recurs in *The Burning World*.

In *The Drowned World* (1962), Ballard abandoned the spectacle and the too obvious moralizing of neo-gothic sf for a form distinctly his own. What the admirers of the New Wave were to call the exploration of *inner* space begins here in the psychology of Robert Kerans, whose withdrawal from civilization, he feels certain, is "symptomatic not of a dormant schizophrenia, but of a careful preparation for a radically new environment, with its own internal landscape and logic, where old categories of thought would merely be an encumbrance."[28] Once again, the origin of the disaster—"A series of violent and prolonged solar storms lasting several years caused by a sudden instability of the Sun had enlarged the Van Allen belts and diminished the Earth's gravitational hold upon the outer layers of the ionosphere"[29]—is unconvincing, and irrelevant. The rising temperatures, the flooding of lowlands by waters from the melting polar ice, and the wave of mutations that brings back the flora and fauna of the Carboniferous Age are seen as projections of the "inner landscapes" of the human psyche as much as external realities. "Innate releasing mechanisms" of mankind's primordial ancestors are now triggered by the changed environment, and Kerans senses the effect:

Beating within him like his own pulse, Kerans felt the powerful mesmeric pull of the baying reptiles, and stepped out into the lake, whose waters now seemed an extension of his own bloodstream. As the dull pounding rose, he felt the barriers which divided his own cells from the surrounding medium dissolving.[30]

Kerans' idyll in a drowned London, where he is part of a research team, is interrupted by the arrival of Strangman, a soldier of fortune with a herd of trained alligators who is fighting back against the jungle. Unlike Hardoon, he is not interested in restoring human pride so much as in simple looting. To that end, he dams off and drains a city square, where Kerans has previously found a wonderland in a submerged planetarium. To Kerans, it is a sacrilege. The marine life which had awed him has become a mass of rotting organic matter: "The once translucent threshold of the womb had vanished, its place taken by the gateway to a sewer."[31] In the end, choosing to abandon civilization and his comrades, he embarks on a quixotic and almost certainly suicidal journey to the South and blows up Strangman's dam as a parting gesture of rejection. There Ballard leaves him, "a second Adam searching for the forgotten paradises of the reborn Sun."[32]

One might at first mistake *The Burning World* for an environmental disaster novel, for the cause of the worldwide drought is the blockage of evaporation by "an thin but resilient mono-molecular film formed from a complex of saturated long-chain polymers, generated within the sea from the vast quantities of industrial wastes discharged into the ocean basins during the previous fifty years."[33] Ballard appears to be concerned more with the disaster as an expression of the psyche of his protagonist. As Charles Ransom watches the water dwindle in the river near Mount Royal, he is "certain that the absence of this great universal moderator, which cast [sic] its bridges between all animate and inanimate objects alike, would prove of crucial importance. Each [individual] would soon literally be an island in an archipelago of time."[34] While most residents are leaving for the coast, where there is a hope of surviving on water distilled from brine and a crazed minister is trying to rally his tiny flock in defiance of the drought, Ransom remains curiously detached. At first he is unwilling to leave with the others, then (with hardly any thought) he joins Catherine Austen, a woman for whom his feelings are ambiguous, in a trek seaward through a landscape of stranded yachts, abandoned cars, and white dunes.

Reinforced by a few other stragglers, they reach the coast, where a grimly social Darwinian struggle for survival, typical of traditional disaster sf, is under way. At first, the military is keeping order of sorts; after the arrival of Ransom and his companions, Ballard cuts to five years later, when all pretense of social order has broken down. Rival gangs fight over pools of water channeled with increasing difficulty through the widening salt barrier along the shore; a few fish and a lot of seaweed constitute the standard diet. For Ransom, the beach is "a zone without time, suspended in an endless interval as flaccid and enduring as the wet dunes themselves."[35] With the sighting of one of the lions released five years earlier from the Mount Royal zoo comes a renewed hope that water may exist inland, and Ransom and his party set out at once across a landscape even more dessicated than before. Sure enough, there *is* water, but it is in a pool carefully hoarded by a madman, one of whose retainers drains it in a fit of pique, and nothing is left but a vain hope that there may be other sources farther north. Ransom, seemingly indifferent to his fate, wanders off across a dry lake bed. He is surprised at a sudden darkening of the sky but fails to register its significance: "It was some time later that he failed to notice it had started to rain."[36]

The Crystal World (1966) is, in effect, the concluding volume of a trilogy that begins with *The Drowned World*; as such, it brings Ballard's philosophy of embracing disaster to its logical conclusion. This time, a progressive crystalization of life is the disaster threatening mankind; only, to Ballard, it is not really a disaster at all, but an escape from the vicissitudes of life and the curse of entropy. Edward Sanders is a doctor at a leprosarium, but as his new acquaintance Ventress tells him, "outside your colony there is merely another larger one."[37] Life itself is only a terminal disease; its cure is heralded by a dimming of the sunlight over

Port Matarre in Cameroon, the appearance of strange jewels in the marketplace, and a military blockade of the road inland to Mont Royal, where his former (as usual, ambiguous) lover has been living with her husband, Max Clair. Whatever is happening upriver, moreover, seems to be part of a universal process. Not only are there other sites in Florida and the Soviet Union, but planets and satellites are giving off strange light, and astronomers "have seen distant galaxies efflorescing."[38] Sanders, of course, manages to evade the blockade and enter the crystallized forest, where he is enraptured by "the crystalline trees hanging like icons in those luminous caverns, the jeweled casements of the leaves overhead, fused into a lattice of prisms, through which the sun shone in a thousand rainbows . . ."[39]

Here, the very line between life and death becomes blurred; here, the semi-living jewels exist in eternal stasis. But that is precisely what attracts Sanders: "I know that all motion leads inevitably to death, and that time is its servant."[40] Ventress, too, welcomes the change, the promise of immunity from time: "You and I will be like them soon, Sanders, and the rest of the world. Neither living nor dead!"[41] There is a lot of frantic action, almost as random as Brownian motion, involving a rivalry between Ventress and Thorenson over a dying woman, and some inconclusive encounters with Max and Suzanne Clair. There is an attempted rescue of a soldier who, when freed from his crystalline armor, cries out in pain, "Take me back!"[42] Sanders, nevertheless, becomes an apostate for a time, fleeing the forest and returning to Port Matarre. In the end, he is determined to go back to the "immense reward to be found in that frozen forest," where "the transfiguration of all living and inanimate forms occurs before our eyes, the gift of immortality a direct consequence of the surrender by each of us of our own physical and temporal identities."[43]

The Crystal World is a reversal on the traditional sf horror tale, such as Jack Finney's *The Body Snatchers* (1954), filmed as *Invasion of the Body Snatchers* (1956), in which loss of identity is the worst fate imaginable. For Ballard, it is rather the human condition—especially in these latter days of threatened nuclear or other apocalypse—that is truly unendurable. In his early short stories, he touches on a number of familiar sf nightmares, such as overpopulation in "Billenium" (1961), where the streets are filled shoulder to shoulder with pedestrians and allotments of living space are being reduced to three square meters per person, and overconsumption in "The Subliminal Man" (1963), where the economy has become dependent on endless sales of look-alike products and huge billboards are erected with subliminal messages compelling people to trade in their cars every month, buy television sets for every room, and so on. But with "The Terminal Beach," Ballard began to elaborate on a far more personal and idiosyncratic vision of human evil. Traven, apparently obsessed with nuclear guilt, maroons himself on Eniwetok, where he undergoes a series of fragmentary, surrealistic, and undoubtedly largely hallucinatory experiences. At one point, the prototype for what was to become Ballard's characteristically cryptic "explanation" appears:

> Traven: In Parenthesis
> Elements in a quantal world:
>   The terminal beach.
>   The terminal bunker.
>   The blocks.
>   The landscape is coded.
>   Entry points into the future = levels in a spinal landscape = zones of significant time.[44]

"The Terminal Beach" itself proved the prototype for a collection of condensed novels, The Atrocity Exhibition (1970). Here, Ballard's bent for cryptic allusions is combined with a more conventional psychologizing of contemporary man—especially the bourgeoisie and its cultural and political idols. Thus, a sketch called "Why I Want to Fuck Ronald Reagan" (1968) concludes: "The profound anality of the Presidential contender may be expected to dominate the United States in the coming years."[45] In "Love and Napalm: Export U.S.A." (1968), the argument that the motivation for the Vietnam War was perverted sexuality is conveyed through "reportage:"

Sexual stimulation by newsreel atrocity films. Studies were conducted to determine the effect of long-term exposure to TV newsreel films depicting the torture of Viet Cong: (a) male combatants, (b) woman auxiliaries, (c) children, (d) wounded. In all cases, a marked increase in the intensity of sexual activity was reported, with particular emphasis on perverse oral and anogenital modes.[46]

Avatars of Traven (Travers, Travis, Talbert, and so on) recur in most of the sketches, which are filled with images of sex, death, and violence—the most obsessive are Hiroshima, John F. Kennedy, and Marilyn Monroe. There is nothing that even resembles a story line, although The Atrocity Exhibition was published, and reviewed, as a "novel."[47] Hints of autobiography appear; as Travers, Ballard's viewpoint character recalls the Lunghwa [sic] internment camp. There are frequent imaginary "studies," assemblages of objects and images with cryptic connections, and cinema-verité vignettes of characters. The last sketch, "The Assassination of John Fitzgerald Kennedy Considered as a Downhill Motor Race" (1966), suggests Ballard's literary intentions, for it is a deliberate homage to "The Crucifixion Considered as an Uphill Bicycle Race" (1902), by Alfred Jarry (1873–1907), father of the theater and literature of the absurd.

When the British New Wave rejected the literary conventions and the Wellsian world view of traditional sf, it found itself in search of a new set of literary forerunners. Jarry was one; another, more immediate, was William S. Burroughs (1914–), whose *Nova Express* (1964) incorporates sf terminology, if not exactly sf ideas, into its vision of a world caught up in conspiratorial madness. Burroughs was praised by Ballard as the "True genius and first mythographer of the mid–20th century,"[48] and he is reckoned to have been an influence of Moorcock, Sladek, and others by critic David Pringle.[49] Peter Nicholls considers Burroughs and Ballard exemplars of a school of absurdist sf that crosses traditional genre boundaries to embrace Kurt Vonnegut, Jr., and Philip K. Dick, on one hand, and Jorge Luis Borges and John Barth, on the other.[50] One can find other precursors to Nicholls' school; perhaps the most obvious was Ward Moore (1903–78), whose *Greener Than You Think* (1947) is disaster of the absurd: science unleashes a mutant grass, which spreads inexorably around the world while scientists make fumbling and futile efforts to control it and the rest of mankind succumbs to panic and confusion. Vonnegut (1922–) may well have been influenced by Moore in *Cat's Cradle* (1963), in which Ice-nine is the occasion of a similarly absurd disaster, congealing all water—and all life—in the finale. Vonnegut had already introduced a note of absurdist cynicism to sf with *The Sirens of Titan* (1959), in which the Tralfamadorians are found to have interfered in human history for fifty thousand years for the sole purpose of obtaining a spare part for a ship carrying a message—"Greetings"[51]—to another galaxy. It was with *Slaughterhouse Five* (1969), in which the all-seeing Tralfamadorians capture Billy Pilgrim and teach him the absurdity of free will in a deterministic block universe, that Vonnegut established himself as a best-selling novelist and literary pundit.

Perhaps the greatest accomplishment of the British New Wave was to revitalize absurdist fiction, already a genre in its own right (even if it is not usually thought of as such), with images and metaphors drawn from science fiction. In Pamela A. Zoline's much praised "The Heat Death of the Universe" (1967), for example, entropy—the stuff of cosmic tragedy in Olaf Stapledon's *Star Maker* (1937)—is recycled as a metaphor for a housewife's nervous breakdown amid the clutter and confusion of her suburban kitchen. The culmination of absurdist sf as a hybrid genre can be seen in the chic decadence of Moorcock's chronicles of Jerry Cornelius. Cornelius is a secret agent and a soldier of fortune in a world of fantastic conspiracies. Or perhaps he is a grubby teenager and would-be rock musician with delusions of grandeur, like the antihero of John Schlesinger's film *Billy Liar* (1963). There is little consistency in *The Cornelius Chronicles* (1977), an omnibus of four novels, from *The Final Programme* (1968) to *The Condition of Muzak* (1977); two other volumes are devoted to even further adventures. A little Cornelius goes a long way;

his escapades are as elaborately absurd as those in Sydney Newman's television series *The Avengers* (1961–9), but with none of the fun; his world is as absurdly dystopian as that in Terry Gilliam's film *Brazil* (1985), but with none of the savage wit. Cornelius' background and even his appearance change, but his message is always the same. In *The Final Programme*, a would-be world savior's harebrained scheme to use hallucinogenic drugs in mass conditioning to restore human "sanity" is quickly torpedoed:

"It's got a familiar ring. Don't you realize it's a waste of time?" Jerry's hand stroked the butt of his S&W .41. "It's over—Europe only points the course of the rest of the world. Entropy's setting in. Or so they say."
"Why should that be true?"
"It's Time—it's all used up, I'm told."[52]

In *A Cure for Cancer* (1969), Europe is invaded by the United States with napalm and official pamphlets on such topics as Sexual Intercourse with Animals and Conditions under Which Allies May Be Killed or Confined. In *The English Assassin* (1972), judgment is passed on Western civilization by one Auchinek:

[It] was out of tempo with the rest of the world. It imposed itself for a short time—largely because of the vitality, stupidity and priggishness of those who supported it. We shall never be entirely cleansed of its influence, I'm afraid.[53]

The very title of *The Condition of Muzak*, with its reference to the insipid recorded music piped into offices, suggests the entropy of middle-class culture. Moorcock himself is a rock musician, and Greenland emphasizes the New Wave's affinity with the alienated culture of rock music in *The Entropy Exhibition*. Yet its world view's roots in absurdist literature make it part of a tradition that antedates both rock and the post-Hiroshima wave of anxiety, guilt, and despair that found expression in the Hollywood sf monster movies of the 1950s before it came part of a higher literary consciousness.

Although it seemed revolutionary to outraged conservative sf fans, not to mention the puritans and censors who made trouble for *New Worlds* on several occasions, Moorcock's movement was also one of accommodation—the magazine won a grant from the British Arts Council with the support of Angus Wilson, hardly a literary outsider.[54] In Moorcock's definitive anthology, *New Worlds* (1983), the similarities of New Wave fiction seem more obvious than the differences; the revolt against sf conventions ended in the embrace of mainstream avant-garde conventions.

FREE RADICAL

The Family/Sygn conflict is the process of creating a schism throughout the entire galaxy concerning just what a woman *is*. And it may mean that instead of one universe with six thousand worlds in it, we will have a universe with one group of some thousands of worlds and another group of some thousands of others, and no connection between the two save memories of murder, starvation and violence.[55]

In Samuel R. Delany's *Stars in My Pocket Like Grains of Sand* (1984), a "woman" is any human being of either sex, except when referred to as a sex object. Aside from that, Delany's passage could apparently have come just as well from some Isaac Asimov Galactic Empire novel. Appearances, however, are deceiving. Delany's plot centers on the homosexual romance between Rat Korga and Marq Dyeth. Although the circumstances that bring the two together have something to do with the machinations of the Family and the Sygn, we never see the prime movers in the galactic conflict. Indeed, the conflict itself seems to be of less importance to Delany than the immediate reality of the cultures in which Korga and Dyeth are raised, and the immediate reality of their relationships within their cultures before their fateful meeting. Delany (1942–) is *not* just a latter-day Asimov. One could hardly find a greater contrast than in their accounts of their early lives—Asimov's in *In Memory Yet Green* (1979) and Delany's in *The Motion of Light in Water* (1987)— even though both biographies relate how their authors came to write science fiction.

Asimov tells of a conventional middle-class upbringing and admits his literary tastes run to Agatha Christie and P. G. Wodehouse. Although Delany's father was a funeral director (Asimov's ran a candy store), at an age when Asimov was just going to school, helping out at the store, and reading science fiction, Delany was reading William Faulkner and other literary heavyweights, meeting W. H. Auden, and living a Bohemian life in the East Village with poet Marilyn Hacker, while coming to terms with being gay and black in a world white and straight. Delany's life is what we have come to expect an artist's life to be like, and it comes as no surprise that there are strong autobiographical elements in his sf. That much is constant, although his literary persona has evolved from the precocious prose-poet of *The Jewels of Aptor* (1962/68) and *The Einstein Intersection* (1967, a.k.a. *A Fabulous Formless Darkness*) to the professorial grey beard of *Triton* (1976), which has an appendix bristling with such terms as metonymy, episteme, syntagm, and signifier. He established himself as a major sf critic with *The Jewel-Hinged Jaw* (1977), and as such can now look askance at his early sf. Why did he write about language in *Babel–17* (1965), about myth in *The Einstein*

Intersection? "I suspect it was because everybody around me was saying how profound and important the topics were, and though I was ready to believe them, I didn't fully understand why."[56]

Delany is hardly the only radical in science fiction, and yet his radicalism is both more profound and more paradoxical than that of his contemporaries. He was often associated with the New Wave by reviewers and critics during the first decade of his career, and he certainly had nothing against the New Wave. In *The American Shore* (1978), he analyzes Disch's "Angouleme" (1971, later incorporated into *334*) lovingly from a structuralist viewpoint; the analysis is several times longer than the story itself. Delany's sf criticism so annoyed Michael Moorcock, who had once published his fiction at *New Worlds*, that Moorcock rebuked him as "fundamentally illiterate . . . a parochial pedant."[57] Delany's work has taken some strange turns. *The Einstein Intersection*, his portrait of the sf artist as a young man, was followed by *Nova* (1968), an extravagant space opera. The intimidating *Dhalgren* (1975), which certainly must be the most experimental novel ever published in the genre, but yet became a best-seller, was followed by *Empire* (1978), a graphic sf novel written in collaboration with comics artist Howard V. Chaykin (imagine James Joyce or Franz Kafka doing that). Delany is familiar with the theory and practice of postmodernism and deconstruction in literature, and he has more right to be alienated from science fiction than any of the white middle-class radicals of the British New Wave. Yet, he seems to have dedicated his life as much as Asimov to science fiction.

What all Delany's science fiction seems to have in common is, not a radical deconstruction, but a radical *reconstruction* of the genre. In Jane Branham Weedman's *Samuel R. Delany* (1982), a critical study written with his cooperation and apparent *imprimatur*, most of his works are seen as parables about aspects of black culture and experience. *The Einstein Intersection* is thus explained in terms of concrete allegory: the strange culture of aliens assimilating human mythology after some sort of holocaust represents rural black society, and the protagonist Lobey is its liberator from the shackles of white science and religion, which are personified by Kid Death (Billy the Kid) and Green Eye (Christ). Yet Delany's work always seems more personal than that, as revealed in the extracts from his journal, which are incorporated into the novel. "I wonder what effect Greece will have on TEI,"[58] he muses while on a pilgrimage to the birthplace of the Orpheus legend used in *The Einstein Intersection*. Of Orpheus himself he writes: "He had a very modern choice to make when he decided to look back. What is its musical essence?"[59] What *is* apparent in Delany's sf, however, even when there are no racial overtones, is a radical shift in cultural perspective. Again and again, he exploits a familiar form of science fiction, yet gives it an entirely new point of view. *The Jewels of Aptor,* his first published work, is a quest novel, set in a post-holocaust world; but the protagonist is a *poet,* rather than the usual warrior or adventurer, and the issue of whether mankind can rebuild civilization without bringing about another holocaust is seen in poetic and mythological terms. The invention and atmosphere of the novel are more those of science fantasy than hard science fiction, but even science fantasy had never been quite like this before.

In *The Fall of the Towers* (1968–9, revised from a 1963–5 trilogy), an empire that arose in a small region of earth still habitable following a holocaust faces a historical crisis centuries later. Once again, Delany's invention is fanciful; the imperial wonder city and the intrigues against it (human and alien) are vaguely reminiscent of pulp classics like A. E. Van Vogt's *The Weapon Makers* (1943). But the sociological theme is more reminiscent of Asimov's Foundation trilogy, turning on a vision of history as a process determined by laws as formal as those in physics. In Asimov's sf, however, history is also influenced by the actions of an all-seeing elite of prime movers who understand those laws. There is no more place for the rest of mankind in shaping the course of history or seeking a utopian social order than there is for the cast of thousands in a Cecil B. DeMille movie in influencing the will of God. In *The Fall of the Towers,* however, there is already a feeling for the plight of the workers and social outcasts. Geryn, a leader of the malcontents, voices a quasi-Marxist analysis of Toromon's woes: "Our science has outrun our economics. Our laws have become stricter, and we say it is to stop the rising lawlessness. But it is to supply workers for the mines . . ."[60] We have already experienced the pain of social injustice in meeting Tel, son of a fisherman, forced to migrate to the city of Toron to look for work after urban fish farms destroy his family's livelihood:

I just got fed up with life at home. We'd work all day to catch fish, and then have to leave them rotting on the beach because we could only sell a fifth, sometimes none at all. Some people give up; some only managed to get it in their heads that they had to work harder. I guess my father was like that. He figured if he worked enough, someone would just have to buy them. But nobody did.[61]

The Devil's Pot, Toron's slum district, is full of people like Tel, who later provide cannon fodder for a war made inevitable by a surplus of wealth that cannot be invested in a consumer economy because Toromon's proletariat is too impoverished to support one. Since Toromon lacks any external enemies (there is nothing beyond it but radioactive desert), the "war" is a colossal hoax, programmed by a military computer that creates illusions of combat in the minds of the soldiers and kills off those arbitrarily chosen to be "casualties." In a Van Vogtian bit of complication, the war and the crisis behind it are manipulated by the Lord of the Flames, an alien creature from another universe; the Triple Being, another alien intelligence, but from our universe, comes to the aid of mankind's saviors: Vol Nonik, a poet; Dr. Clea Koshar, a physicist; and Dr. Rolth Catham, a historian. Nonik is an archetypical outlaw poet, whose origins lie in the underclass and whose insights into the wounds of society are essential to the healing process, as Catham, the archetypical Hari Seldon, realizes. In perfecting his own theory of the historical interpretation of individual action, Catham has found Nonik invaluable. As Nonik himself puts it:

It's happened before; you make a beautiful theory about society and psychology; then some guy in the street who doesn't know anything about either comes along and says, "Hey, you forgot all about such and such," and there goes your work. I was Catham's guy in the street.[62]

Already, however, without their help, the City of a Thousand Suns is rising in the wilderness: the dispossessed of Toron are laboring to save themselves without waiting for their saviors. It is here that the seed of a new culture is being nurtured, and Catham and the others can refine their theories to assist in an evolutionary process that others have already begun. Toron itself is destroyed, as the great computer, deprived of its "war," takes out its frustrations on mankind. Although the mood at the end is similar to that in Jack Williamson's "Breakdown" (1942), with Clea Koshar's revolutionary unified field theory primising mankind will be able "to reach out and touch the stars,"[63] we can see a distinctly new world view even in such an early Delany work. Mankind has already touched many stars in *Nova*, and again there are obvious touches of Asimov—even a planet named Trantor. But the novel turns out to be as much *bildungsroman* as space opera or sociological sf. The real hero is Mouse, a gypsy artist whose perspective as a poetic outsider sets him apart from a formal protagonist, Lorq Von Ray, starship captain extraordinaire and seeker of the new Holy Grail of Illyrion, a complex of transuranic elements essential to interstellar travel.

Cheaper Illyrion would end the virtual monopoly Red-shift Ltd., and old earth corporation, has enjoyed over starship construction since the dawn of the starfaring age. It would also upset the balance of power between earth's Draco hegemony, the Pleiades, and the Outer Colonies. The Von Rays are already allied with the Outer Colonies in developing an Illyrion mining industry, but Lorq Von Ray would take his ship through the heart of a supernova to capture seven tons of the substance at a stroke. *Nova* thus takes on overtones of Herman Melville's *Moby Dick* (1851): Von Ray has already failed once in his quest, and he has even been maimed (but by the vengeful Prince Red, rather than the nova/whale). Is Katin, an intellectual whose own quest is to revive the lost art of the novel, Delany's Ishmael? A man of thought, rather than of action or emotion, his motivation for taking part in Von Ray's expedition is that it may assist him in his own search for "an awareness of my time's conception of history"[64] on which to found his literary labor. If Katin seems to be relatively conventional, however, convention itself has changed radically by the year 3172. Take the ancient bourgeois obsession with cleanliness, which reflected a fear of infection that was valid, Katin admits—once:

But after contagion became an obsolescent concern, sanitation became equally obsolescent. If our man from five hundred years ago, however, saw you walking around this deck with one shoe off and one shoe on, then saw you sit down and eat with that same foot, without bothering to wash it—do you have my *idea* how upset he'd be?[65]

Even Mouse, despite his gypsy origins, finds it hard to accept the fact that tarot reading has become an accepted means of "[propagating] an educated commentary on present situations,"[66] by using "symbols and mythological images that have recurred and reverberated through forty-five centuries of human history."[67] And this is all in the same novel that discourses on the social stratification of the galaxy—the worlds of the Draco hegemony were settled by either national governments or megacorporations, the Pleiades by private business and the middle class, and the Outer Colonies by the proletariat—in a manner reminiscent of both Asimov and Robert A. Heinlein. It is the same novel that anticipates, after a fashion, one of the obsessions of cyberpunk with its vision of an industrial workplace transformed by the cybernetic symbiosis of man and machine. Delany builds on the literary traditions of science fiction, yet turns the conventions of traditional sf on their heads. Even at its most daring, traditional sf—consciously or otherwise—had remained stolidly middle-class in its cultural assumptions. Customs, mannerisms, even the arts themselves, as imagined in science fiction, tended to just propagate those cultural assumptions into the indefinite future. Delany, however, subverts and transforms the conventions of sf. Nevertheless, he also respects those conventions—there is never a sense that science fiction is being held up to contempt or ridicule, as other popular forms of fiction have been in, for example, Robert Coover's novels.

Outsiders are the protagonists in a number of Delany's short works. "The Star Pit" (1967) even has a futuristic working-class setting: sort of a galactic Gasoline Alley, where starships put in for repair. Vyme works as a drive mechanic there, and he considers himself lucky. In his youth, he had to scrounge for jobs from world to world, got drunk a lot, and lost his communal family in some pointless war. Ratlit, his teenage apprentice, has been in trouble with the law since the age of seven. Both are trapped not only by the old bars of social injustice, but also by exclusion from the new genetic aristocracy of the galaxy: the golden. The golden, thanks to their hereditary hormonal imbalances, are the only humans who can travel to other galaxies; the alien reality of inter-galactic space is fatal to normals. Their temperaments are usually as freakish as their imbalances, and they aren't very bright, either—once they brought back a deadly fungus from Andromeda that was used in a war, but it never occurred to them to bring back the antitoxin as well. What they lack in intelligence, they more than make up for in arrogance; they are essential to commerce between the galaxies, and they never let anyone forget it. That "commerce" includes a drug trade worse than any we know, whose victims, such as the teenage girl Alegra (old and worldly-wise in ways we can hardly imagine) Ratlit briefly befriends, are treated with utter callousness. His love-hate relationship with the golden eventually leads Ratlit to the suicidal gesture of hopping an intergalactic ship with a stolen golden I.D. belt, and even the stabler Vyme is driven to despair, which ends with a revelation that there are places the golden themselves cannot go.

Proletarian outsiders figure again in "Driftglass" (1967), in which sur-gically created amphibious men are exploited for dangerous underwater work, and in "Cage of Brass" (1968), which is perhaps unique as a fusion of science fiction and prison literature. Brass, a prison cruel beyond present belief or present technology, is a prison without guards, where inmates are sealed in coffins that serve their every physical need but deny them any contact with outside reality. Only a freak occurence lets three of them (for a time) communicate with each other. The theme of the alienated outsider is carried to its limits in *Dhalgren*, which has to rank as a literary landmark for having made a popular success of the experimental novel. *Dhalgren* was Delany's breakthrough novel, a novel which reached a mass audience after years of critical and reader acclaim for other works that were limited to the sf audience. That breakthrough seems as hard to explain as the novel itself, which begins and ends— like James Joyce's *Finnegans Wake* (1941)—in the same passage, as the Kid, a.k.a. Kidd, a.k.a. Dhalgren, has "come to wound the autumnal city."[68] The Kid is the apotheosis of the artist-criminal outsider, and Bellona is the city overwhelmed by some disaster that never quite be-comes clear. Much of the text is devoted to a clinically naturalistic account of the Kid's activities, from moving furniture for a middle-class family, which tries to pretend everything is still normal, to taking over the leadership of a violent street gang called the Scorpions. But there are also such bizarre episodes as the sudden appearance of a second moon, named George after a notorious rapist, and then practically forgotten amid the detail of everyday chaos. There is a metafictional scenario, with the Kid seen as the author of *Dhalgren* itself, as well as journals and poetry embedded in the text. Despite the often baffling complexity of the novel, however, Weedman's seemingly reductionist reading may be the best key to *Dhalgren*: one can recognize the temporal dislocations as references to Delany's own dyslexia and the unnamed disaster as the black rebellion in the cities, for example. Bellona itself can be seen as symbolic of the grim reality that comfortable, white, middle-class society cannot or will not see: "Very few suspect the existence of this city. It is as if not only the media but the laws of perception themselves have redesigned knowledge and perception to pass it."[69]

If *Dhalgren* is topical allegory and autobiographical metafiction, *Triton* marks a return to pure science fiction, but a science fiction shorn of the romanticism of *Nova* and founded on Delany's increasingly theoretical approach to sf and the language of sf. Apparently related to "Time Considered as a Helix of Semi-Precious Stones" (1969), which mentions some of the same locales as it follows the desperate life of a high-class interplanetary smuggler in a dystopian future, *Triton* is an "ambiguous heteratopia," a reference to the "ambiguous utopia" of Ursula K. Le Guin's *The Dispossessed* (1974), which Delany thought too simplistic.[70] Delany's social order on Triton and other far satellites is pluralistic in the extreme: there are dozens of political parties, and none of them ever wins an election. Well, actually, all of them do, as an envoy from Triton explains during a mission to earth:

You're governed for a term by the governor of whichever party you vote for. They all serve office simultaneously. And you get the various benefits of the platform your party has been running on. It makes for competition between the parties, which, in our sort of system, is both individualizing and stabilizing.[71]

Triton offers welfare services, but without a huge welfare bureaucracy—in any case, nobody is on welfare for long, and there are no ghettoes or other manifestations of social stratification. Pluralism is practiced in manners, mores, and living arrangements—preference classifications run to "forty or fifty sexes, and twice as many religions."[72] In this best of all possible worlds, "all you have to do is know what you want: no twenty-first-century-style philosophical oppression; no twentieth-century-style sexual oppression, no nineteenth-century-style economic oppression."[73] At least, this is how Bron, Delany's protagonist, sees it. Only, he does not quite see truly—not his society, not even himself.

Despite the General Information system that supposedly guarantees an open society, much important decision making seems to go on in secret councils or counsels. After a seemingly accidental disruption of Triton's artificial gravity, handbills appear that suggest it was not accidental—"Here are Thirteen Things *your* government does *not* want you to know,"[74] the dissident broadside reads. Before Bron can finish reading the handbill, a cop appears and collects the flyers in the name of combatting "pollution." Of course, Bron can take one home and read it if he *really* wants to, but no mass distribution is allowed. And what about the war that is developing between the Outer Satellites on one hand, and Earth and Mars on the other? Bron is an immigrant from Mars himself, but he does not take the threat seriously; he does not even pay much attention to it—although Sam, the envoy from the Liaison Department whom he eventually accompanies to Earth, is in his immediate circle of acquaintances. Before the novel is over, the war has killed billions, including three quarters of the population of Earth. The Outer Satellites have "won"; Triton got off lightly, even though Lux on Iapetus was wiped out.

Born considers himself a "reasonably happy man," [75] comfortable with both his profession (which involves resolving problems by application of "metalogic") and his personal life (he lives in an all-male, unspecified co-op). But his seeming adjustment begins to unravel after his encounter with the Spike, whose troupe picks him out as an audience of one for its experimental "micro-theater" (an intense, brief, mixed-media presentation akin to contemporary performance art). Bron becomes fixated on the Spike, who brings out the male chauvinist pig in him—much to her chagrin. In a fit of pique over his rejection, and believing her to have been killed in the war in any case, he overcompensates by having a sex change—only to become more miserable and alienated than ever. Long before that, he has become tiresome; Bron and his personal fate never seem as interesting as the world around him. Perhaps Delany himself is overcompensating for what now seems to him the romantic excess of earlier works like *Nova*. But in *Stars in My Pocket Like Grains of Sand*, it is not the protagonists themselves, but their relationship that becomes tiresome.

Prolonged delay in the publication of a sequel, *The Splendor and Misery of Bodies, of Cities*, originally scheduled for 1985, makes it impossible to assess Delany's intended work as a whole, but the background concepts are fascinating. In a far-future galactic civilization, bound by a General Information system called the Web, there is a struggle between two basic ideologies:

with the Family trying to establish the dream of a classic past as pictured on a world that may never even have existed in order to achieve cultural stability, and with the Sygn committed to the living interaction and difference between each woman and each world from which the right stability and right play may flower.[76]

The two ideologies are apparently also distinguished by their attitudes toward death: for the Sygn, the reality of death means that the only fulfillment for the living lies in living each moment as intensely as possible; for the Family, it lies in concentrating on whatever is "eternal" rather than on the "trivialities" of everyday existence. For either side, "the other is considered the pit of error, the road to injustice, and the locus of sin."[77]

Drawn into this conflict are Rat Korga, a delinquent sentenced to the slavery of Radical Anxiety Termination on a world so reactionary it is not even tied into the Web, and Marq Dyeth, an industrial diplomat (job$_1$) and history professor (job$_2$) from Velm, a world on which humanity and the native evelm have evolved a symbiotic (well, not everywhere, not all the time) culture. Korga, a member of the underclass, and deliberately kept stupid (except for a brief interval when a woman introduces him to the wonders of galactic literature by a computer link), is the only survivor when his world is destroyed (possibly by Cultural Fugue, which rival factions had called in the Family and the Sygn to prevent or possibly by the Xlv, aliens nobody has been able to communicate with). Dyeth is part of the seventh "ripple" (as opposed to generation) of a "nurture stream" (as opposed to family) that adopts both human and evelm infants and was founded by Gylda Dyeth, a Sygn adherent who nevertheless enjoyed the patronage of an interstellar tyrant and Family proponent named Vondramach Okk. The Dyeths have a colorful and somewhat mysterious past, and the machinations of the Family and the Sygn are even more mysterious, so intriguing that we are frustrated by the focus of the novel on gay romance, Dyeth domestic life, and the like.

Still, Delany's radical transformation of sf, and the truly radical world view behind it, remain fascinating. One need only compare his sf to that of Norman Spinrad (1940–), whose *Bug Jack Barron* (serialized, 1967–8, in *New Worlds*) seemed *the* radical sf novel of its time. Full of explicit sex, hip dialogue, and aggressively experimental style, *Bug Jack Barron* concerns the exposure by an ex-radical television personality of the sinister plot of a billionaire to achieve immortality for himself and a favored few by killing black children and using their irradiated glands in transplants. Even two decades ago, the plot seemed melodramatic, too much like that of *The Man Who Could Cheat Death* (1959), a Hammer Films camp classic. But today, the explicit sex and experimental style that once seemed daring have actually become quaint, and the "hipness" even quainter:

The ass is always greener, Barron thought. Village days, Berkeley was the place; Berkeley days, Strip City, and back to here in goddamned Coast-to-Coast incestuous daisy chain. Hey, which way to the action, man? And baby, when you're a loser, the action's always somewhere else.[78]

Spinrad has gone on to do better; yet even in *Little Heroes* (1987), his political and cultural radicalism remain those of the 1960s. Sometimes it seems that nothing is as old-fashioned as yesteryear's revolution.

6

Angry Young Men—and Women

UP AGAINST THE WALL, CAPTAIN FUTURE!

The Jack I present is the Jack of all of us, of course. The Jack that tells us to stand and watch as Catherine Genovese gets knifed, the Jack that condones Vietnam because we don't care to get involved, the Jack that we need. We are a culture that needs its monsters.[1]

Puritan New England had its Jonathan Edwards; science fiction has its Harlan Ellison. Ellison (1934–) wears his heart—and his social conscience—on his sleeve. The Ellison who, in "The Prowler in the City at the Edge of the World" (1967), shows how a near-future society even more morbidly voyeuristic than our own gives Jack the Ripper the kind of public recognition and acclaim denied him in his own Victorian England, is the same Ellison who ends his afterword with: "That is the message of the story. You are the monsters."[2]

"The Prowler in the City" was Ellison's own contribution to what was meant to be, and became, the most controversial anthology in the history of science fiction: *Dangerous Visions* (1967). Although Ellison's anthology was a rallying point for what was called the American New Wave, the movement in American sf was never as coherent as the British New Wave under Michael Moorcock. Even though Ellison encouraged relevance and taboo-breaking in both *Dangerous Visions* and *Again, Dangerous Visions* (1972), he has never attempted to impose an ideology on sf. Both his anthologies include stories that can hardly be called controversial, and his other projects include *Medea: Harlan's World* (1985), a created-world symposium-anthology. But he has always chafed at the traditions of science fiction when they seem to limit his own freedom, or that of any writer, to say what needs to be said and to try to awaken people's minds to the evils and dangers surrounding them.

Ellison loathes being typed as an sf writer: when he speaks of "sf," he means speculative fiction, an alternate name for the genre, apparently introduced by Robert A. Heinlein.[3] Heinlein simply thought it a better name for science fiction as traditionally understood, but speculative fiction has since come to mean something much broader—just how much broader is hard to determine. Like others who use it, Ellison is impatient with definitions and distinctions. Still, the historiographer of science fiction must make them, even when they complicate discussion of stories that are clearly related. Ellison's "Along the Scenic Route" (1969), for example, is purest science fiction in the traditional sense, but his "Shattered Like a Glass Goblin" (1968) is purest supernatural horror. Yet the two stories, in complementary ways, define Ellison's position as a moralist in contemporary society.

"Along the Scenic Route" is a savagely satirical attack on macho attitudes in America. Like gunslingers in the Old West, drivers on the freeways of the near future are always looking for a showdown; and now society has sanctioned their violent passions. There is none of the wry detachment Robert Sheckley once brought to a similar situation, in "Seventh Victim" (1953); Ellison means to hit you in the gut from the very start, when we witness George's explosion of anger when another car cuts in front of him:

> George slapped the selector control on the dash, lighting YOU STUPID BASTARD, WHAT DO YOU THINK YOU'RE DOING and I HOPE YOU CRASH & BURN, YOU SON OF A BITCH. Jessica moaned softly with uncontrolled fear, but George could not hear her: he was screaming obscenities.[4]

Needless to say, cars of the future are equipped with a lot more than electronic insults: lasers, machine guns, armor, and g-suits to protect the driver and passengers while taking 250-miles-an-hour turns during duels. George, the more fool he, takes on an opponent with coded options that totally outclass his own. Only dumb luck saves him in a desperate last chance maneuver, but not for long. Having dispatched the duelist "rated number one in the entire Central and Eastern Freeway Circuit,"[5] he hears the challenges pouring in over the Sector Control radio.

We have all seen this sort of social criticism before, and we know where it usually comes from. But then we read "Shattered Like a Glass Goblin," which is set in a den of the drug culture. As we also know, all right-thinking liberals who condemn violence and injustice are convinced (or were in 1968, at least) that the drug culture is (or was) the very incarnation of peace, love, and enlightenment. All except Ellison. When Rudy gets out of the Army in the story (one need not ask what Ellison thinks of the Army), what he finds at a decrepit gothic mansion in Los Angeles, where he goes to look for his girl friend Kris, is pure *hell*. Nevertheless, for her sake, he moves in: "It was a self-contained little universe, bordered on the north by acid and mescaline, on the south by pot and peyote, on the east by speed and redballs, on the west by downers and amphetamines."[6] One of the other women there is so indifferent to anything but immediate gratification that when her boyfriend has a bad trip, the first thing she does is offer to fuck Rudy: "When Jonah trips, he turns off. I been drinking Coca-Cola all morning and day, and I'm really horny."[7] Kris, indifferent to anything but dope, refuses to budge; she will not even talk to Rudy, except to urge him to "get heavy." Eventually, she gets him to "make it, heavy behind acid."[8] What happens after that, when Rudy and the others literally turn into the monstrous images of their addictions (Rudy himself is the goblin, who is smashed to pieces by the hairy thing that was once Kris), is so terrifying that it makes the moralizing of the Moral Majority seem every bit as shallow as it actually is.

In "Croatoan" (1975), Ellison comes out against abortion and promiscuous sex. A womanizer who gets his girlfriends in trouble and has them get abortions finds himself compelled to descend into the sewers, where he is adopted into a netherworld community of aborted children:

> I am the only adult here.
> They have been waiting for me.
> They call me father.[9]

Ellison's moral fervor is always intensely personal, always completely sincere, but it is never merciful. Perhaps his most controversial story, "A Boy and His Dog" (1969), which became the basis of a 1975 film by L. Q. Jones, shows Ellison at his nastiest. Vic is a survivor, in a grim post-holocaust world where survival comes hard indeed. His only real friend, Blood, is a mutant dog: a genetically engineered breed from some prewar military research and development program; he is as intelligent as a man and is able to communicate telepathically. Blood taught Vic to read and write, taught him history, and has always looked out for him whenever the going got tough. Vic is not a nice person; he enjoys stopping by a gang outpost to watch movies, for which the admission price

is foraged canned goods, like *Smell of a Chink* ("Beautiful scene of skir-
misher greyhounds equipped with napalm throwers, jellyburning a
Chink town"[10]). He also likes to get laid, and for that a girl named Quilla
June seems to be made to order—except for her social background: she
comes from the downunders, where survivors of the old middle class
maintain a fantasy of a Norman Rockwell America:

Southern Baptists, Fundamentalists, lawanorder goofs, real middle-class squares
with no taste for the wild life. And they'd gone back to a kind of life that hadn't
existed for a hundred and fifty years. They'd gotten the last of the scientists to
do the work, invent the how and why, and then they'd run them out. They
didn't want any progress, they didn't want any dissent . . . [11]

Against Blood's advice, and his own better judgment, Vic lets his
gonads lead him after Quilla June when she returns to her hometown
of "Topeka," where he is soon imprisoned by the Better Business Bureau
and subjected to attempted brainwashing. He escapes, of course; Quilla
June even goes with him, still whiningly professing her "love." In the
meantime, Blood, having been left back on the surface, has really been
having a hard time of it. Vic returns from downunder to find him starving
and near death. Who deserves his love, Quilla June or Blood? Vic must
choose; a sacrifice must be made. Guess who gets fed to whom. In Jones'
screen version, Vic himself shares the meal, during which Blood makes
a revolting remark about how Quilla June "may not have had particularly
good judgment, but she sure had good taste."[12] Ellison, a feminist by
the time the film was made, protested its "sexist aspects";[13] yet Jones
was basically faithful to the story. In both versions, Quilla June is a
stuck-up middle-class bitch who *deserves* to be fed to the dog. It was her
kind, after all, that was responsible for World War III and most of the
world's evils before that.

Ellison's rage against the moral blindness and utter stupidity of the
so-called common man explains his frequent impatience with science
fiction itself, which often seems hopelessly naive and conservative in its
values even when it professes to be a literature of the future. His complaint was anticipated by Robert Bloch, best known as the author of
Psycho (1959). Indicting sf at a 1957 seminar for its almost total lack of
social criticism, Bloch complained that most of its "rebellious" heroes
seek "merely to restore the 'normal' culture and value standards of the
mass-minds of the twentieth century:"

You won't find [the hero] fighting in defense of incest, homosexuality, free love,
nihilism, the Single Tax, abolition of individual property rights or the castration
of the tonsils of Elvis Presley. Stripped down to the bare essentials, our hero
just wants to kick the rascals out and put in a sound business administration.[14]

Bloch's "A Toy for Juliette" (1967) was the lead-in for Ellison's "The Prowler in the City" in *Dangerous Visions*; and in several of the other stories in the anthology, the heroes—or at least the authors—fight for some of the proscribed causes enumerated by Bloch. Sturgeon's "If All Men Were Brothers, Would You Let One Marry Your Sister?" with its argument for incest appeared therein. So did Philip José Farmer's "Riders of the Purple Wage," a novella full of Joycean experimentalism and irreverance anent the doings of an antihero named Winnegan during the coming social upheavals. As explained in an afterword (each author contributed an afterword which, with Ellison's forewords, made each story the filling in a sandwich of commentary), the novella was really an argument for the Triple Revolution: a neo-technocratic movement, then current. Other stories concerned the use of hallucinogenic drugs to reveal a malevolent universe and its evil God (Philip K. Dick's "Faith of Our Fathers"), or to cure a man's cancer but leave him catatonic (Norman Spinrad's "The Carcinoma Angels"). Also included are such misanthropic sf stories as Robert Silverberg's "Flies," in which the message is that we are all vampires—(what else can the cliché that "People need people" possibly *mean*, Silverberg asks in his afterword.[15]) At times, contributors had to strain themselves to introduce shock elements. In Samuel R. Delany's "Aye, and Gomorrah," the theme is a new form of sexual perversion: frelks seek the company of astronauts, who have been surgically neutered in order to prevent them from having any children (radiation in space has damaged their genes). The required social end could have been achieved just as well by mere sterilization, in which case the astronauts could fuck like rabbits without any risk of deformed offspring.

Again, Dangerous Visions (1972) also shows signs of straining for effect. In "With the Bentfin Boomer Boys on Little Old New Alabama," Richard A. Lupoff tells a wickedly inventive story of how a transplanted black nationalist society on N'Haiti uses updated voodoo to conduct a war against the transplanted rednecks of neighboring N'Alabama—the only problems are with the premise. How did such fossilized cultures manage to survive unchanged long enough to reach the stars, and why would they, given their mutual hatred, settle on planets within fifty parsecs of one another? Ben Bova, a basically conservative writer, rang in with a rather trite story of sex in space, "Zero Gee"; Kurt Vonnegut, Jr., got the F-word into a title with "The Big Space Fuck," which relates the launching, by an exhausted world, of a starship carrying "eight-hundred pounds of freeze-dried jizzum"[16] to spread our unworthy kind to distant worlds. Ellison, in his quest for "relevant" sf, boasted about how he "stole" a couple of Bernard Wolfe stories, one an anti-Vietnam war piece called "The Bisquit Position," away from *Playboy*.[17] No doubt that was a coup; however, Wolfe's story, with the sure-fire sentimental impact of its lovable dog being burned with napalm, would have surely reached a larger audience and thus been more effective, if it *had* run in *Playboy*.

In their time, *Dangerous Visions* and *Again, Dangerous Visions* certainly seemed to be revolutionizing science fiction. Only a year after the appearance of the first anthology, Farmer's *Image of the Beast* (1968), with its explicit, often sadistic, sex and its pervasive sense of evil broke whatever taboos remained in science fiction, even though it had to be published by Essex House, which specialized in pornography. Among other Essex House imprints, the best received by critics—and almost impossible to find today—was Hank Stine's *Season of the Witch* (1968), a psychological sf novel centering on a rapist-murderer who, thanks to a brain transplant, is sentenced to live as a woman in the body of his victim. Even more conventionally published science fiction felt the impact of Ellison's revolution. Silverberg's *Thorns* (1967), published by Ballantine, was a thematic expansion of "Flies": the corrupt world of the future revels in the exploitation of human pain for mass entertainment, with the sadistic Duncan Chalk the chief purveyor. The only alternative to sadism is masochism. Two of Chalk's victims, Minner Burris, an astronaut whose body has been mutilated by aliens for reasons never really explained, and the naive orphan Lona Kelvin, find meaning in sticking thorns in themselves. "Pain is instructive,"[18] remarks Burris, echoing Chalk's epigram from the opening of the novel. With the book publication of Spinrad's *Bug Jack Barron* (1969) and its nomination for a Hugo award, it might have seemed that the radicalization of sf was complete. Paralleling the Ellison revolution were such developments as the appearance of original paperback sf anthology series, particularly Damon Knight's *Orbit* (1966–80), which were receptive to short stories by writers like James Sallis, Carol Emshwiller, and Kit Reed whose work was too literary or too pessimistic for traditional sf magazines; and the growing popularity of writers' workshops like Milford and Clarion, often sympathetic to the New Wave, as proving grounds for new talent.

Ellison himself seemed to mellow at times. When he got a chance to sell a hard science fiction story to the archconservative editor John W. Campbell, Jr., collaborating with Ben Bova (hardly a radical either) on "Brillo" (1970), he actually took pride in confounding expectations based on his reputation. Mike Polchik, protagonist of "Brillo," is a sympathetic cop, like one of the Hill Street blues, who is threatened with replacement by a robot. Ellison's other collaborations, collected in *Partners in Wonder* (1971), included "The Human Operators" (1971), with A. E. Van Vogt, surely as Old Guard an sf writer as there could be. It is hard to imagine J. G. Ballard or Thomas M. Disch in such company—Michael Moorcock would doubtless have thundered against the idea from his editorial pulpit. Yet Ellison remained true to his vision of radical protest in a society—even a universe—ruled by oppressive evil. In "Silent in Gehenna" (1971), the two aspects of that vision come together. Joe Bob Hickey is a revolutionary in a near-future Amerika. He fights the good fight, planting bombs at a militarized UCLA campus and exhorting students to rebel against the varks, as the fascist police are called, all to no avail. Then he is killed and goes to his reward, only to learn that Heaven itself is run by capitalist pigs and that its workers as cowed and apathetic as the students back on earth.

Ellison describes "Silent in Gehenna" as the expression of his own "self-disillusionment" with the social revolution of the 1960s[19]—not its goals, but with the hope that it stood any chance of achieving them, in the face of Nixon and Reagan and "the loathsomeness of The Common Man,"[20] as personified in a creep from Georgia who wrote Ellison a letter calling the victims of the Kent State massacre Communist-led hooligans who "deserved to be shot."[21] It is hard to find stories in which Ellison held out much hope even when the revolution was at its height; the most outstanding exception is " 'Repent, Harlequin!' Said the Ticktockman" (1965), with its amalgam of social consciousness—an extract from Henry David Thoreau's "Civil Disobedience" introduces the story—and whimsy—Harlequin's brand of guerrilla warfare against a regimented society includes sabotaging an expresstrip with millions of jelly beans. Of course, Harlequin gets caught in the end, and he is brainwashed, but not in vain. A short time later, at the entrance to the Master Time-keeper's office:

"Uh, excuse me, sir, I don't know how to uh, tell you this, but you were three minutes late. The schedule is a little, uh, off."

He grinned sheepishly.

"That's ridiculous!" murmured the Ticktockman behind his mask. "Check your watch." And then he went into his office, going mrmee, mrmee, mrmee, mrmee.[22]

More typical of Ellison are his theological fantasies on the nature and significance of evil. In "Paingod" (1964), he attempts to justify endless pain and suffering: the god whose mission is to inflict torment on all living creatures learns that, without misery and ugliness, there can be no joy or beauty. In "The Beast that Shouted Love at the Heart of the World" (1968), there is no such comfort; evil is only a wave of madness unleashed on the rest of the universe by a distant world intent on securing its own peace and sanity at any price. In "The Whimper of Whipped Dogs" (1973), a woman afraid of urban violence but unwilling to take a stand against it is enlisted into the worship of a new God—"a deranged blood God of fog and street violence. A God who needed worshipers and offered the choice of death as a victim or life as an eternal witness to the deaths of *other* chosen victims."[23] Another woman,

whose life has been filled with bitterness, becomes a goddess herself
when her spirit takes possession of a slot machine in "Pretty Maggie
Moneyeyes" (1967) and lures other greedy victims to their doom. There
is no escape, save death—and sometimes not even that. In "I Have No
Mouth, and I Must Scream" (1967), a few survivors of World War III
are trapped in the subterranean world of AM, an artificial intelligence
created for the war by the military-industrial complex. AM's hatred for
humanity, which has given it life without any reason for living, knows
no bounds; it gives its human captives endless life to subject them to
endless torture in a technological Dante's Inferno. One of them finally
finds the chance, and the courage, to free the others—by killing them
so swiftly that AM is caught off guard. His fate is to be transformed
into a monstrous, sluglike thing that cannot kill itself, that cannot even
take much comfort in having put the others beyond the machine's reach:

> AM will be all the madder for that. It makes me a little happier. And yet . . .
> AM has won, simply . . . he has taken his revenge.
> I have no mouth. And I must scream.[24]

Ellison can and does scream, only nobody will listen. Or, if anyone
does, it is in the wrong way. The taboos are broken, but their breaking
has become a matter of routine, from the routine incest and sex changes
of John Varley's Eight Worlds stories to the routine homosexual romance
of Jeffrey M. Elliot's anthology *Kindred Spirits* (1984). Having spurred
women's liberation in sf by publishing Joanna Russ' controversial "When
It Changed" in *Again, Dangerous Visions*, he has seen that cause escape
the bounds of the New Left Movement to become an ideology unto
itself, which at its most extreme must regard Ellison himself (theoreti-
cally, at least) as a demon incarnate by virtue of his Y chromosomes. In
science fiction, as in society at large, the attempt at radicalization seems
to have brought about the antithesis of its aims. The generation of Ronald
Reagan in politics has become the generation of Jerry Pournelle in sf.
Whereas it once seemed that the New Left militancy of Ellison, Spinrad,
and others would be the wave of the future in sf, even if neither the
British nor the American New Wave reshaped its literary value system,
the momentum has now shifted to the militancy of the New Right.
    Pournelle (1933–), the New Right's leading angry "young" man (a
year older than Ellison), first reached a wide audience with *The Mote in
God's Eye* (1974), a collaboration with Larry Niven. Although it is en-
riched by Niven's vivid imagination in its portrayal of the Moties, an
alien species that threatens the Second Empire of Man, the novel's political line is pure Pournelle. That is hardly surprising, since it is part of
Pournelle's CoDominium future history, the foundations for which are
established in his *West of Honor* (1976, revised 1978) and *The Mercenary*

(1977). The CoDominium is an unwieldy U.S.–Soviet hegemony, which collapses in face of nationalistic rivalries after a century but gives mankind enough time to settle planets of the nearer stars and thus survive the nuclear armageddon back on earth. The lesson learned from that destruction is the need for a universal state: the Empire of Man, founded on the feudal social order that has evolved on colonial worlds and in the CoDominium fleet. It is the feudal patriarchy of the Empire, and its successor after an interregnum of civil war and barbarism, that is seen as the only salvation for mankind. Only lords and admirals can appreciate the threat of the Moties in *The Mote in God's Eye;* traders and scientists (especially *women* scientists) tend to muck things up. Under the Empire's cruel internal security policy, rebellious worlds "might be reduced to glittering lava fields," reflects a commander, but "it was the only possible way"[25] to ensure galactic peace and order.

Superficially, Pournelle's world view appears close to Heinlein's, and Heinlein might have agreed, since they shared a number of New Right causes such as the Star Wars space defense. *Farnham's Freehold* (1964), Heinlein's post-holocaust novel, even seems to anticipate survivalist sf of the New Right like Jerry Ahern's *Total War* (1981). Yet Heinlein was always more abstractly Darwinian, even in *Starship Troopers* (1959). For Pournelle, even the Darwinian struggle for existence seems of less importance than the survival of a classical tradition of the universal state that dates back to ancient Rome. His patrician conservative world view seems akin to that of Allen Drury, whose *Advise and Consent* (1959) and its sequels are obsessed with the decadence of liberal democracy in its struggle with world communism. In *Lucifer's Hammer* (1977), *Oath of Fealty* (1981), and *Footfall* (1985), all in collaboration with Niven, he follows a consistent neoconservative line: there are always military and technological solutions to our problems, and the only obstacles to order and progress come from fanatical environmentalists, pacifists, and bleeding-heart liberals. Pournelle has become the center of a school of neoconservative and martial science fiction, typified by such works as David Drake's *Hammer's Slammers* (1979), Janet Morris' and Drake's *Active Measures* (1985), and Timothy Zahn's *Cobra* (1985). In its single-mindedness, even its alienation, the neoconservative school is a virtual mirror image of the New Wave.

BIOLOGY AND DESTINY

Katy drives like a maniac; we must have been doing over 120 kilometers per hour on those turns. She's good, extremely good, and I've seen her take a whole car apart and put it together again in a day.[26]

Katy is not some tomboy, allowed to take part in earthly drag races to amuse the men. She is not some token woman, accepted grudgingly into the man's world of racing, like Shirley Muldowney in Jonathan Kaplan's film, *Heart Like a Wheel* (1983). She's a normal, everyday woman, living on Whileaway in Joanna Russ' "When It Changed" (1972). While-awayan women can do anything they want, be anything they want. There is nobody to stop them, because, for generations, *there haven't been any men.* When the first starship to visit the planet in 600 years makes its landing, there is a sense of foreboding for it is crewed by men, and the implication is clear: once again, women are doomed to become second-class citizens. As Katy's lover Janet puts it:

I doubt very much that sexual equality has been reestablished on Earth. I do not like to think of myself mocked, of Katy deferred to as if she were weak, of Yuki made to feel unimportant or silly, of my other children cheated of their full humanity or turned into strangers.[27]

None of the visiting men have any idea of this; they are convinced that they are about to restore the natural order of things and are certain that the women are just *dying* to let them, ah, "use Whileaway's genes."[28] It is the sort of arrogance men have traditionally taken for granted, and have not even *noticed* they were taking for granted. Russ (1937–) is only one of a number of contemporary feminists who mean to put them on notice and, more important, to raise the consciousness of women themselves, who have often taken sexism as much for granted as have men.

Something must be said at the outset concerning language, for in the contemporary feminist movement, it is not simply laws or customs that are being challenged, but the most fundamental assumptions of history, culture, and language itself. It is already controversial to continue using such terms as "man" and "mankind" in the generic sense; the trend has been to replace then with "person" and "humanity." Language, we are reminded, does not reflect perceptions, but controls them. Perhaps this is so, but there is a bit of the chicken-and-the-egg paradox in this. Which came first, the decline of women's status in the later Roman Empire or the etymological evolution of the generic Latin *homo* (as opposed to *vir*) into the romance language words (*homme, hombre,* and so on) applying only to males? Was there sexual equality in old England, when "man" was still a generic word, and "woman" really meant "*female* man" (not "out of man" from the Hebrew *ishshah* of Genesis)? Has the status of women been higher in Russia, where there has always been the generic *chelovek* in addition to *muzhchina* and *zhenshchina* for the male and female genders? (Any improvements under the Soviet government do not count, since the language was the same for centuries under the tsars.) Moreover, however politicized, language is still *literary*. It is not only a question of awkward terms like "chairperson," but of literature itself: are we to purge the classics of "sexist" language as they were only bowdlerized of vulgarisms? Perhaps that is what it will come to. Still, there might be a literary advantage to at least trying to restore the generic sense of "man" and "mankind" and introducing new gender words, as David Brin has done with "mel" and "fem" in *Startide Rising* (1983), or even going back to the Indo-European "wiros" and "gwen." We could then keep Shakespeare's "What a piece of work is a man!"[29] and universalize its meaning, while making his "Frailty, thy name is woman!"[30] seem merely archaic. In any case, as used in *When World Views Collide* and its companion volumes, "mankind" is to be construed generically, and "man" is also used generically unless the specific context indicates otherwise.

Russ' "When It Changed," which was the kernel of her controversial novel *The Female Man* (1975), signaled a revolution in science fiction—a revolution more far-reaching than even that of the New Wave. Even neoconservative sf writers have given at least a grudging support to the equality of women. More important, women themselves account for an increasing share of sf readership, and it has become a cliché to observe that most of the best new sf authors are women. Even before the rebirth of the feminist movement, of course, there were some prominent women authors in sf, such as C[atherine] L. Moore (1911–87) and Leigh Brackett (1915–78), not to mention André Norton (1912–), Marion Zimmer Bradley (1930–), and Judith Merril (1923–). Also, there were major male authors who portrayed competent women as heroines or even raised feminist issues: Stanley G. Weinbaum, John Wyndham, and James Schmitz.

The androgynous pen names of Catherine L. Moore, Leigh Brackett, and others might seem evidence of sexism. Actually, Moore used her initials in order to conceal her literary identity from the bank she worked for.[31] Brackett's given name really was Leigh; in any case, readers could know her sex from a biographical sketch, with photo, in *Startling Stories.*[32] Because Moore and Brackett both wrote heroic adventure stories, usually with male protagonists, it is easy enough today to dismiss them as mere victims of a male-dominated genre, even as traitors to the women's cause. Not true; by their own accounts, they wrote what they wanted to write. In their marriages to Henry Kuttner and Edmond Hamilton, respectively, they were equal partners and, in Moore's case, equal collaborators. Jirel of Joiry was as much a part of Moore as Northwest Smith. As for Brackett's Eric John Stark, he was hardly a male chauvinist. Ciaran, his partner at the end of "People of the Talisman" (1964), has won his admiration for fighting as a man to regain her heritage, for *earning* her victories: " 'With these two hands, Stark,' she said, holding them up. 'With what I am myself, and what I can do, not what I can trick and wheedle and whore out of others by the ancient usages of the bed-chamber.' "[33]

Weinbaum, Schmitz, Wyndham, Moore, Brackett, and others were active long before the contemporary women's liberation movement, and none seems to have suffered for having introduced either strong heroines or clearly feminist viewpoints. Yet science fiction has gained a sexist reputation, and much of it is deserved. There are any number of sf classics that are embarrassing by contemporary standards. Lester del Rey's "Helen O'Loy" (1938), in which a functionally female robot finds conventional love and marriage, is a favorite target of critics—including born-again male feminists, who presumably never noticed the story's sexism until their conversions.[34] Harlan Ellison, one of the born-agains, found an example of more recent vintage to excoriate in his introduction to Russ' "When It Changed": Keith Laumer's *Dinosaur Beach* (1971), in which the female lead is a secret agent who ought to be cool and competent, but who is instead portrayed as "weak, sniveling and semi-hysterical."[35] But these are examples of unconscious sexism; one can find the conscious variety in modern science fiction. Richard Wilson, in *The Girls from Planet 5* (1955), ridicules a feminist movement which, at the time the novel was published, hardly existed: in a future of reversed sex roles, men have been reduced to "household engineers" by dominant women who have taken over all the professions and positions of authority. Then there is John Norman, author of the notorious Gor novels, in which women just love to be treated as sex slaves, as demonstrated ad nauseam in *Nomads of Gor* (1969), *Captives of Gor* (1972), and so on.

Why should Russ be angered by this sort of thing? Why are blacks angered by *Birth of a Nation* (1915) or *Gone with the Wind* (book 1936, film 1939)? Anger can produce its own excesses, but among sf's radical feminists, Russ has actually begun to seem conservative. *The Female Man* is an assault on the idea that biology is destiny, at least for women. "Women can't" and "Be ladylike" are sexist clichés that drive Russ, and Janet, up the wall. For that matter, men in general drive them up the wall, for there is not a single male of the species in the novel (except a sex slave in one alternate reality where the tables have been turned) who does not seem to devote every waking thought and action to putting down women. Rape and murder are the universal and automatic response to any sign of resistance. A traumatized woman vows revenge:

> For every drop of blood shed there is restitution made; with every truthful reflection in the eyes of a dying man I get back a little of my soul; with every little gasp of horrified comprehension I come a little more into the light.[36]

Russ does not reject civilization; Whileaway enjoys the comforts of technology; the assumption is that women can manage it more sanely and rationally than men. In *The Female Man*, Whileaway is the future of earth rather than a remote planet. Apart from the extinction of men in a plague, its capsule history reads pretty much like any other future history: advances in nuclear power and genetic engineering, colonization of other planets, the revolution of the industrial workplace with induction helmets, and so on. "Humanity is unnatural!"[37] exclaims Whileawayan philosopher Dunyasha Bernadettson: a sort of Wellsian, she. There is no sugary sentimentality about either nature or human nature; it is a matter of common sense, rather than devotion to the Earth Mother, that Whileawayans practice recycling and the like. They love their children, but they also fight duels. Russ' world view is an evolutionary feminism, close to the evolutionary humanism of traditional sf.

James Tiptree, Jr.'s "Houston, Houston, Do You Read?" (1976), which is probably the best-known feminist utopia of genre sf, shares the same world view. Three male chauvinist pig astronauts are flung through some sort of time warp to a future earth which, although they do not realize it at first, is inhabited entirely by women: after a plague sterilized the human race, the only salvation was in parthenogenesis. When the men finally do understand the situation, two of them go off the deep end, resorting to violence; the third whines about the women's ingratitude to his kind—who, after all, built their civilization and "protected" them for thousands of years? Well, maybe there was some use for men when women were menaced by lions and tigers and bears, but later on, as Lady Blue points out, "what you protected people from was largely other males, wasn't it?"[38] Still, the women appreciate men's inventions and have even developed a technological culture of their own which is very sophisticated, considering the fact they have a population of only two million based on a scant eleven thousand genotypes (a new technique for combining haploid nuclei is introducing more variety). They believe in progress; they are just not as frenetic about it. When one of the doomed astronauts concludes that evolution has stopped, he is contradicted by a Constantia Morelos clone: "No, why? It's just slowed down. We do everything much slower than you did, I think. We like to experience things *fully*. We have time. There's all the time."[39]

Tiptree, of course, was actually Alice Sheldon (1915–87), whose pen name caused understandable confusion until her identity became known the year after "Houston, Houston" was published. Tiptree wrote a number of other brilliantly feminist sf stories, including "The Women Men Don't See" (1973), in which two women decide that setting off for a distant world aboard an alien ship beats having to live in a male world here, and "Your Faces, O My Sisters! Your Faces Filled of Light!" (1976), in which a courier on a mission for some future feminist utopia somehow strays into our time and gets raped and murdered. Even so, she never entirely despaired of civilization and progress, or even of men.

Suzy McKee Charnas (1939–), by contrast, represents an important shift in the entire direction of feminist sf, although the significance of that shift was not entirely apparent in her first novel, *Walk to the End of the World* (1974). The setting is a post-holocaust earth on which the only survivors, so it seems at first, live in the Holdfast: a dreary environment of tidal flats and marshes in which an insanely patriarchal society subsists mostly on seaweed and hemp. Women are enslaved; men devote themselves to ritual dominance games. Women are held to blame for the Wasting, although it was entirely men's fault. Contact between the sexes is kept to a absolute minimum: male children are all raised in Boyhouses to eradicate the "fem-taint." Even among men, blood ties are kept secret, lest jealous fathers slay their sons:

It made sense, after all: sons, fresh from the bellies of fems, were tainted with the destructiveness which characterized their dams. Therefore they were dangerous. It was natural for fathers to protect themselves from their sons' involuntary, irrational aggression by striking first.[40]

Eykar Bek knows his father's name, and he wants to learn why. Thus begins an odyssey that takes him and his companions—including a fem, Alldera, who represents a secret women's underground—to Troi, a city in the foothills from which strange tales have come. Raff Maggomas, the charismatic leader of the city, has somehow restored man's pre-holocaust technology almost overnight: electricity, iron foundries, paved streets, the works. It's the sort of thing that would be considered a return to progress in traditional post-holocaust sf; at first, Maggomas seems to have some sensible ideas, like restoring grain production in the face of a famine that threatens the seaweed harvests. It soon becomes clear, however, that he is a megalomaniac psychotic: he has had all Troifems killed for their meat, and he intends to do away with fems altogether. The Ancients, he reveals, had almost done so: "they were about to cut through the tie of dependence on this mortal bitch of a world and become gods."[41] With immortality, who would need even sons, let alone women?

You can see that the fems couldn't have that. They were committed—still are—to an endless, pointless round of birth and death. They knew that once they were no longer needed for reproduction they would be dispensed with altogether. So they attacked first.[42]

For Charnas, this is not a paranoid fantasy: this is how men think, always have thought, and always will think. Not only are good and evil sex-linked characteristics, but the good or evil of any artifact, idea, philosophy, or institution can be determined solely by its historical or cultural associations with women or men. Civilization—at least since the matriarchal Golden Age—has been an absolute evil because it has proceeded from the absolute evil of men. Telephones and electric lights are as diabolical as nuclear weapons and toxic wastes, for they are all tainted by hatred of women, hatred of nature, and limitless power lust—the only motivations known to *man*kind. There is a Manichaean dichotomy between the linear male thought of science and the natural intuition of women; even the complementary functions of the left brain and the right brain are reduced to an antithesis of right brain and *wrong* brain.

In *Walk to the End of the World*, Bek's only possible redemption is to recognize the evil of his own kind. Summoned by his father to rule at his side and to be his heir, he is disgusted by the works of Maggomas, and he brings the evil of Troi crashing down in a fiery apocalypse. That leaves Alldera free to find her way to the Riding Women, a nomadic folk of the plains beyond Holdfast, in *Motherlines* (1978). Here, the absence of men, even men like Bek, defines good. Tribes may raid each other, and individual women seek dominance within them; children may be raised with seeming callousness—yet these cannot be evils as practiced by women; at worst, they are lingering effects of the patriarchal past. Even the practice of mating with horses, which can be as dangerous as it sounds, but is necessary to trigger parthenogenesis, finds its justification in its advantages over heterosexual intercourse:

The stud horse doesn't attack anyone, he means no harm, no abuse or degradation. He's innocent. He has to be led and coaxed and trained to do his part with our help. It's nothing at all like a man overpowering a fem just to show her who's master.[43]

Just why truly liberated women should choose such a means of reproduction just to score points against men who are no longer there to listen remains obscure. But the Rousselian lesbian utopia, free of men and their evil science and technology, seems to have become a litmus test for commitment to the women's cause among some radical feminists. One of the most extreme examples is Sally Miller Gearhart's *The Wanderground* (1980), in which an outbreak of virgin births signals the revolt of the Earth Mother herself against male domination. Before long, some magical force brings *man*kind's wicked technology to a standstill and makes men themselves impotent beyond the confines of their cities. Why hasn't the Earth Mother finished the job, by destroying the cities? To keep a constant reminder of men's evil before women, so it seems. Women spend a lot of time on intelligence missions in those cities and in reliving past atrocities by men in their memory rooms. Of course, they do not need any of men's evil works themselves; they practice telepathy, telekinesis, and even levitation, and they never seem to have to do any hard work to make their farming and hunting economy flourish.

Within genre sf, some feminists have come up with more imaginative approaches to the theme of women's liberation. In *Native Tongue* (1984), for example, Suzette Haden Elgin (1936–) portrays the evolution of a new language called Láadan among the cloistered women of the Linguists: families who handle negotiations with alien species in a future in which all women have been disenfranchised and made wards of fathers, husbands, or other nearest male relatives on the grounds of a never-defined "scientific" proof of their inferiority. One of the key concepts in the creation of Láadan is Encoding: inventing words for ideas or experiences never before recognized. As an underground training manual puts it:

We mean the making of a name for a chunk of the world that so far as we know has never been chosen for naming before in any human language, and that has not just suddenly been made or found or dumped upon your culture. We mean naming a chunk that has been around a long time but has never before impressed anyone as sufficiently important to *deserve* its own name.[44]

In *Native Tongue*, we follow the career of Nazareth, from a childhood of cruel exploitation in the acquisition of alien languages to serve men in the cause of interstellar commerce, through an equally cruel marriage in the cause of breeding more Linguists, to an old age in which she can at last learn the secret of Láadan and take part in its creation. It is she who persuades the others to put it into *use*, instead of waiting for it to be "finished." In *The Judas Rose* (1987), we see how the new language begins to spread through a worldwide underground, and how it subtly influences the consciousness of men as well as women.

Language is also a key element in Joan Slonczewski's *A Door into Ocean* (1986), but only one element. Slonczewski has created a true epic of utopian feminism, with a fully realized world that offers a real alternative to traditional civilization, rather than mere denunciations. Her Shora is an ocean world, reminiscent of C. S. Lewis' Perelandra in the innocent splendor of its raft-like islands. Its people, the Sharers, are females who have lived for millenia in harmony with nature. Yet it is anything but a primitive harmony, for the Sharers have developed an incredibly sophisticated biological technology. Their lifeshapers have created everything from breath microbes, enabling fellow-Sharers to swim underwater, to clickflies to carry their messages across the sea. Their knowledge of genetic engineering is recorded, not in books, but in their very habitats, which double as laboratories. A visitor encounters:

A chromosome library. Trillions of bits of data on molecular chains, coiled up so small you can't even see it. In every cell of raft-wood. Billions of cells in every raft seedling, each the seed of an entire Sharer life and culture.[45]

Their ecological consciousness is equally sophisticated. They have developed fingershells to control the parasites that attack silkweed, a basic Shoran resource, rather than exterminate the pests; without them, silkweed would choke their rafts, tubeworms would die off, leaving fish and octopi with nothing to eat, and the Sharers themselves would face starvation. Slonczewski (1956–), a Quaker as well as a molecular biophysicist, is as much concerned with ethical as cultural evolution. The Sharers have made a virtual science of nonviolence; when violence threatens, they can go into whitetrance, which renders them immune to coercion, physical or mental, though it may lead to death. Their language admits no concepts of ownership, dominance, or precedence; all resources are truly shared, all decisions are made in concert. When they cannot agree on policy, for the Sharers are not perfect, the worst sanction they can imagine is unspeaking—Coventry.

Shora is part of a double-planet system with Valedon, a dry world bound to a galactic empire doubtless modeled on Jerry Pournelle's: only centralized authority and ruthless force hold it together. Its patriarch rules ninety-three worlds, but as a starship pilot remembers: "There used to be more. Nine out of ten are congealed chunks of rock today; some still smolder. Weed out the bad ones, you know. What else is the Patriarch for?"[46] Shora has engaged in trade with Valedon for several years, although its benefits are dubious. Coldstone cables for binding starworms, creatures used for both transport and long-distance communication—farsharing—prove a poor substitute for native shockwraiths. Motorized surface craft deplete fisheries and otherwise disrupt the environment. Trinkets of gem stone afflict some Sharers with an addiction called stonesickness, much as alcohol once corrupted Indians. But predatory trade is only an opening wedge, as the Patriarchy of Torr moves to assert its authority. Sharers oppose the military invasion in the only manner they know: nonviolent witness. Slonczewski adds complication to what might otherwise be merely a radical feminist set piece. Spinel, a Valan who accepts an invitation to Shora out of curiosity, wins acceptance and even sexual love, although he is an alien malefreak; in the final test, his moral integrity is as strong as any Sharer's. The most repellant character, by contrast, is Colonel Jade, a woman who serves General Realgar as chief of staff and chief torturer. Realgar himself is a more tragic figure than villain, forsaking his only chance at love for what he actually believes to be an ideal. Merwin the Impatient, as close to a spiritual leader as there is on Shora, must endure the sufferings of Job as her people sacrifice their lives again and again with no assurance that her courage, or theirs, can avail.

Shora wins its victory, but it may be only a reprieve: Valedon and the Patriarchy are still out there. Spinel, who considers returning to his homeworld as a missionary for nonviolence, chooses at the last to remain on Shora with his loversharer Lystra. Although his final message to Valedon is that "the door is still open,"[47] his voice seems to be only one crying in the wilderness, with no hope of answer.

In *The Shore of Women* (1987), Pamela Sargent portrays an entire culture of men crying in the wilderness, for it is thence that they have been exiled by the women, who have assumed guardianship of the world after the devastation of a nuclear war. Women live in the comfort of their walled cities, with all the material blessings of pre-holocaust science and technology; men are forbidden all knowledge, and they are condemned to life in a Hobbesian state of nature: poor, nasty, brutish, and short. It is all they deserve, as far as the women are concerned: the evil of the past is in their very genes. But, for the sake of diversity, they still need those genes; and women have therefore bound men by superstition to the cult of the Lady, who appears at shrines in various guises (often erotic) and summons a few to the cities to donate their semen.

Male children, stripped of their memories, are exiled in childhood. Women are also occasionally exiled for serious crimes. Birana, who allowed her mother to commit murder, is such an exile. Against all odds, she not only survives, but finds love with Arvil, a primitive hunter who has seen the powers of the Lady unleashed against those of his kind who presumed to build a new civilization of their own, yet still trusts her. As their love grows, they learn to trust each other, yet every hand seems raised against them, and they can nowhere find peace. Sargent (1948–) has established her feminist credentials, not only through her own novels and short stories, but also as the editor of a series of anthologies of sf by and about women, beginning with *Women of Wonder* (1975). Yet, she is also very much a Wellsian in her sympathies. *The Shore of Women*, as it follows the wanderings of Arvil and Birana, becomes a meditation on the Wellsian dream and the feminist dream, and whether they can ever be reconciled. Perhaps the lovers only die at the end, and any hope for the future dies with them; yet Laissa, a chronicler of the city who befriends them to her cost and who raises their child, longs for a better ending: "I imagine them on a distant shore near a refuge they have built for themselves dreaming of the oceans we might sail again and the stars we might seek. Perhaps we will join them on that shore at last."[48]

7

For the Good of the Cause

UP FROM STALINISM

The old human conflict between the end and the means of its attainment had arisen, and the experience of thousands of generations teaches mankind that there is a certain boundary limiting the means to an end that must not be overstepped.[1]

So reflects Mven Mass, as he himself oversteps that boundary in Ivan Yefremov's *Andromeda* (1957). Mass' soul-searching hardly seems the stuff of revolution, but *Andromeda* was nevertheless a revolutionary work. When it first appeared, the Soviet Union was only beginning to emerge from the terrible legacy of Stalinism. Yefremov's novel must be seen in that light, whatever its faults; and they are many. By contemporary standards of sf, *Andromeda* is clumsy. Its heroes are pompous, and their conversations are as stilted as the dialogue of bad Hollywood sf films. Interstellar ships encounter cliché menaces like meteors; even the few moments of wonder are marred by awkward prose, aggravated in English by a translation that compounds its sins of gracelessness with such ludicrous renderings as "circles" for orbits and the "Geisenberg principle of indefiniteness."[2] By Western standards, Yefremov ranks at best with Edmond Hamilton—his "science" is just as quaint, and even his naming of names (Mven Mass, Erg Noor, Renn Bose) is reminiscent of Hamilton's (Zarth Arn, Vel Quen, Shorr Kan) in *The Star Kings* (1947).

Yet *Andromeda* is more than a space opera; it is a utopian sf novel, and its vision of the future of mankind is a complex and challenging one—especially in the context of Soviet science fiction, which, like Soviet literature generally, had been conscripted into the service of a totalitarian state for more than two decades. It was almost inevitable that the following passage found its way into Aleksei Tolstoy's science fiction thriller, *The Garin Death Ray* (1925): " 'Everything that leads towards the establishment of Soviet power throughout the world is good,' said Shelga. 'Everything that hinders it is bad.' "[3] That paean to the end justifying the means may actually come from some later, revised edition of the novel,[4] which pits the heroic Soviet agent Vasily Shelga against Pyotr Garin, a crazed engineer who uses a death ray to try to conquer the world. Tolstoy (1882–1945) was, in fact, a fellow traveler, rather than a Bolshevik; but he found it expedient to adopt a Bolshevik stance in his fiction. Even so, science fiction during the ten years immediately following the Russian Revolution was surprisingly diverse and free spirited, as witness the works of Aleksandr Belyayev, which reveal a liberal humanist world view and even flirt with anarchist sentiments. But with the campaign of vilification against sf as a "harmful genre,"[5] which was organized in the late 1920s by the Russian Association of Proletarian Writers (RAPP), the genre was virtually destroyed. What finally emerged after another decade of uncertainty and even terror (some major science fiction writers were caught in the purges[6]) was a sanitized, juvenile, pedagogical form of science fiction with a world view as fundamentalist in its own way as that of the most dogmatic Christian.

Vladimir Nemtsov (1907–) exemplifies the conservative imagination of fundamentalist sf in *A Splinter of the Sun* (1955):

This summer no interplanetary spaceship left the earth. On the railways of the country there traveled ordinary trains, without nuclear energy. The Antarctic remained cold. Man had not yet learned to control the weather, to get bread from the air, and to live for three hundred years. There were no advertisements for a lunar flight either. All these things did not exist for the sole reason that our story is about the events of the present day, which we like no less than we do the future.[7]

A Splinter of the Sun, which deals with a solar power project, is part of a series about Soviet engineers Vadim Bagretsov and Timofei Babkin. Like the heroes of juvenile series novels here, they never change. What is more striking is that their background never changes. Series like the Hardy Boys and Nancy Drew stories have been updated several times, in order to relate to the drastic changes that have occurred in American culture and mores. Nothing seems to have been updated in Nemtsov's series, nor does it need to be: the social background in *When Distances Approach* (1975), which involves near-future advances in housing construction, is the same as that in *The Seven Colors of the Rainbow* (1950), which is set on a near-future model collective farm. True, in a 1978 edition of *A Splinter of the Sun*, Nemtsov's opening lines are changed slightly—it's a flight to Mars that hasn't been advertised yet.[8] Perhaps sensing that the times have overtaken him, Nemtsov characterizes *When Distances Approach* as a "novel of practical dreams,"[9] rather than sf. But he isn't in the least apologetic; in a preface to the same novel, he cloaks himself in the mantle of Lenin and Vladimir Mayakovsky to justify his fundamentalist approach.[10] Like American religious fundamentalists, Nemtsov is alarmed by liberal ideas: in 1966, he attacked the new generation of Soviet sf writers in *Izvestia* for leading young people astray through stories tainted by naturalism, ESP, and ideological deviation.[11] Even in *A Splinter of the Sun*, written before that new generation appeared, he was denouncing the pernicious influence of foreign sf. It is obvious that one youth, Kuchinsky, is a rotter because he wears a green jacket and lilac trousers, slicks his hair, and tries to impress the girls thusly:

Well, for instance, have you heard about Atlantis? It happens there's a city on the bottom of the sea, and people live there. What a life! All the girls go around in golden tunics! And a glass dome over them. . . . Or I read a foreign book somewhere about a voyage through the Galaxy. It's packed with starships there.[12]

Nemtsov's novels are full of patriotic sentiments. In *Golden Bottom* (1948), engineers Aleksandr Vasilyev and Ibrahim Hassanov are pursuing rival approaches to exploiting the oil resources of the Caspian seabed: seabed installations vs. floating platforms. Vasilyev's seabed approach seems like a long shot at first, and he is regarded as rather eccentric and impractical; yet he is vindicated in the end. Hassanov's approach is more conservative, and he is rewarded by initial success. Rustamov, a Communist Party organizer, is the first to give credit where credit is due, but he reserves the right to find favor with Vasilyev should he succeed:

Comrades! We can congratulate engineer Hassanov and all his remarkable collective for a great victory. It's a victory of the creative mind—our government's strongest weapon. When faced with any glorious task, every Soviet must and can be an innovator. The creative, originating mind is the most contemporary of weapons; it never becomes obsolete.[13]

Later, Rustamov tells Hassanov privately that he is sure he can be counted on not to feel jealous toward his rival: "You understand, you understand very well, how important Vasilyev's experiments are. You're a Communist, Ibrahim. And how can you look at Vasilyev as a competitor?"[14] But Vasilyev has another problem: his missing son Aleksei, who has turned up in the West after having been captured by the Germans in World War II. A letter from America contains a veiled threat and suggests it might be helpful for Vasilyev to publish the secrets of his technology in a U.S. journal. Vasilyev resists the blackmail attempt, but he suffers a nervous breakdown. Rustamov assures him that the son will survive his ordeal—"They [the Americans] don't understand that a Soviet, even if he has for years been breathing the poisoned air of foreign lands, will still want to return home."[15]

Return home he does in *When Distances Approach*. We learn that Aleksei was taken to South America, which Nemtsov confuses with the American South, where he was put to work with blacks picking bananas, pineapples, tobacco, and so on. When he runs away, he is caught and put on a chain gang. Again he runs away, lives as a tramp, and finally makes his way to a seaport. There he accosts some well-dressed Russians, only to learn that they are nasty emigrés; they beat him up. Once again, he is arrested and sent back to a plantation in chains. By this time, he is so ill he cannot work; he is finally freed and even given an American passport as "William James." Eventually, he gets to New York, a den of capitalist iniquity, where he searches in vain for the Soviet consulate, the location of which is kept secret by the authorities. He tries to stow away on an outbound ship, but he is discovered and brought back. As the fog rises over New York Harbor on his return journey, there appears "a terrifying green hag—the Statue of Liberty."[16] How does he finally return to the Soviet motherland? He joins the American army, which is sent to intervene in Afghanistan, and he manages to slip across the border!

What might be called the socialist gothic was a popular form of sf during the Stalin years, and even afterward. Lazar Lagin's *Patent A.V.* (1948) is typical: an apolitical scientist in Argentia, a fictionalized America, develops a growth hormone and dreams of using it to solve the problem of world hunger. However, evil monopolists steal the invention in order to raise muscular morons for grunt work and cannon fodder. A plot by the United States to breed soldiers with a silicon biochemistry in a Middle Eastern country is the subject of Anatoly Dneprov's "Clay God" (1964). Dneprov (1919–75), who specialized in socialist gothic, may be best known for "The Island of the Crabs" (1959), in which a British scientist, Cookling, develops mechanical crabs that can process metal and replicate themselves to the limit of available resources. Naturally he, and the Admiralty, are interested in military applications:

These crabs can, in a short time, eat up all the metal the enemy has, all his tanks, cannon, airplanes. All his machine tools, devices, equipment. All the metal on his territory. In a month there wouldn't be a scrap of metal left on Earth. It would all go to the reproduction of these crabs.[17]

Cookling's crabs begin to mutate, which is fine with him—survival of the fittest will produce more efficient weapons against the enemy. But when they run out of resources, they start gobbling up each other, like the figures in a Pac Man game. In a parody of dog-eat-dog capitalism, there can be only one victor—a huge, dinosaur-like creature to which Cookling becomes the ultimate victim when, still searching for metal, it senses his false teeth.

Naturally, such gothic scenarios are possible only in the West. An episode involving a Soviet robot that gets out of control and tries to operate on its maker's brain to find out what makes humans tick leads to a reassuring conclusion on Dneprov's "Siema" (1959): the scientist will build in proper safeguards next time, "So we would soon be hearing about a new Siema. Splendid!"[18] Sever Gansovsky (1918–) hews closer to pure gothic tradition in "A Day of Wrath" (1964), in which the Frankenstein theme is replayed on an epidemic scale: the bear-like Otarks, created in an ivory-tower scientist's laboratory, escape to commit murder and mayhem. "Those scientists have grown very proud and can't see further than their experiments,"[19] complains a Canadian forester who becomes one of their victims shortly afterward. In "A Part of the World" (1974), Gansovsky brings an element of Kafkaesque nightmare to the socialist gothic. The story is set in a huge underground city that is run by the military-industrial complex, but the attitude toward the world beyond the Soviet orbit remains that of Dneprov in his cruder works: Here There Be Tygers. During the depths of Stalinism, "bourgeois cosmopolitanism" meant virtual treason, and that was the charge one critic brought against Aleksandr Kazantsev for having written Arctic Bridge (1946), in which the United States and the Soviet Union work together to build a railway tube-tunnel under the Arctic Ocean between Alaska and Siberia.[20]

But the winds of change were soon blowing. Shortly after the death of Stalin, there began to appear such idealistic utopian science fiction as Stanislaw Lem's The Magellan Nebula (1955) in Poland and Jan Weiss' The Land of Our Grandchildren (1956) in Czechoslovakia.[21] But it remained for Yefremov (1907–72) to bring the post-Stalin cultural revolution home to the Soviet Union with Andromeda.

Set a thousand years in the future, long after the achievement of world socialism, it sees that achievement, not as the culmination of social evolution, but as its true beginning. A fundamentally Wellsian, rather than Marxist philosophy, can be seen in an account of the further evolution from the Age of Alliance to the Age of the Cosmos, as mankind advances culturally and spiritually. A new sense of happiness and brotherhood is found in the "never-ceasing struggle against nature, the overcoming of difficulties and the solution of ever new problems arising out of the development of science and economy."[22] One can see echoes of Wells' *Men Like Gods* (1923) and *Things to Come* (1936) in all this. As Mark Hillegas points out, even some of the physical details of Yefremov's utopia, such as the Spiral Way, a world-girdling railway which links all the continents with electric trains travelling at 200 kilometers an hour, hark back to Wells' *A Modern Utopia* (1905).[23] The spiral is a recurrent metaphor for Wellsian evolution in *Andromeda*; it is seen in natural forms ranging from shellfish to galaxies, even in the development of "cochlear calculus," explained in a footnote as "a division of bipolar mathematics dealing with progressive spiral movement."[24]

Much attention is devoted to the physical transformation of earth. With the disappearance of nations, urban concentrations are now limited to the temperate zones; the tropics are devoted to forests that supply both timber and food; the former arctic areas, after the climatic changes of applied technology, have become prairies grazed by domestic animals and wildlife. There is also a political transformation: the state has withered away, and the affairs of the world are managed by an Economic Council, which works with a number of consultative organs such as the academies of Productive Forces, Stochastics, and Prognostication, Psychophysiology of Labor, and so on. Veda Kong, a historian, likens the council and the academies to the "inhibition center" and "associative centers" of the human brain:

Our brain and our society, both of which are persistently advancing, have this dialectic interplay of opposing forces brought into harmonic action. There was a time, long ago, when this was incorrectly termed cybernetics, or the science of control, in an attempt to reduce the most intricate interplay of inhibitions to the relatively simple functioning of a machine.[25]

One of the checks on the Economic Council is an Academy of Joy and Sorrow, which examines policy from the standpoint of its impact on men's spiritual well-being. There are also such public services as a "Vector of Friendship, a system of direct communication between people linked by the ties of profound friendship that enabled them to contact each other at any moment."[26] Yefremov stresses the variety of options open to utopian man. With longer life spans, for example, one career is not enough: Darr Veter takes a sabbatical from the Astronautical Council, where he serves as Director of the Outer Stations, to work with Kong on paleontological research and, later, does a stint at a seabed mining complex. While the prevailing custom is communal raising of children, women who wish to be mothers in the traditional sense are allowed that right at a reservation in Java. The sanctity of private emotions is respected: faced with what seems an unrequited passion for his astrogator, Erg Noor, the commander of an interstellar expedition, can refuse a chemical "cure" offered by his ship's physician: "I would not give up the wealth of my emotions, no matter how much suffering they cause me. Suffering, so long as it is not beyond one's strength, leads to understanding, understanding leads to love and the circle is complete."[27] It is a crude approximation of Arthur C. Clarke's approach to the same issue in *The Songs of Distant Earth* (1986).

Most important, there is still moral conflict. When Mven Mass, in his obsession with achieving faster-than-light travel, proceeds with a dangerous experiment without consulting the Astronautical Council, it is clear that the ethical question of ends and means is at stake. When that experiment ends in death and disaster, Mass is overwhelmed by guilt and he accepts exile to the Island of Oblivion, an institution similar to Coventry in Robert A. Heinlein's History of the Future. While there, he meditates pointedly on the "bulls," authoritarian personalities whose dogmatic fanaticism once plagued the world:

The sufferings, quarrels and misfortunes of mankind in the distant past had always been aggravated by such people in various guises who proclaimed themselves the sole holders of the truth, the rulers who claimed the right to suppress all those whose opinions did not agree with theirs, the right to eradicate all other ways of thought or of life.[28]

Eventually the council forgives him his transgression—his motives, after all, were noble, and those who were killed were volunteers. Even so, never again will he be trusted with a position of authority.

Meanwhile, there is also the conflict with the cosmic process that is typical of Wellsian sf, symbolized in the expedition of the *Tantra*, which comes across the grim derelict of the *Parus* on the bleak planet of a dark star. Against the forces of cosmic entropy stands the community of the Great Circle, a growing network of intelligent species in the galaxy. Unfortunately, Yefremov's anthropocentrism sentimentalizes what should be a powerful concept, comparable to Clifford D. Simak's galactic community in *Way Station* (1963). When earth broadcasts its world history to a newly contacted planet of 61 Cygni, Veda Kong wears a Minoan costume for the occasion, and Darr Veter explains the rationale: "Communications for the different planets are always read by beautiful women. This gives them an impression of the sense of the beautiful."[29] Later, when earth receives its first transmission from a planet of Epsilon Tucanae, that world's red-skinned ultra-humanoid natives dance nude for the edification of their Terran audience.

Those who followed Yefremov made short work of his chauvinism, however. In "Ballad of the Stars" (1960), for example, Genrikh Altov and Valentina Zhuravlyova built on the foundations of *Andromeda* but went beyond its limitations. Their heroic astronaut Shevtsov comes to the rescue of "an unusual world, whose beauty was totally different from Earth's."[30] Its benign environment has led to the evolution of a Rousselian culture that has never known war or class struggle; but that culture is threatened by a change in the planet's orbit that will bring a harshly cold climate. Native flora and fauna, adapted to the radiation of Sirius A and Sirius B, resemble nothing earthly; and the pale, ghostly sentients who call themselves Seers-of-the-Essence-of-Things are so alien that communication is difficult; "In such a complex situation, mistakes are almost inevitable."[31] The Seers cannot be judged by human (even Marxist) standards, nor we by theirs.

In the growing liberation, Sergei Snegov even brought space opera to Soviet sf with *Men Like Gods* (1966), in which a Communist earth is part of a galactic alliance of many species against the dread Destroyers. Others have infused their utopian visions with social and psychological complexity. Yevgeny Voiskunsky (1922–) and Isai Lukodyanov (1913–), in such early works as "The Black Pillar" (1962), combined the cosmopolitan spirit of Kazantsev's *Arctic Bridge* with the heroic humanism of Yefremov. Aleksandr Kravtsov, hero of "The Black Pillar," gives his life to save the world after a column of material from earth's mantle erupts from a boring drilled for scientific research; his fellow heroes come from the United States and other Western countries, even if the countries as such are not portrayed in a favorable light. In *The Splash of Starry Seas* (1967), however, Voiskunsky and Lukodyanov depict a Marxist utopia in which there are still conflicts. A colony on Venus is breaking away from the mother planet, and relations are so strained that earthmen are expelled and an embargo on trade is imposed. Meanwhile, the protagonist devotes his life to the cause of interstellar travel, but he is constantly frustrated by lack of adequate funding and personal disappointments such as the failure of his first marriage. By the time a breakthrough is achieved, he is too old to travel to the stars himself, and the interplanetary rift induces him to abandon his career and return to his native Venus.[32]

Social criticism, even biting satire, has gone far beyond the smug denunciations of capitalist evils that characterized fundamentalist sf. One of the funniest sf stories ever published—in the Soviet Union or anywhere else—is Vadim Shefner's "A Modest Genius" (1968). The hero is a young inventor who never receives any recognition from his bureaucratic society, even for devices like a Local Effect Anti-Gravitation machine. His only reward seems to be the fun of invention, whether it's a set of water skates so he can go skimming across a lake with his love, or a Quarrel Measurer and Ender to help maintain the peace at his community house. Meanwhile, an establishment inventor is showered with honors for such idiotic inventions as a can opener that weighs five tons and costs four hundred thousand rubles. Of course, no housewife can afford one; instead, there'll be a United City Can-Opening Center (UCCOC):

It will be very handy. Suppose you have visitors and want to open some sardines for them; you don't need a tool for opening the can and you don't have to do a lot of work. You just take your can to UCCOC, hand it in at the reception desk, pay five kopeks and get a receipt. . . . You go to the waiting room, settle down in an easy chair and watch a short film on preserves. Soon you're called to the counter. You present your receipt and get your opened can.[33]

Even the fundamentalist Dneprov varied his socialist gothics with such anarchic pieces as "Interview with a Traffic Policeman" (1965); and a bitter edge comparable to Mikhail Bulgakov's appears in stories like Vladimir Grigoriev's "The Horn of Plenty" (1964), in which a Soviet bureaucrat, unimpressed with an invention that produces consumer goods out of scrap, manages to wreck the machine, killing himself and the inventor in the bargain. Still more important, perhaps, Soviet science fiction began to take a revisionist attitude toward the basic tenets of collectivism as laid down by revolutionary writers such as Aleksei Gastev, who promoted the idea of a mechanized proletariat, with psychological manifestations "so foreign to personalism [and] so anonymous, that as these collectives-complexes move they resemble the movement of objects, with individual human faces gone."[34] In *World Soul* (1964), for example, Mikhail Yemtsev and Yeremei Parnov threaten the world with the "biotosis," an artificial life-form that begins to bind mankind into a collective consciousness, much like that of Isaac Asimov's Gaia in *Foundation's Edge* (1982). Only, Yemtsev (1930–) and Parnov (1935–) are *against* the biological version of Gastev's mechanistic collectivism. When a Western intellectual, who evidently considers himself progressive, hails the biotosis as harbinger of a multiorganismic Great Man, one of their Soviet heroes protests:

But that's a lot of nonsense, professor! Man is not a cell, and he can never be one! When you speak of the communists' desire to create such an organism, you mock us! You predict the total annihilation of the individual. I assure you that I have no desire to be the Great Man's earlobe. No one in my country would want to be. We are free people, and we believe in free man in a free communist world.[35]

It was this new intellectual climate that fostered the emergence of the two greatest stars of Soviet science fiction.

THE ARCHITECTS OF CONSCIENCE

I am an animal, you see that. I don't have the words, they didn't teach me the words. I don't know how to think, the bastards didn't let me learn how to think. But if you really are . . . all-powerful . . . all knowing . . . then you figure it out! Look into my heart, I know everything you need is in there. It has to be.[36]

Redrick Schuhart's desperate prayer for justice and decency, which comes at the end of *Roadside Picnic* (1972), is addressed to a "god" that is only one of the baffling pieces of technological debris left on our planet by passing aliens as we ourselves might leave trash behind after a picnic. The visitation zones are as fiendishly indifferent to mankind as the alien artifact in Algis Budrys' *Rogue Moon* (1960), but in the sf of Arkady (1925–) and Boris (1933–) Strugatsky, the indifference and uncaring inertia of human society are as cruel as the cosmos. In their science fiction, they have struggled unceasingly against that inertia and indifference to reawaken the moral and social conscience.

In their early work, the Strugatskys seem orthodox enough. A future history that begins with *The Land of Crimson Clouds* (1959) follows what was then the Khrushchev scenario for the victory of socialism through economic and ideological competition, rather than violence. *The Land of Crimson Clouds* introduces Aleksei Bykov, Vladimir Yurkovsky, and Grigory Dauge, three comrades who prove their mettle while risking their lives to develop a uranium golconda on a hellish Venus for the greater good of the Soviet Union. It is a period of international competition in space, but in their first mission, the Soviet heroes never come face to face with their counterparts from capitalist countries, who remain voices on the radio. In "The Way to Amalteia" (1960), Bykov commands the *Takhmasib*, a photon freighter on a relief mission to a research base on Jupiter's innermost moon; planetologists Yurkovsky and Dauge are part of his crew. By this time, the three are legend for their exploits on Venus years earlier; young Ivan Zhilin, who has just signed on, fresh out of the Advanced School of Cosmogation, as flight engineer, is ecstatic at the chance to serve with them. When the *Takhmasib* comes to grief in the Jovian atmosphere, Zhilin finds himself working to the point of exhaustion by Bykov's side to repair the photon reflector so that the ship can escape and bring its vital supplies to J-Station.

Foreign astronauts and scientists such as Charles Mollart, a French crewman aboard the *Takhmasib*, begin to appear in "The Way to Amalteia," but there is no sign of any ideological conflicts until *Space Apprentice* (1962). The apprentice, Yura Borodin, is a vacuum welder trainee assigned to Rhea, who misses his own ship and hitches a ride with Bykov and his comrades on the *Takhmasib*. At Mirza-Charle spaceport, his initial encounter with Zhilin takes place at Your Old Mickey Mouse, a bar-café run by a man named Joyce who prides himself as being his own boss but who is seen by the Russians as a pathetic figure, sacrificing himself to a life of boring work for the sake of providing himself with an economic security that would be his birthright under socialism. The aging Dauge has retired by this time, but Zhilin is still flight engineer with the *Takhmasib* under Bykov. Yurkovsky has moved up in the world—he is now the inspector general of the International Administration of Cosmic Communications (IACC), with powers to "reduce rank, chew out, deride, fire, replace, appoint, and even, it seemed, use force"[37] to maintain law and social justice on the space frontier. On the asteroid Bamberga, Yurkovsky shuts down a gangster-ridden gem-mining operation, Space Pearl Ltd., that endangers the miners (and their unborn children) through exposure to cosmic radiation. The pay is fabulous, however, and most of the miners, philistines to the end, when offered construction and technical work elsewhere, are interested only in how much it will pay.

"Naturally, about five times less than here," Yurkovsky said. "But you will have work for the rest of your lives, and good friends, real people who will turn you into real people too! And you'll be healthy and be part of the most important work in the world."[38]

On Dione, a Soviet research station has fallen under the sway of Vladislav Shershen, a careerist who has exploited his power as director to play his subordinates off against each other, to claim credit for their work, and so on. Morale has been destroyed, and Yurkovsky must set things right by getting rid of Shershen and his chief toady, but not without giving the staff a tongue-lashing:

I didn't expect this of you young people. How easy it was to make you revert to your prehistoric condition, to put you on all fours—three years, one glory-hungry maniac, and one provincial intriguer. And you bent over, turned into animals, lost your human image. . . . You should be ashamed of yourselves![39]

Much else happens in *Space Apprentice*, from a roundup of flying leeches on Mars to the tragic deaths of Yurkovsky and one of his other comrades in an accident exploring Saturn's rings. As in juveniles here by Robert

A. Heinlein, Borodin comes of age by learning from older and wiser heads. The novel ends with Zhilin's decision to give up the chance for a berth on a Transpluto expedition in order to work for mankind at home: "The most important thing is on Earth," he reflects. "The most important thing always stays on Earth, and I will stay on Earth, too."[40]

In *The Final Circle of Paradise* (1965), we meet Zhilin again; now a secret agent for the United Nations, he is investigating a mysterious social disorder in the Country of the Boob, a prosperous—in itself enough to make the novel controversial[41]—capitalist state in the Mediterranean area. Although the Strugatskys' approach to near-future sociological sf is clumsy compared to that common in the West—the imaginary country has too much of a fairy-tale quality about it; and the "secret," a device to stimulate the brain with electric current, as in Larry Niven's "Death by Ecstasy" (1969), could *never* be kept secret in an open society—the moral vision of their novel still comes through. Zhilin emerges as one of their archetypical heroes of utopian conscience in his struggle against the philistinism endemic in a materialistic culture, which has been unable to find any goals beyond immediate sensual gratification. A decadent intelligentsia, personified in the "neo-optimist" philosopher Sliy Opir, sanctions this state of affairs. "Satisfy love and hunger," prescribes Opir. "All the utopias of all times are based on this simplest of considerations."[42] But alcoholism and drug addiction are widespread, and alienated youth take part in orgiastic street dances, or "Shivers," which are subject to disruption by guerrilla attacks from the even more alienated Intels. Eventually, Zhilin exposes the ugly secret of "slug," the current addiction device. But that is not enough, he realizes:

What a labor lies ahead, I thought. . . . I didn't know where to begin in this Country of the Boob, caught unprepared in a flood of affluence, but I knew that I wouldn't leave here as long as the immigration laws permitted. And when they stopped permitting it, I would break them . . .[43]

We never see the final crisis of capitalism, for a Communist world utopia has become reality in *Noon: 22nd Century* (1967)—"in the square in front of Finland Station in Leningrad, Lenin held out his arm over this city and over this world, this shining and wonderful world that he had seen two centuries before."[44] In its broad outlines, the Strugatskys' vision of utopia resembles Yefremov's. Automated farms and factories serve mankind's economic needs, and a network of moving roads links the far-flung parts of the world together. There is no sign of centralized power or administration (for that matter, the Communist Party is never referred to again after *The Land of Crimson Clouds*); everything seems to just run itself. Children are raised in boarding schools, but the relations between teachers and pupils are as warm and intimate as those in some

of the best families of old. Although meals are usually communal, utopians often have their own homes and, to keep in touch with their
friends, sophisticated videophone networks and easy access to ptero-
cars.

It is a time of revolutionary advances in science and technology. Faster-
than-light D-ships have brought worlds of other stellar systems within
mankind's reach, and a sophisticated medical procedure involving both
immunization and radiation therapy at birth has freed mankind from
disease and has given ordinary men an almost superhuman vigor. Philistinism and other social disorders are a thing of the past, it seems, and
only the frontiers of space and the challenge of alien contact present
any ethical problems. Leonid Gorbovsky, a recurring hero in the Strugatsky future history, represents the antithesis of Yefremov's anthropocentric philosophy. In *Noon: 22nd Century*, he is an astroarchaeologist
with the Commission on Contacts; when we first encounter him, he is
organizing an expedition of assaultmen to Vladislava, a planet with two
artificial satellites and possibly a hidden city on the surface—all left by
the Wanderers, an apparently long-vanished race like Niven's Thrintun
in the Known Space series. Later, we find Gorbovsky pondering such
mysteries as the Voice of the Void, which few like to talk about because
it cannot be explained. Still later, he orders the abandonment of a research station on Leonida, where his Pathfinders have disturbed a biological civilization ("Not machines, but selection, genetics, animal
training. Who knows what forces they've mastered?"[45]) without real-
izing it *is* a civilization.

Sergei Kondratev, whose mission on the slower-than-light *Taimyr* has
carried him through time as well as space (an old convention in Western
sf), represents the traditional outsider in utopian sf, but he finds a new
career with the Oceanic Guard and is happily integrated at the end. But
in "Escape Attempt" (1962), there is the first close encounter between
a utopian earth and a dystopian society beyond. In a scenario akin to a
television episode of *The Twilight Zone*, two young adventurers about to
set out for an unexplored planet are approached by a mysterious
stranger, Saul Repnin, and they agree to take him along. The planet
turns out to be a cross between a feudal autarchy and a fascist police
state, with a new wrinkle of its own: there is a moving road, filled with
vehicles left by the Wanderers, and political prisoners are forced to risk
their lives by pushing and probing controls at random to try to find out
how they work. Vadim and Anton, the young adventurers, can recognize Wanderer technology when they see it, but they are too innocently
utopian to understand the sort of society they have run into, until Repnin
rubs their noses in the facts. Repnin, it eventually develops, is a World
War II Red Army tank commander who has somehow psychically "escaped" in time after being taken prisoner, but who decides to return in
the end.

Strugatsky protagonists similarly confront dystopian worlds in *Hard to Be a God* (1964, independent of their future history) and *Prisoners of Power* (1969, revised and expanded in 1971). Although the social systems on those worlds are invariably likened to feudalism and fascism, it is readily apparent that they also represent the dark heritage of Stalinism in the Soviet Union itself. In *Hard to Be a God*, for example, a coup by an alliance of storm troopers and religious fanatics on Arkanar is accompanied by an alleged doctors' plot; the persecution of intellectuals, including stage-managed confessions and show trials; and the familiar cult of personality. Anton, in the guise of Don Rumata, has been working undercover there for six years. Like his fellow agents from earth, he finds it increasingly difficult to maintain his role as a dispassionate observer, especially when the events now unfolding belie the officially sanctioned Basic Theory of Feudalism:

For as far as I am concerned, this is equivalent to scientific justification of inactivity. I know all your arguments! And I am well acquainted with our theories. But theories do not work in such a situation, where every minute human beings are attacked by wild beasts in a typical fascist manner! Everything is going to pieces, going to rack and ruin. What good is our knowledge and our gold? It always comes too late.[46]

Yet, as Anton himself realizes, mankind cannot intervene, it cannot bring about a golden age on Arkanar: social consciousness is at too low a level. In a dialogue reminiscent in its power of Fyodor Dostoyevsky's parable of the Grand Inquisitor in *The Brothers Karamazov* (1879–80) Anton tries to explain as much to Dr. Budach, an intellectual he has managed to rescue from the new order—the sort of small favor he *is* allowed to perform. Having realized who and what Anton really is, Budach begins to ask all the hard questions. Why, for example, cannot the alien God provide his world with material abundance? "This would be no blessing for mankind. For the strong of your world would take away from the weak whatever I gave them and the weak would be as poor as ever."[47] Then enlighten the cruel rulers, Budach begs. "Cruelty is a mighty force," Anton replies. "Once the rulers rid themselves of their cruel ways they would lose their power. And other cruel men would take their place."[48] On it goes, until Budach can think of nothing more than to pray that God might remake his race, or at least ordain that it can follow a better path. "My heart is heavy with sorrow," answers Anton, "but this is not within my power."[49] Anton himself suffers a mental breakdown when Kyra, a native woman with whom he has been living, is killed by a mob.

In *Prisoners of Power*, mankind does intervene on Saraksh, a world at a much higher level of technological development, too high for its own good. An atomic war has already devastated this world: "millions upon millions had perished; thousands of cities had been destroyed; dozens of large and small nations had been wiped off the face of the planet."[50] Out of the ensuing chaos, famines, and epidemics, emerged the All-Powerful Creators, a military-technological elite that has restored order in the Central Empire and has managed to run the economy well enough to win widespread popularity among all classes. Or so it seems, for the real secret of the Creators is their broadcast mind-control system—an old concept in Soviet sf, going back at least to Aleksandr Belyayev's *The Master of the World* (1929):

The field was everywhere. Invisible, omnipresent, all-pervasive. A gigantic network of towers enmeshing the entire country emitted radiation around the clock. It purged tens of millions of souls of any doubts they might have about the All-Powerful Creators' words and deeds.[51]

The only people immune to the mind-control broadcasts are the despised degens, political dissidents. The same radiation that brainwashes an ordinary man paralyzes a degen with pain, and degens caught in the open are easily rounded up. All this and more is revealed gradually, through the eyes of Maxim Kammerer, a young explorer stranded on Saraksh, who believes he is the only earthman there. In order to learn more about the world and what he can do, he joins the Fighting Legion, an elite force charged with defending the frontier regions from post-nuclear barbarians; later he joins the dissidents (socialists, technocrats, neo-Rousselians), who seem to be weak and divided among themselves. Some dissidents hope to take advantage of another war that is breaking out with neighboring Khonti, but they cannot come up with any real plans. Kammerer, despairing of the underground, decides to strike out on his own: a James Bond reborn, he manages to outwit everyone, including the secret police of the dread Strannik, to locate and destroy the broadcast center—only to learn moments later that Strannik is actually an agent of Galactic Security, whose careful plans for the salvation of Saraksh have just been disrupted by his impetuous action. Kammerer is abashed, and yet he is not repentent: the mind-control broadcasts should never have been allowed to continue, even if they did make Strannik's work easier. He is willing to work with Strannik's mission in any capacity he can, he says. "But I'm damned sure about one thing; I'll never permit another Center to be built as long as I live. Even with the best of intentions."[52]

The Strugatsky treatment of the intervention theme has influenced other sf works, including Yefremov's *The Hour of the Bull* (1970), and has aroused criticism in fundamentalist quarters for casting doubt on the legitimacy of wars of liberation.[53] Even more radical has been the criticism that turns inward, at the institutions of the seeming utopian order itself, rather than outward at the confrontation with pre-utopian worlds. "Far Rainbow" (1963) was a harbinger of this new direction in the Strugatskys' work. Rainbow is a world devoted entirely to research, especially in Zero-Transport (matter transmission), it has become a warped society; its scientists think of nothing but their work. One of them, Camill, is the last of the Devil's Dozen: scientists with grafted computer implants, which made them totally rational and also totally inhuman. The others destroyed themselves, recalls Leonid Gorbovsky, who is on a mission to the planet when disaster strikes: an experiment goes wrong, creating deadly waves that spread toward the equator from both poles. Only the children can be evacuated in the one ship available; the rest face their doom. All but Camill, who has risen from the dead before and will again, "alone on a dead planet, covered with ashes and snow."[54] Yet he has always been alone: "You tear out the emotional half of humanity and leave only one reaction to the world surrounding you— doubt."[55]

At one point, Gorbovsky tells the story of the Massachusetts Machine, an artificial intelligence that almost took over the world a hundred and fifty years earlier: "Leonid, it was terrifying,"[56] one of its creators told him. In *Beetle in the Anthill* (1979–80), the heretofore invisible machinery of the state begins to seem more ominous. Rudolf Sikorski—whom Maxim Kammerer encountered on Saraksh as Strannik—is now head of a security agency, COMCON-2, that grew out of the original Commission on Contacts but is concerned with threats from other worlds. For it seems that the Wanderers are still active, after all. In "Space Mowgli" (1973), we get an inkling of them, through their influence on a youth marooned for years on a desert planet. But their intervention is more far reaching on Hope, a planet from which they have removed nearly all the population after the local civilization succumbed to an ecological disaster of its own making. One of those who investigated the Hope mystery, Lev Abalkin, a mystery himself, is one of thirteen foundlings, raised from fertilized human ova found in a sarcophagus at an abandoned Wanderer installation. Mankind has its Progressors, who guide the social evolution of Saraksh and other primitive worlds; what if the Wanderers are similarly attempting to intervene in *our* evolution?

To neutralize any such threat, Sikorski uses his influence with the World Council on Social Problems to have the foundlings raised apart from each other and kept away from earth afterward, although this violates their fundamental rights and personal dignity. When Abalkin nevertheless suddenly returns to earth and then disappears, Sikorski is alarmed, and he puts Kammerer on the case without telling him what the case is really about. In a brilliantly ambiguous narrative; we never learn whether the threat of the Wanderers is real or mankind is simply succumbing to atavistic paranoia. We do learn that the Tagorians destroyed a similar sarcophagus with larvae of their own kind and that their progress has since come to a dead end—or has it? What *is* progress? More important, we learn how little Kammerer himself—a trusted agent of COMCON–2—knows. In the course of his investigation, for example, he learns of Operation Mirror, a series of "top secret global maneuvers, for repulsing an attack from outside (an invasion by the Wanderers, supposedly),"[57] which involved millions of unwitting participants and killed some of them. We learn of an ongoing rivalry between COMCON–2 and Isaac Bromberg, the leader of a group that opposes restrictions on scientific research, even when it involves the creation of androids. We learn that Sikorski and other world leaders (including Gorkovsky, inexplicably returned from his seemingly certain death on Rainbow) are in fact all-powerful, although they *know* they are not all-wise. Sikorski has his doubts—perhaps the Tagorians were wrong to have destroyed the Wanderer-engineered larvae—but when he confronts Abalkin at the end, he shoots him with hardly a moment's hesitation.

What had seemed a classless utopia, founded on humanistic values, now seems a managerial society—one, moreover, in which the creative minority may be, in Arnold Toynbee's sense, turning into a mere dominant minority as it faces historical crises beyond its competence. *The Time Wanderers* (1985–6), which deals with the successful resolution of another crisis—the emergence of a breed of supermen called the Ludens—is less convincing for that very reason. Kammerer has succeeded Sikorski, and all is right with the world; humanity faces a strange destiny but faces it openly and unafraid. In other novels, the Strugatskys are less sanguine. The technological marvels left by those passing aliens serve only the black market and the military in *Roadside Picnic*, and Schuhart can survive only by looting the visitation zone for them. The universe itself seems to conspire against all human hope in *Definitely Maybe* (1976–7), an almost Dickian nightmare. The conspiracy is pointedly close to home, and all too human, in *The Snail on the Slope* (1972).

On some nameless world, not part of the future history but close to contemporary earth in its obvious allegory, a faceless bureaucracy (the Forest Study and Exploitation Authority) seeks to impose its will on a seemingly endless forest and its primitive inhabitants. In alternating chapters, we follow the lives of two protagonists: Pepper, who finds a place of honor and authority in the system at the end, and Kandid, who is adopted by the forest people after the crash of his helicopter. If *Noon: 22nd Century* expresses the Strugatskys' hopes for communism, *The Snail on the Slope* reveals their darkest fears. The Directorate seems at first absurdly comical, but its ominous reality is clear by the time Pepper is asked to sign a directive prohibiting "involvement in chance effects (probability)—as a criminal activity."[58] Meanwhile, in the forest, Kandid confronts the brutality of a war of liberation, which is evidently at least aided and abetted by the Directorate. Although the language is Aesopian, with its references to the parthenogenetic Maidens and their holy cause of Accession (telepathic broadcasts through "Ears" in each village speak of "the Great Harrowing in the Northern lands . . . new advances in Swamp-making,"[59] and so on), its meaning becomes all too clear as Kandid witnesses the devastation visited on the natives—one, called "Buster" in translation, is *Kulak* in the original. Kandid, although he has always believed in progress, cannot accept a cause that has forgotten common *humanity*, that has come to regard the villagers as expendable:

If those Maidens had picked me up, cured me and showed me kindness, accepted me as one of themselves, taken pity on me—well, then, I would probably have taken the side of this progress easily and naturally, and Hopalong and all these villages would have been for me an exasperating survival, taking up too much effort for too long. . . . But perhaps not, perhaps it wouldn't have been simple and easy, I can't stand it when people are regarded as animals. But perhaps it's a matter of terminology, and if I'd learned the women's language, everything would have sounded different to me: enemies of progress, gluttonous stupid idlers. . . . Ideals. . . . Great aims. . . . Natural laws. . . . And for the sake of this annihilate half the inhabitants! No, that's not for me. In any language, that's not for me.[60]

8

From Left Field—and Right

Starhome—as you damned well know—is a force-grown society. It's not exactly regimented, but it's sure as hell disciplined. It was planted by the spiritual descendants of the twentieth-century totalitarians. I know that's a dirty word, but it's an accurate description. Their supreme goal is efficiency. It's the most workable compromise ever achieved between the laxity of individual freedom and the rigidity of a corporate state.[1]

That's the verdict of a well-rounded man in *The Long Result* (1965), a utopian sf novel by John Brunner. Micky Torres is hardly a Starhomer himself; his comfortable apartment on earth is filled with objets d'art and volumes of literature, including recently imported poetry from that other colony world, Viridis, which we have already learned was settled "by a group of neo-Rousselians who wanted to return to a pre-technological civilization."[2] But the future lies with Starhome, the only society that has ever surpassed our own. It was founded on the basis of cooperation, rather than evolving to that stage after thousands of years of wasteful competition; with that foundation, it can progress beyond anything possible on earth. That's enough for Torres—and for Brunner (1934–).

The Long Result is not Brunner's best known work, but it is perhaps his most revealing one. Roald Vincent, the hero, is an official with earth's Bureau of Cultural Relations, which faces an interstellar crisis when a fanatical group called the Stars Are for Man League attempts to kill an alien delegation from Tau Ceti brought by the Starhomers with no advance notice. The league zealots are obviously off the wall, as an official of the world police observes: "Anyone who really believes men could set up an interstellar empire is ripe for psychotherapy, and somebody who commits a criminal act in support of that belief is not just ripe but rotten."[3]

But where is the league, once a minor nuisance, getting the funding to pose a major threat now? Where did it get what turns out to have been a weapon beyond earth's technological capacity? The answer is obvious, but even after Kay Lee Wong, the courier assigned by Starhome to the Cetian delegation, admits being the agent provocateur, neither she nor Starhome is ever held culpable. Ringleaders of the league, including Vincent's old girlfriend, are rounded up and the league is banned. Yet Vincent not only accepts Wong's explanation that Starhome's actions were justified by its struggle for political independence—which earth was about to grant anyway—but also emigrates to Starhome himself, marries Wong, raises a family, and heads up a Bureau of Cultural Relations that helps the Cetians establish their own world government. Fifty years later, he is éminence grisé of a collectivistic society that has demonstrated its worth through "maximum utilization of its human resources."[4]

If this sounds rather Marxist, so be it. Brunner is very much of the Old Left; he shares the admiration for the Soviet system typical of such Old Left intellectuals as Bernard Shaw—an admiration based not so much on ideology as on discipline, the feeling that totalitarianism is essential to real social justice and social progress. Eric Ambler expressed that admiration by casting a Soviet agent in a heroic role in *A Coffin for Demetrios* (1939); Brunner does the same in *The Wrong End of Time* (1971). Even Brunner's borrowing of the techniques of John Dos Passos' *U.S.A.* trilogy (1930–36) for *Stand on Zanzibar* (1968) is as much a political as a literary statement. For Brunner, as for intellectuals of the Red Decade, the Soviet Union is a beacon of hope for the world, and Afghanistan means no more than the purges or gulags. Yet Brunner is a Wellsian, for H. G. Wells' own objections to Marxist-Leninist ideology were always tinged by personal resentment: the Bolshevik Revolution had upstaged his own crusade for a modern state on "scientific" lines. It is ironic that, at a time when Soviet sf was beginning to question Marxist-Leninist orthodoxy in Wellsian terms, Brunner was attempting to purify the Wellsian world view of its evolutionary mythology and return to the basics of the modern state. As Torres complains in *The Long Result*, "We shy away from that—we say 'totalitarianism!' and run a mile."[5]

By Brunner's standards, most science fiction is reactionary, or at least naive. Wells would doubtless feel the same way, but he might consider Brunner's sf just what the doctor ordered. *Stand on Zanzibar* is, for all its stylistic innovation, a "fantasia of possibility" on the same model as Wells' *When the Sleeper Wakes* (1899). Like its model, Brunner's novel is dystopian, with a faint gleam of hope at the end. World population is at least close to the planet's carrying capacity; hunger and poverty are widespread; and, even in the industrialized West, homelessness is endemic. But the pressures of population are as much psychological as physical, a growing lack of privacy—even business executives share apartments—is making daily life more and more intolerable. As Chad C. Mulligan, the antiestablishment sociologist, and Brunner's viewpoint character, puts it in *You: Beast*, one of his imaginary tomes:

You're a predatory beast shut up in a cage of which the bars aren't fixed, solid objects you can gnaw at or in despair batter against with your head until you get punch-drunk and stop worrying. No, those bars are the competing members of your own species.[6]

Most seek refuge in tranquilizers, some in outright insanity. Worst of all, Western capitalism exploits and aggravates the ills of mankind. General Technics, an international conglomerate, spreads its tentacles to the farthest parts of the world, with the strategic advantage of its own artificial intelligence, Shalmaneser. Among the corporation's influences on the world at large is Scanalyzer, a news service edited and processed by Shalmaneser that keeps the airwaves filled with a sanitized version of reality. *Mr. and Mrs. Everywhere*, in which average couch potatoes can see "themselves" as participants in world affairs, is a top-rated show that serves to keep the bourgeoisie spiritually lobotomized. Eugenic laws in most of the United States prohibit children for carriers of even the most minor hereditary defects, such as color blindness; whereas the benefits of genetic engineering are available only for business applications, such as tailored bacteria to produce sulphur from low-grade sludge. The United States, meanwhile, is fighting another imperalist war in Southeast Asia, having annexed the Sulu Islands to create a fifty-second state, Isola (Puerto Rico, of course, is the fifty-first).

Stand on Zanzibar conveys such details through a series of vignettes organized as "context," "the happening world," and "tracking with closeups." The main plot, or "continuity," is quite straightforward. It centers on Norman Niblock House, a black executive for General Technics, and on his roommate Donald Hogan, who does not seem to do anything for a living but is actually a sleeper for U.S. intelligence awaiting the call to duty. As a black man in a white world, House leads an essentially false life; as a seeming dilettante, Hogan hardly leads a life at all. Both become drawn into critical events that may determine the future of the world—House through General Technics' development project in Beninia, a basket case in Africa; Hogan (as "eptified" into a killing machine) through his mission to the Southeast Asian nation of Yatakang to investigate reports that a native scientist has learned how to breed supermen. Both imaginary countries represent ideals dear to Brunner. Yakatang, which calls itself a "guided socialist democracy," is full of collective determination—at a university, Hogan is impressed by the sense of energy:

There was an air of almost frantic busyness unlike the atmosphere at any American university he had ever visited. Even the few students he saw who were just standing about were talking—he heard them—about studies, not about shiggies or what to do at the weekend.[7]

Part of Hogan's mission, however, is to discredit the government, which has in fact exaggerated the work of Dr. Sugaiguntung, in order to bring about a counterrevolution. Too late, the doctor realizes he has betrayed his country, "doubting the word of those who knew better than I myself did,"[8] by allowing himself to be used by the counterrevolutionaries. A tantalizing mystery, meanwhile, surrounds Beninia: although its poverty is abysmal, it has never known hatred or violence. Shalmaneser refuses to believe such a country can exist, and the evidence that it obviously does touches off an investigation to find out why. The answer, it turns out, is a dominant mutation among the Shinka people that causes them to secrete a suppressant for the territorial-aggressive reaction. No matter how poor, no matter how crowded, the Shinka respond to one another with love, rather than hatred. Now the secret belongs to a corporation, which can exploit it at a profit. Perhaps it will save the world, after all, but Mulligan is aghast at the circumstances:

It's not something to be made in a factory, packaged and wrapped and sold! It's not something meant to be—to be dropped in bombs from UN aircraft! That's what they'll do with it, you know. And it isn't right. It isn't a product, a medicine, a drug. It's thought and feeling and your own heart's blood.[9]

For Brunner, *Stand on Zanzibar* is a relatively dispassionate work. In *The Jagged Orbit* (1969), the near-future United States is a nightmare of racist paranoia in which typical middle-class whites cower behind the bolted doors of their apartments, while blaring television commercials urge them to buy Guardian burglar traps that promise to skewer intruding blacks on metal prongs. Rather than the pressures of overpopulation or even the aggravations of cultural or ideological conflict, the cause of the world's ills can be reduced to the machinations of the Gottschalks, who sell heavy weapons to whites and blacks alike and fan the flames of hatred to maximize sales and profits. So thorough is the brainwashing of America that the South African terms *blanke* and *nie-blanke* have become standard idioms as "blank" and "knee-blank"; so debased is its culture that television is almost round-the-clock commercials. All that prevents an armageddon, it develops, is a Gottschalk computer's analysis that it would not be good for business.

In *The Sheep Look Up* (1972), pollution is destroying the world, and the blame falls entirely on one country. As one guest on a television talk show during the accelerating environmental collapse puts it:

We can just about restore the balance of the ecology, the biosphere, and so on—in other words we can live within our means instead of on an unrepayable overdraft, as we've been doing for the past half century—if we exterminate the two hundred million most extravagant and wasteful of our species.[10]

Even in the more dispassionate *Total Eclipse* (1974), in which a human expedition investigates the remains of a vanished alien civilization, it is clear (to Brunner, at least) that the root cause of their extinction is the same as that which seems to have doomed mankind at the end: "the besetting sin of greed."[11] Individualism and collectivism are matters of black and white, regardless of species or any other considerations—one leads to inevitable destruction, the other to salvation. For Frederik Pohl (1919–), however, it is not quite that simple. Pohl, once a member of the Communist-leaning Futurians, has always been of the Left, and as science fiction's best-known satirist, he has always savaged the evils of plutocracy in works like *The Space Merchants* (1952, in collaboration with Cyril M. Kornbluth) and its sequel, *The Merchants' War* (1984). Not since a Communist wanted him to join in a toast to the 1940 "liberation" of Paris by Nazi Germany, however (remember the Nazi-Soviet pact?), has Pohl trusted the totalitarian Left.[12] He still opposes the militaristic Right, especially in regard to the Star Wars program; but he has come to distrust all concentrations of power as dangerous. In his response to a survey of sf writers by *Soviet Literature* on the question of the "most important problem" facing humanity, Pohl declared that it is not nuclear war as such, but rather "the tendency of governments to reflect the most aggressive and grasping characteristics of their people rather than the kindly and altruistic ones."[13]

In *Chernobyl* (1987), his novelization of the nuclear disaster, Pohl cites the parallel between the accident at the Soviet power plant and the American *Challenger* disaster: both were the result of what British social critic Grahame Leman calls the "Technical-Bureaucratic-Political system of decision making,"[14] in which rational considerations are subordinated to the collective interests of the system. Like Brunner, and many others, Pohl remains a Wellsian. Like Arthur C. Clarke, he retains Wells' *Things to Come* (1936) as one of his personal icons. But he is clearly a revisionist Wellsian, and his revisionism is the opposite of Brunner's: a rejection of the bureaucratic-totalitarian temptations of the modern state. In one of his columns, Pohl recalls that, in *Things to Come*, the sculptor Theotocopulos is granted the right of free speech only because he is a master craftsman—ordinary citizens are evidently expected to keep their mouths firmly shut.[15] And it is no accident that in his most recent utopian sf work, *The Years of the City* (1984), his social ideal is a decentralized participatory democracy.

Pohl, like Wells himself and many social Wellsians since, feels torn between utopian optimism and dystopian pessimism. The latter comes out, not only in his own fiction, but also in *Nightmare Age* (1970), an anthology of disaster sf he edited, and in which his introduction rings a change on Rudyard Kipling's "If":

> If you can keep your head when all about you
> Are losing theirs—
> Then you really ought to consider the possibility that you
> Just haven't understood what the problem is.[16]

In the same introduction, Pohl recalls how he and Kornbluth concocted a number of horrors for *The Space Merchants*, believing at the time that they were only satiric exaggerations:

We talked about people needing "soot extractor plugs" to walk in the city streets; we didn't think it would really happen, but since then, in the streets of New York and Los Angeles, I've seen people wearing absorbent masks for the same purpose.[17]

In more recent works, he has brought a grimmer tone to similar scenarios. "Rem the Rememberer" (1974), for example, is the story of a Long Island youth of the next generation who dreams every night of a utopian world of ecological consciousness and small-is-beautiful technology; for example, bicycles have replaced cars for short-distance transportation and algae from sewage treatment plants and waste heat from power stations are the basis for a flourishing mussel industry in the Sound. But Rem awakens each day to the real world: a polluted desert, in which a sulfur-laden smog pervades the air and the rain comes down in sticky black blobs, except once in a while, during a hurricane, "and then for a few days Long Island might look queerly green and fresh for a while."[18]

Jem (1978/79) remains the most fully realized vision of the tension between Pohl's utopian dreams and dystopian fears. It begins as a novel of the rivalry among the great power blocs to exploit a newly discovered planet of the red dwarf NO-A Bes bes Geminorum 8426, or Jem for short. The rivalries are much the same as today's, only the rivals aren't: the three blocs are Food ("Fats"), Fuel ("Greasies"), and People ("Peeps")—based, as the names imply, not on ideology but on command of resources in a world where most are dwindling. Jem could be a golden opportunity for mankind; only there are a few drawbacks. The planet's sun is so dim that only a dull, reddish light illuminates it. The climate is hot and humid on the sunward side, eternally frigid on the dark side; Jem is tidally locked to its primary. The weather is violent and unpredictable, and the native biochemistry seems incompatible with our own. But the most important barrier, practically and ethically, to exploitation is the existence already of intelligent life on Jem—not just one species, but three: the crab-like Krinpit, the aerial balloonists, and the elusive subterranean Creepies. Compared to mankind, of course, they are all very primitive; they even prey on each other. Jem is not exactly Eden, but it has a sort of innocence to lose, just the same.

Mankind is not exactly the serpent, either, but its institutions and their amoral imperatives always seem to get the worse of individuals, however well-intentioned. And they are not always well-intentioned. Take Marge Menninger, whose behind-the-scenes lobbying (including seduction of a key senator) secures funding for the first Food Bloc expedition to Jem. She does not mince any words about her motivations:

I think there's goodies on this planet. I want them for us. Us being defined as the Food Bloc, the United States, the state of Texas, the city of Houston, and all the other subdivisions you named or want to name. . . . I think that's what they call patriotism, senator.[19]

Since the Food Bloc also includes the Soviet Union and its dependencies, one of the other protagonists is Ana Dimitrova, a Bulgarian with a more idealistic dream of what Jem could mean: "a new world where things could be done properly. Where the mistakes of earth could be avoided. Where one's children would have a future to look forward to."[20] That dream is shared by Danny Dalehouse, a scientist with the first expedition. Earth may be doomed, he fears, but Jem could be a second chance for mankind, if only . . .

Planning. Thought. Preparation. Control of growth so that scarce resources would not be pissed away irrevocably on foolishness. A fair division of Klong's treasures so that no nation and no individual could profit by starving others. An attempt to insure equality to all—[21]

And in the struggling camp of the People Bloc, Feng-hua Tse feels much the same way, but the very existence of rival camps on Jem is an ominous sign. Back on earth, the Fuel Bloc (Great Britain, the Arabs, and such other energy exporters as Venezuela) has touched off a crisis with its plan to monopolize the harvest of Antarctic krill; on Jem, its camp is as profligate as its refineries back home, arousing enmity in both the Food and People bloc camps. And as the rivalries mount, all three camps are reinforced.

Among the reinforcements are Menninger, loaded for bear, and still naive Dimitrova, who has trouble understanding why it is not considered proper for her to try to contact a former lover in the People camp. For that matter, the equally well-intentioned Dalehouse is slow on the uptake, even after Menninger puts the Food camp on a military footing. All the while on Jem, he has been working with the balloonists, gaining their trust, arming them against their natural enemies—little understanding that the Food Bloc's only interst in them is to conduct aerial reconnaissance against the Greasies, just as the Peeps have used the Krinpit for hit-and-run attacks and the Greasies have trained the Creepies for subterranean commando raids. Menninger soon whips the Fats into shape; almost to the end, she is a dark inversion of Robert A. Heinlein's competent man. But Dimitrova, a translator whose brain hemispheres have been severed from each other to make her more efficient at her work, is depressed by the new militaristic camaraderie of the Food camp: "Her own brain had been divided by a surgeon's knife. What divided theirs, so that they could plot genocide in an afternoon and drink and cavort and play their sexual games at night?"[22]

War comes, to Jem as it does to Earth. The high ground to be seized turns out to be a secret Greasie base on Farside, for Jem's sun is about to flare and incinerate life on the sunward side. But Menninger blunders in the placement of a small atomic bomb to kill off the Greasies so that the Fats can use their aircraft to escape. Dalehouse and Dimitrova surrender, and that is the last we see of them. Six generations later, we get a glimpse of a utopian society that realizes their ideals—sort of. Under their Six Precepts, the Jemman Republics have forsworn war, strong centralized government, and abuse of the environment. A quarter of a million Jemmans share in a culture that is seemingly carefree and hedonistic; Christmas is now the occasion for orgies around the manytree. But it is immediately apparent that this "utopia" is utterly dependent on exploitation of the sentient natives, who do all the hard work (even the balloonists, tethered, sing Christmas carols and spray aphrodisiacs for the orgies). All this is "voluntary," of course, and it is "deceiving" to look on the utopian matriarch Muskrat Greencloud AnGuyen as "like a Virginia planter overseeing slaves, or perhaps like a Shensi landlord accepting squeeze from the tenant farmers in her paddies."[23] Ironic? No more so than the United States having been founded on the ideals of the enlightenment—and also on the brutal enslavement of blacks and the virtual genocide of Indians.

George Orwell once summed up Charles Dickens' message as: "If men would behave decently the world would be decent."[24] Pohl a Dickensian? It is not as far-fetched as it sounds, for while nothing in his science fiction resembles Dickens in any outward way, there is a pure Dickensian sensibility to some of his works, especially in "Happy Birthday, Dear Jesus" (1956), an afterthought to *The Space Merchants*, in which a sales-obsessed department store executive learns the true meaning of Christmas from a missionary family just back from Borneo. Pohl's social criticism is, like that of Dickens, what Orwell calls "generously angry," rather than a mask for a hidden agenda of any of the "smelly little orthodoxies which are now contending for our souls."[25] A recurrent theme in Pohl's work is that of men trying to live decently in an indecent world, even trying to improve that world, however slightly. Dalehouse and Dimitrova try to behave decently in *Jem*, and they and others of like mind do affect history, they simply do not affect it enough.

Yet both Pohl's sense of anger and his sense of decency are always integrated with the Wellsian long view of science fiction. In *The Space Merchants*, he is angry at abuses such as strip mining of farmland by an insane culture devoted to consumption at any price. Yet the ravaging of Wyoming for food mines in *Gateway* (1976) is more saddening, for the very survival of a fifth of the world's population depends on protein rations grown in shale oil, "and what are we going to do with all those people when the last drop of hydrocarbon is converted to yeast?"[26] The utopian society of *The Age of the Pussyfoot* (1965–6) is just as materialistic as those of the Fats and Greasies in *Jem* and as hedonistic as that *on* Jem at the end; but at least it does not depend on abuse of the environment or the enslavement of human or other beings. Perhaps even its seemingly all-powerful computers serve the ends of freedom and democracy: "Was it possible that a state had been reached in which fundamental decisions made themselves—not by acts of a legislature, but by the actions of sovereign individuals, viewed en masse?"[27] Pohl is never a puritanical dog in the manger; he is willing to forgive mankind its foibles, as long as it can overcome gross social evils, outgrow what the protagonist of *Syzygy* (1982) calls its "childish vices":

Nuclear war.
Waste of irreplaceable resources.
Lack of prudence.
Failure to learn.[28]

That may be the kind of perspective we need most.

WAITING FOR RIGHTY

I swear—by my life and my love of it—that I shall never live for the sake of another man, nor ask another man to live for mine.[29]

With that credo, broadcast nationwide, John Galt seals the doom of a tottering civilization, from which he has already withdrawn the support of its most creative minds, in Ayn Rand's *Atlas Shrugged* (1957). Almost needless to say, that credo was Rand's own. With one sweeping concept, she sought to overthrow the prevailing moral and social traditions that have guided mankind for millenia; with its elaboration into objectivism, she sought to cut through the knotty problems of philosophy as Alexander the Great once cut through the Gordian knot. In keeping with her egoism, there was nothing modest about her ambitions; she acknowledged no rivals as a novelist save Victor Hugo and believed she had made the only real advances in philosophy since Aristotle.

Rand (1905–82) seemed at times to delight in the controversy she aroused; at other times, she was paralyzed by depression at the failure of her work to receive greater recognition. She lent her support to the Nathaniel Branden Institute, which worked to spread her teachings, but then purged Branden, until then her chief disciple, over what turned out to be his rejection of her sexual advances rather than a betrayal of her philosophy as she claimed at the time. Her movement shattered and deserted by most of her intimates, those not already purged, Rand died lonely and embittered. All this and more is revealed by Barbara Branden (once wife of Nathaniel) in *The Passion of Ayn Rand* (1986). If there is a syndrome peculiar to prophets and would-be prophets, Rand suffered it more than any other contemporary novelist who comes to mind: the wild mood swings between creative enthusiasm and cynical apathy, liberating insight that was frozen into instant dogma, joy in intellectual companionship turned to rage at real and, often, imagined slights. One can see the parallels with the careers of other prophets, including science fiction's own H. G. Wells—and Rand went far beyond Wells in asserting her claims to have *the* answer to the crisis of mankind.

None of this would be relevant to science fiction but for the real influence Rand has had as a catalyst for the libertarian movement, which is reflected in a small but growing school of libertarian sf. While Rand herself wrote science fiction—*Atlas Shrugged* is at least a borderline case and *Anthem* (1938, revised 1946) clearly falls into the category of anti-utopian sf and was even reprinted in an sf magazine[30]—she certainly never thought of herself as an sf writer, any more than she thought of herself as the fountainhead of libertarianism (which, in fact, she rejected[31]). Rand hardly took notice of sf, except to dismiss it, in *The Romantic Manifesto* (1969), as associated with the decline of romantic fiction.[32] For Rand, the summit of literature was the romantic movement of Friedrich von Schiller and Victor Hugo, just as the peak of social evolution was nineteenth-century capitalism. Both expressed a confidence in free will and the human capacity for greatness, and both were betrayed: romanticism by the dreary determinism of Leo Tolstoy, Émile Zola, and other exemplars of realism and naturalism; capitalism by the philosophy of altruism and collectivism, which led to the nightmare of totalitarianism in the Soviet Union.

Born Alisa Rosenbaum in Saint Petersburg, Russia, Rand lived through the early years of the Bolshevik Revolution, and she never forgot them. For her, it was never a noble experiment nor a perversion of a noble ideal by an excess of fanaticism, but an obscenity: the immolation of individual man on the sacrificial altar of the state. Only the altruistic doctrine that the highest purpose in life is to serve others could sanction such an evil; altruism, therefore, was the root of all evil. Egoism was then the root of all good. Rand was not the first to reach this conclusion; Friedrich Nietzsche had preached an egoistic philosophy decades before. While she flirted for a time with Nietzsche, whose influence is still apparent in her first novel, *We the Living* (1936), Rand—who already saw herself as a champion of reason—could not accept his mysticism. What was needed was a rational philosophy to define, and defend, all the values she cherished, from the heroic vision of man in romantic fiction to the role of capitalism as the only social incarnation of freedom and progress. That philosophy, already obvious in *The Fountainhead* (1943), was detailed at length in *Atlas Shrugged*, especially in Galt's 30,000-word speech, which is filled with the sort of arguments that Bernard Shaw would have left for a preface but which Rand insisted on working into the plot of a vast, romantic suspense novel because, she said, it was the only way to project her vision of the ideal man.[33]

What can one say of *Atlas Shrugged?* That it is the most denounced novel of our time? That it must be the most successful work of didactic fiction in our time, enjoyed by millions, revered by Rand's followers as sacred writ? These are commonplaces. What strikes anyone trying to read *Atlas Shrugged* as science fiction is that, like Wells' time machine, it is singularly askew. We see what purports to be a near-future world, in which there is no such thing as nuclear power or the threat of nuclear war; where commercial air travel appears to be uncommon, but the heroic age of railroads still obtains; where Galt's revolutionary engine, which he withholds from the world rather than allow it to be exploited by social parasites, is an atmospheric electricity motor like that in Jules Verne's *Robur the Conqueror* (1886). Great industries are still run by individual entrepreneurs like Hank Rearden, who is also the inventor of a fantastic alloy called Rearden metal, far stronger than steel; but none of the familiar American corporate names appears anywhere. Congress has given way to a National Legislature, and the chief executive is called simply the head of state instead of the president, with no explanation. There is no mention of the Soviet Union, or of international power rivalries; but Europe has become a continent of people's states that are economic basket cases, sustained only by American relief ships, which are regularly attacked by Ragnar Danneskjold, a Robin Hood in reverse who has his own commerce raider (not even a submarine) to rob from the looters, giving their ill-gotten gains back to the producers.

Rand would have considered these cavils irrelevant; the task of the novelist is not to reproduce concrete reality, but to project a "selective re-creation of reality according to [the] artist's metaphysical value-judgments."[34] Rearden and Dagny Taggart—the real brains of the Taggart Transcontinental Railroad—are projections of businessmen as they might and ought to be. The villains, from Dagny's brother James and Orren Boyle of Associated Steel (the chief competition to Rearden Steel to the extent that it can be considered a functioning business at all) to Wesley Mouch, who betrays his trust as Rearden's Washington lobbyist to become the country's economic czar, are distillations of the mediocrity Rand saw as inherent in the values of altruism and collectivism. Still, one can imagine even the philosophy of Objectivism being expressed in a different manner; the real key to Rand is her Promethean world view. It sprang into her mind, when she was nine, from the pages of an adventure serial, Maurice Champagne's *The Mysterious Valley* (1914). Champagne (1868–1951) was a truly prolific French author of sf, lost-race fiction, and exotic adventure in the tradition of Verne. Cyrus Paxton, hero of *The Mysterious Valley*, is a British officer in India, but he is more than that: he is a Promethean hero, as confidently larger than life as Verne's Captain Nemo, but without any tragic flaw. Captured with his comrades by an evil rajah (who has been using trained tigers in raids on British forces), brought to the rajah's hidden temple in chains, and kept in a cage, he remains nonetheless proudly defiant. Threatened with torture, Paxton hurls insults at his captors, even laughs at them. He seems to dominate the novel, even though he comes on stage only toward the end, when a rescue expedition mounted by other comrades reaches the valley.

Decades after she had read it, the motifs of *The Mysterious Valley* recur in *Atlas Shrugged*. John Galt, like Cyrus Paxton, remains a man of mystery, never seen through most of the novel; like Paxton, he is captured by the villains and defiantly insults his torturers, he even advises them how to fix their torture machine when it breaks down. When he first conceives his strike of the mind—at a mass meeting of Twentieth Century Motors employees who have been called to approve reorganization of the plant along collectivist lines—he is every bit as confident as Paxton (or as Frank Reade or Tom Swift, promising some astounding new invention or exploit): "I will put an end to this, once and for all," he declares. "I will stop the motor of the world."[35] In the original myth, Prometheus was punished by the gods for stealing fire; he was chained to a rock and his liver was devoured anew each day by an eagle. In Rand's fiction, however, the jealous gods are only the social and economic mediocrities among mankind, who bind the creative and productive heroes with guilt feelings of a false morality, even as the Lilliputians bound Gulliver with ropes. What she called "the sanction of the victim"[36] was, for Rand, the ugly secret of our whole civilization. Her complaint is not entirely unknown in science fiction, as witness the confrontation between the Big and the Little in Wells' *Things to Come*, or the vision of earth's most gifted minds sacrificed to the needs of morons in Frederik Pohl and C. M. Kornbluth's *Search the Sky* (1954). It is simply more obsessive.

In *Anthem*, people are burned at the stake for having rediscovered the Unspeakable Word; and while Rand's protagonist, Equality 7–2521, is a familiar sf archetype as rediscoverer of lost science and technology in a primitive post-holocaust culture, his real quest—although even he does not realize it at first—is for that Unspeakable Word: *I*. When he finds the sacred word in ancient books at a pre-holocaust house in the Uncharted Forest, to which he has fled with his mate from persecution by the puritanical collectivists of the World Council, he changes his name to Prometheus and dedicates himself to a new cause: "The word which will not die, should we all perish in battle. The word which can never die on this earth, for it is the heart of it and the meaning and the glory."[37]

Envy of Promethean man is the motivation of most of Rand's villains, such as Ellsworth Toohey, the cultural critic who harries Roark in *The Fountainhead*. James Taggart, in *Atlas Shrugged*, is forced to face that motivation in the end: "he knew that it was Galt's *greatness* he wanted to torture and destroy."[38] And *that* is Rand's interpretation of history: the criticism of capitalism and the advance of collectivism, ever since the industrial revolution, have had nothing to do with actual abuses in mines or factories or with immoral (even by Rand's standards) behavior of those who call themselves capitalists—such as invoking the power of government to smother competition or suppress labor unrest. Marx and Dickens alike were imagining things; their protests reflect nothing but mean-spirited envy of the heroic entrepreneurs who were actually making life better for all as they made fortunes for themselves. The same sort of envy, directed at the material successes of capitalism, underlies the contemporary environmentalist movement, she argues in *The New Left: The Anti-Industrial Revolution* (1971). In all her works, nonfiction as well as fiction, there is only one kind of good and one kind of evil—

there can be no important conflict in the world other than that between a world view of egoism, reason, and capitalism on one hand, and altruism, mysticism, and collectivism on the other. The only reference in *Atlas Shrugged* to the Wellsian struggle between evolution and entropy, for example, comes in an exchange between Dagny Taggart and Hank Rearden:

"I keep thinking of what they told us in school about the sun losing its energy, growing colder each year. I remember wondering then, what it would be like in the last days of the world. I think it would be . . . like this. Growing colder and things stopping."

"I never believed that story. I thought by the time the sun was exhausted, men would find a substitute."

"You did? Funny, I thought that, too."[39]

But it would never have occurred to Rand to write *that* story; the only function of the (scientifically outdated) Wellsian vision of the last days of the world is as a metaphor for the social breakdown taking place as, one by one, the producers and creative intellects vanish. Rand is at her best in her panoramic vision, supported by countless telling details, of the sort of social and technological devolution that has since become a staple of the Mad Max films. But she never seemed to realize where her greatest strengths lay. When Jeff Allen, a tramp who once worked at the Twentieth Century Motors plant, tells about the human cost of the social experiment that was the catalyst for Galt's rebellion, it is a far more powerful indictment of collectivism than Galt's own marathon speech—indeed, the smaller, more intimate scenes are often more effective than the harangues. Galt's utopia in a mountain fastness is, like nearly all utopias, a perfect community of true believers; and the grand climax, in which Galt is delivered into the hands of his enemies in order to prove his heroic mettle, seems patently contrived. Rand's ambivalence toward ordinary men, portrayed by turns as loyal workers or faceless whiners, becomes repellently condescending in the treatment of Eddie Willers, Dagny Taggart's right-hand man at the railroad. Faithful to the end, Willers' only reward is a hopeless passion for the woman who has left his world for Galt's Valhalla and left him in the lurch.

Rand's increasing dogmatism, exemplified by her pronouncements on a widening range of psychological, esthetic, and cultural issues she knew little about, alienated even many of those basically receptive to her literary and philosophical vision. Her very reference to the virtue of an *"unbreached rationality"*[40] (as if rationality were a wall against reality, rather than an active engagement with it) was more revealing than she realized. Nevertheless, her influence on libertarianism and on science fiction has been more crucial than one might think. There was libertarian sf before *Atlas Shrugged*, as witness Robert A. Heinlein's "Coventry" (1940), Eric Frank Russell's " . . . And Then There were None" (1951), and Kornbluth's *The Syndic* (1953), just as there were libertarian thinkers before Rand. But what Wells brought to evolutionary humanism—"an overwhelming vigor, vitality and comprehensiveness,"[41] in the words of Mark Hillegas—is what Rand brought to libertarianism. She was the first to offer what at least *seemed* to be an integrated world view in support of rational individualism, as opposed to the rationalistic collectivism of Marx on one hand, and the religious or tradition-based ideologies that had failed to effectively oppose Marxism on the other. One can begin to see her influence in works like Richard C. Meredith's *The Sky Is Filled with Ships* (1969), in which a corrupt and tyrannical Terran Federation is crumbling in face of a rebellion of the Alliance of Independent Worlds; but in which the real hope lies with neither of the warring parties, but with the Solar Trading Company, which, through production and trade, created the basis for interstellar civilization in the first place.

Among those influenced by Rand, the most successful in building a genre sf base for libertarian science fiction has been L. Neil Smith (1946–), whose *The Probability Broach* (1980) is the first of a series set in the parallel universe of the North American Confederacy—where the Whiskey Rebellion of 1794 overthrew the Constitution and led to a libertarian world under a revised version of the Articles of Confederation as conceived by Albert Gallatin. Win Bear, a Denver cop in our universe, who chafes at the increasingly restricted life in the United States, is drawn into a cross-time conspiracy involving the Hamiltonians—statist diehards who are receiving aid and comfort from our world in support of their conspiracy against the Confederacy. Along the way, we learn a lot about Confederate society and history. As in Rand's philosophy, private property is sacrosanct; Smith calls his philosophy propertarian, and a Propertarian Party is active in Colorado on the U.S. side. But Smith's idea of government is much more limited than Rand's; in the Confederacy, the state has withered away to the point that the major political debate centers on the abolition of the Continental Congress, which rarely meets any more in any case. From Heinlein's *Beyond This Horizon* (1942), he borrows the idea of an armed citizenry, each man responsible for his own defense. But there are also such innovations as recognition of sapience, and all the rights thereof, for simians and dolphins. All this and more has its origins in a small, but decisive change in the Declaration of Independence: in the Confederate universe, Thomas Jefferson used it to argue in favor of *unanimous* consent of the governed as the only basis of government. For Smith, that is an illustration of Rand's concept of free will: "To think or not to think. . . . History isn't determined by some mysterious impersonal machinery, but by people *deciding* whether to use their minds or slough it off. In this world, Jefferson *decided* to insert that one little word."[42]

More improbably, Bear concludes that free will accounts for the fact that, despite their divergent histories, the worlds of the Confederacy and the United States are inhabited by avatars of the same individuals. Win Bear has his own double, Ed; there is a Richard Milhous, a burglar, and a peanut salesman named Jimmy Carter. A rather annoying weakness in Smith's universe is the lack of any real conflict, beyond that inspired by Hamiltonian conspiracies. After two centuries of utopian evolution, which has brought universal peace and prosperity, the very existence of such a movement seems as improbable as that of the Secret Loyalists who try to bring back British rule in Curtis Steele's *Scourge of the Invisible Death* (1935), an *Operator No. 5* thriller. One would also expect crime and other signs of social disaffection to have withered away, yet the Confederates seem to have frequent need for their guns. In *The Venus Belt* (1981), there is a Hamiltonian conspiracy again, this time involving an unctuous newscaster (Voltaire Malaise, get it?), to create statist colonies on planets of other stars with 150,000 kidnapped women as breeding stock. *The Gallatin Divergence* (1985) has to do with yet another conspiracy, as Hamiltonians travel in time to undo Gallatin's victory in the Whiskey Rebellion. But there is more complication in *Tom Paine Maru* (1984), in which two soldiers from a Hamiltonian planet, Vespucci, are rescued by the Confederacy and face a challenge to their fundamental beliefs similar to that confronting the barbarian world warrior in Arkady and Boris Strugatsky's "The Kid from Hell" (1976). Finally, in *The Wardove* (1986), Smith even explores the conflict *within* a libertarian society caught up in a divisive interstellar war.

Most successful in broadening the themes of libertarian sf is J. Neil Schulman (1953–), who made his debut with *Alongside Night* (1979). Set in the near future, it follows the conventions of Heinlein juveniles and the favorite libertarian scenario for economic apocalypse: runaway inflation is running the United States into the ground, and opposition from groups like Citizens for a Free Society has the government worried. Fearing the worst, free-market economist Martin Vreeland makes plans to flee the country with his family, only too late—he seems caught in an FBI crackdown, along with his wife and daughter. And Elliot, his teenage son, finds himself trying to stay alive, free himself, and, hopefully, rescue the rest of his family. After some narrow escapes, Elliot manages to make contact with the Revolutionary Agorist Cadre, which supervises the portable (literally) underground libertarian utopia of Aurora—comes a police raid, it just picks up and *moves*. Instead of a government, its social contract is a General Submission to Arbitration, and it does not even offer Elliot the standard utopian Grand Tour ("You know: 'Here is the food-production facility. It produces three times the food of the old, reactionary system.' "[43]), but it is a lot of fun. But things become grim: Martin Vreeland, blackmailed into aiding the government by its threats against his wife and daughter, nevertheless appeals to the cadre, which mounts a climactic commando raid against the FBI's underground political prison—only to watch in horror as the helpless prisoners are killed by the installation's self-destructive devices (fortunately, the Vreeland women had already been transferred). In a Randian bit of complication, Elliot's partner in the raid is Lorimer Powers, the daughter of the mad FBI director, whom Elliot himself must kill to defend his father after exposure of the holocaust at the gulag has brought down the government.

If *Alongside Night* is an amalgam of Heinlein, Rand, and the modern libertarian economic theoreticians, *The Rainbow Cadenza* (1983) is even more ambitious. Joan Seymour Darris is a brilliant young artist, whose passion for lasegraphy matches Howard Roark's for architecture. What is lasegraphy? A totally original art form, akin to music, which uses the colors of the spectrum rather than the notes of the scale, except in a mixed-media, vulgarized form called roga. That in itself would make provocative subject for an sf novel. There is also the bizarre world Darris inhabits. Thanks to a drug that enables parents to choose their offsprings' sex, combined with the militaristic pressures arising from the thirty-year world civil strife of the Brushfire War, the sex ratio has become totally unbalanced. Men outnumber women seven to one, and even though it would be possible to restore the balance, hardly anyone wants to; the new order has become institutionalized. The World Federation is ruled by an elite of Gaylords (gay and celibate men) and Ladies; straight men are represented only in the lower house of a Federation parliament. Since the War of Colonial Secession, in which earth's space colonies broke away, there has been no serious threat to the peace of mankind, but there is the World Federation Peace Corps.

All women, when they come of age, must serve in the corps, in order (so the theory goes) to eliminate rape in a society where most men have no other hope of sexual companionship. Joan Darris' sister (actually, her mother's cloned twin; relationships get complicated here), Vera Collier Delaney, conceives an enmity toward Joan for showing such promise in the artistic career at which she herself has failed. Schulman sets up a truly Randian conflict of wills: "Her fundamental choices were now to bring about—for herself and those she affected, but particularly Joan— just those sorts of destiny which only the possibility of free choice allowed."[44] Although Darris has gone to Ad Astra, a libertarian colony, to pursue her studies, Delaney contrives—through her influence as a judge—to have her drafted into the Peace Corps almost as soon as she sets foot on earth again for a family visit. What follows is more than an exposé of an evil system, even after Darris is "liberated" from grunt sex into a special assignment with a high-ranking politico who has a shit fetish. Deserting the corps, she hides out among the Touchables, offenders who have been deprived of virtually all civil rights and who may be hunted and raped for sport—more serious offenders get broiled, on live television, in microwave ovens. There she meets Hill Bromley, a priest of the Mere Christian Church (C. S. Lewis has been canonized, and a space colony has been named for him) who ministers to his fellow Touchables at the risk of his own life. In an affair that ensues, their philosophical dialogue attempts what Lewis and Rand alike would have surely thought impossible: a synthesis of the Christian and Objectivist world views. Even after the events of the plot—their capture and her daring action to save his life and her own and her career—are wound up, Bromley's words haunt us:

Christianity against Judaism against Hinduism against Witchcraft against Objectivism against Scientism. If we all ever started *listening* to each other instead of squabbling all the time, we might learn something—the password St. Peter needs to let us through the gates.[45]

9

The Synthetists

THE REDISCOVERY OF MAN

We were drunk with happiness in those early years. Everybody was, especially the young people. These were the first years of the Rediscovery of Man, when the Instrumentality dug deep into the treasury, reconstructing the old cultures, the old languages, and even the old troubles. The nightmare of perfection had taken our forefathers to the edge of suicide. Now under the leadership of Lord Jestocost and the Lady Alice More, the ancient civilizations were rising like great land masses out of the sea of the past.[1]

It is 15,000 years from now, more or less, when Paul and his lover Virginia are transformed from faceless, numbered utopians into romantic individuals. "I had known her well, but never known her," Paul recalls. "I had seen her often, but never seen her with my heart, until we met just outside the hospital, after becoming French."[2] Their liberation, although it ends in tragedy, is a reaffirmation of the values restored to mankind in Cordwainer Smith's "Alpha Ralpha Boulevard" (1961).

Smith was the pseudonym of Paul Myron Anthony Linebarger (1913–66), a professional scholar, soldier, diplomat; an authority on Oriental cultures and psychological warfare; and much else. Smith's science fiction is like nothing else in the genre; he was the most distinctive stylist

in sf of his own or any other generation, but his legacy does not depend
on style alone. For Smith was a synthetist, a man of ideas, and—more
important than that—a reconciler of ideas. Yevgeny Zamyatin may have
been the first to apply the Hegelian dialectic to the evolution of art. In
"On Synthetism" (1922), written two years after his anti-utopian classic
We, Zamyatin was concerned with schools of writing: realism as the
thesis, symbolism as the antithesis, and neorealism as the synthesis.
"Tomorrow we shall be gone," he declared of his own school of neo-
realists. "Tomorrow a new circle will begin. . . . The equation of art is
the equation of an infinite spiral."[3] But that spiral can involve the substance as well as the esthetics of art. *We* is the antithesis of the Wellsian
utopia, even though Zamyatin considered himself part of a synthetist
school. Perhaps he would have appreciated the dialectical conflict of
world views in science fiction, having already recognized in the early
sociological sf of H. G. Wells a negation of the traditional static utopias.[4]
It is that conflict of world views that is the foundation of Smith's synthesis.

Smith was a romantic visionary, and in some passages he achieves a
synthesis of the vision of sf and the vision of poets and mystics. When
Helen America, in "The Lady Who Sailed *The Soul*" (1960), asks the star
sailor Mr. Grey-no-more what it is like out there, his reply seems to sum
up the essence of both visions:

"There are moments—or is it weeks—you can't really tell in the sail ship—
when it seems—worthwhile. You feel . . . your nerve endings reach out until
they touch the stars. You feel enormous, somehow." Gradually he came back
to her. "It's trite to say of course, but you're never the same afterward."[5]

Yet Mr. Grey-no-more also longs to return to New Earth, a planet "like
Earth must have been in the old days,"[6] where life has not become too
artificial, where the ocean is actually sometimes too cold to swim in,
where "We have music that doesn't come from machines, and pleasures
that come from inside our own bodies without being put there.'"[7] Smith
finds romance in both the Wellsian dream of science fiction and the old
human values defended by the anti-Wellsians. It is always *hard* romance,
too. Science fiction has a reputation for cheap heroics, but nothing is
cheap about the heroism of the star sailors, who must endure journeys
of forty years literally wired into the controls and support systems of
their ships, while drugged to make the subjective duration seem only
a month. When Helen America qualifies as a sailor, so she may join Mr.
Grey-no-more on New Earth, a medical officer lays it out for her: "So
what you face is a month of being absolutely wide awake, on an operating table and *being operated on without anesthetic,* while doing some
of the hardest work that mankind has ever found."[8]

Paul Linebarger came to science fiction by a strange route. Son of Sun Yat-sen's legal advisor, he spent much of his childhood in China, or in Japan, or Germany, or France. Raised as a Methodist, he had a brief teenage infatuation with communism, returned to nominal Methodism, and, after his second marriage, became a High Church Episcopalian. Like most sf writers, he discovered the classics of Jules Verne and H. G. Wells in his formative years, not to mention Edgar Rice Burroughs and the entire pulp magazine tradition; but his international upbringing also brought him in touch with such exotic fare as *Mountains, Seas and Giants* (1924), a visionary chronicle of the rise and fall of a machine civilization in Europe by Alfred Doblin, the German novelist better known for *Berlin Alexanderplatz* (1929).[9] Doblin may well have influenced the conception behind "Scanners Live in Vain" (1950), the story with which Smith burst onto the science fiction scene, having seemingly come from nowhere ("War No. 81-Q," his first published sf story, had appeared in a high school newspaper in 1928).

"Scanners Live in Vain" is the story of a guild of cyborg pilots, whose monopoly over space travel is threatened by a discovery that makes their living sacrifice and the rituals that justify it obsolete. In the background, there is a larger story: the story of mankind's emergence from a terrible holocaust, suggested in allusions to the Wild with its Beasts and man-shonyaggers—revealed in "Mark Elf" (1957) to be mutant animals and ancient German killing machines—and to isolated cities, guarded by electronic pales. In an unpublished revised version of "War No. 81-Q" (1961), we learn that an attempt to limit conflicts to ritual wars fought by remote-controlled machiens broke down under pressures of population: "When [the *real* war] was over, hideous new creepers covered the wreckage of cities, saints and morons camped in the overpasses of disused highways, and a few man-hunting machines scoured the world."[10] We meet one of the morons in "Mark Elf," and it must be the saints whom the E'Telekeli speaks of in *Norstrilia* (definitive version, 1975), when he tells of the others in the earth, after the Ancient World fell:

They conquered death. They did not have sickness. They did not need love. They sought to be abstractions, lying outside of time. And they died, E'lame-lanie—they died terribly. Some became monsters, preying on the remnants of true men for reasons which ordinary men could not even begin to understand. Others were like oysters, wrapped up in their own sainthood. They had all forgotten that humanness itself is imperfection and corruption, that what is perfect is no longer understandable.[11]

Smith's historical cycle begins in the aftermath of one nightmare of perfection and ends with the dismantling of another. Presiding over that cycle is the Instrumentality, which emerges from the Ancient Wars. Paul Linebarger's widow, Genevieve, gives it a more definite origin in "The Queen of the Afternoon" (1978), which she expanded from her husband's uncompleted story, but that is strictly her conjecture. (The Fighting Trees, which remove radioactive poisons from the soil, the ocean full of weeds, and the puppy people are from the original fragment.) In part hereditary, in part selective, the Instrumentality has the aura of both a political elite and a priesthood. Like the Communist Party, it is the power behind the the formal institutions of government. Its ruling lords are reminiscent of Plato's philosopher kings, or of Chinese mandarins. In terms of science fiction, they are the ultimate incarnation of Wells' New Samurai: the all-seeing wise men who hold the destiny of mankind in their hands. Their original mission is to stop war, and their world-state is a means to that end. In the end, however, the mission becomes a mission of social perfection, even as the mission of the saints had been spiritual perfection. We can sense their ruthless dedication in the ritual that initiates Roderick Eleanor as a lord in *Norstrilia*:

> That you have earned this status by survival capacity, and that the strange and difficult lives which you have already led with no thought of suicide have earned you a place in our terrible and dutiful ranks—
> That in being and becoming the Lord Roderick Eleanor, you shall be man or woman, young or old, as the Instrumentality may order—
> That you take power to serve, that you serve to take power, that you come with us, that you look not backward, that you remember to forget, that you forget old remembering, that within the Instrumentality you are not a person but a part of a person—[12]

In an abandoned partial draft of what became "The Ballad of Lost C'Mell" (1962),[13] there is an account of the successive rulers of earth which refers to the Dwellers, the Originals, the Bright, and the Pure. It conflicts in several respects with references in published stories, but it seems likely that the Dwellers are the true men of "Mark Elf," who leave the government of the Wild to the morons, in order that they themselves may pursue "the quiet and contemplation which their exalted but weary temperaments demanded."[14] (In S. Fowler Wright's *The World Below* [1929], the Dwellers were a similarly austere and enervated race of giants; Smith may have borrowed the term from Wright.) Into their world comes Carlotta Vom Acht, the daughter of a German rocket scientist, who has orbited earth since World War II, and whose destiny is "to bring the gift of vitality back among mankind."[15] Her descendants become the Vomacts, who figure in Smith's fiction again and again. "Acht" is a German word with a double meaning: "care" or "attention," and "proscribed" or "forbidden." Like the life force itself, the Vomacts are amoral, alternating as benefactors or outlaws throughout the cycle.

The return of vitality to mankind ushers in a heroic age, an age of reconstruction on earth and exploration of other worlds. "Scanners Live in Vain" takes place during the dawn of this age; by the time of "The Lady Who Sailed *The Soul*," the Wild has long since been tamed, and the Beasts and the manshonyaggers are no more. In "When the People Fell" (1959), we witness the conquest of Venus by the Chinesians, the last of the old nations of an increasingly homogenized mankind. The discovery of planoforming, a means of faster-than-light travel, opens rapid communication with other stars, once long decades away by sail-ship. We share the adventures of the pinlighters who fight the dragons of Space$_2$ with their feline partners in "The Game of Rat and Dragon" (1955) and share the tragedy of the Go-Captain who must make an incredible sacrifice to bring his lost planoforming ship to port in "The Burning of the Brain" (1958). Perhaps the apogee of the heroic age is represented by the Inter-World Dance Festival related in "No, No, Not Rogov!" (1959). Watched by a thousand worlds, a golden shape on the golden steps of the festival hall is a living synthesis of human and nonhuman cultures:

> *Out of meeting inhuman art, out of confronting non-human dances, mankind had made a superb esthetic effort and had leapt upon the stage of all the worlds.*
> *The golden steps reeled before the eyes, Some eyes had retinas. Some had crystalline cones. Yet all eyes were fixed on the golden shape which interpreted* The Glory and Affirmation of Man *in the Inter-World Dance Festival of what might have been A.D. 13,582.*[16]

" 'There is a music which underlies all things,' " Lady Ru quotes some "ancient lord" in "Under Old Earth" (1966). " 'We dance to the tunes all our lives, though our living ears never hear the music which guides us and moves us.' "[17] Music was a powerful symbol to Smith, a symbol of the underlying divine order and purpose in the universe. That is hardly a fashionable view in literature; today, the prevailing view in fiction (including New Wave sf) is that the universe is chaos—orderless and purposeless. Yet, even if we do not believe in a divine origin for the universe, contemporary evidence suggests there is an order in the form of self-organizing principles that appear to govern phenomena ranging from the flocking of birds to the unfolding of evolution itself. As to purpose, we still interpret that for ourselves. Nikolai Rogov, a Soviet scientist in Smith's story, works on a telepathic weapon to probe the minds of Western leaders, but what he tunes in on instead is that dance festival of the year 13,582: "The rhythms meant nothing and everything to him. This was Russia, this was Communism. This was his life—indeed it was his soul acted out before his very eyes."[18]

Rogov's conviction, although the overpowering experience evoking it drives him mad, foreshadows that of the Instrumentality itself. But the order gradually imposed by the Instrumentality is a poor imitation of what Smith regarded as the real order of the universe. It is purely mechanistic and materialistic. We see signs of a cultural decline into hedonistic decadence in the epilogues to "When the People Fell" and "The Lady Who Sailed *The Soul*," where injections of a drug (later identified as stroon, derived from the sick sheep of Norstrilia) have extended the human life span to hundreds of years, but there seems to be less and less to live for. In "Golden the Ship Was—Oh! Oh! Oh!" (1959), we first meet the Go-Captain Tedesco when he is lost in the pleasure of current addiction, like one of Larry Niven's wireheads; only when he is summoned to serve in the war with Raumsog does he learn that real experience can bring him "even greater pleasure than that of the electric current."[19] Beyond the pleasure revolution itself, however, comes a stifling utopia of enforced happiness in the tradition of Zamyatin's *We*: "The citizens were happy. They had to be happy. If they were found sad, they were calmed and drugged and changed until they were happy again."[20] No true man is responsible for his own life; except for a few fighters and technicians, nobody goes anywhere or does anything: ordinary work is performed by underpeople.

Derived from animal stock, but unable to breed true like the Beasts of the dark age, the underpeople are paradoxically more human than true men—their lives are real, even if they are not free. They have no rights, only hope: the hope of the Old Strong Religion, the religion of the First Forgotten One and the Second Forgotten One and the Third Forgotten One, of "the love that will give them a clean death and true."[21] In "The Dead Lady of Clown Town" (1964), they put that faith to the test; yet the workings of Providence are paradoxically ambiguous—for while "The Dead Lady of Clown Town" is an intensely religious story, as shown in the exegesis of Sandra Miesel,[22] it also seems a pure sf story, in which everything that happens can also apparently be explained by chance and human intervention. It begins with Elaine, erroneously programmed from fertilization for the career of lay therapist on Fomalhaut III—a world with a settled, post-Riesmannian society that has no need for such frontier skills. There are no humans to treat, only underpeople, which would be illegal; sick or injured underpeople are simply sent to the slaughterhouses because it is cheaper to breed new ones. Lost and confused, she wanders through a forbidden door and into a destiny that is ordained by a higher power—or perhaps only by the dead Lady Panc Ashash, once of the Instrumentality, whose personality now animates an information booth.

"You're *Elaine*!" it exclaims. "The worlds wait for you."[23] Before she can take any of it in, Elaine is being groomed for an encounter with her destined lover, the Hunter, who knows the Old Strong Religion, and whose own destiny is to prepare the dog-girl D'joan for her role as the martyr of the underpeople's revolution. Imprinted with all the memories of the Hunter and Elaine and, through them, of mankind to its antiquity, she becomes Joan, ready to beam her telepathic message to the world as she dies on the pyre to which she has been condemned by a tribunal of the Instrumentality: "Loved ones, you kill me. This is my fate. I bring love, and love must die to live on. . . . I die for all of you now, dear ones—"[24] The transcendental purpose behind the events of Fomalhaut III seems as obvious as the parallels with Joan of Arc, and yet God seems to work in ways even more mysterious than we are accustomed to. Charley-is-my-Darling, one of the fugitive underpeople who will die in a revolution that lasts six minutes and reaches barely a hundred meters, is so frank about it that he would seem cynical, if we did not know he *believes*:

We have all our information from the Lady Panc Ashash. . . . Since she has not had much of anything to do, she has run through billions and billions of probabilities for us . . . [she] found that perhaps a person with a name like yours would come, a human being with an old name and not a number name, that that person woud meet the Hunter, that she and the Hunter would teach the underchild D'joan a message and that the message would change the worlds. We have kept one child after another named D'joan, waiting for a hundred years.[25]

Divinely inspired, or humanly engineered, the martyrdom and legend of Joan have their effect: among the underpeople, in the diffusion of the Old Strong Religion and the later Holy Insurgency of the E'Telekeli; among true men, through Lady Goroke, whose anguish over her own role in the tribunal leads her to name her son Jestocost ("cruelty" in ancient Russian) so that "he, or his son, or *his* son will bring justice back into the world and solve the puzzle of the underpeople."[26] Generations later, the seventh Lord Jestocost does just that in "The Ballad of Lost C'Mell." But he is also one of the architects of the Rediscovery of Man, and the plight of the underpeople and the plight of mankind can be seen as the two polarities of social existence. Mankind lives in the absolute security of utopian socialism, knowing neither want nor suffering:

But the lords of the Instrumentality had decreed that underpeople . . . should live under the economics of the Ancient World; they had to have their own kind of money to pay for their rooms, their food, their possessions and the education of their children. If they became bankrupt, they went to the Poorhouse, where they were killed painlessly by means of gas.[27]

In "The Dead Lady of Clown Town," in the insanely brutal treatment of the underpeople, like the rat woman whose children are dashed against the pavement before she herself is clubbed to death, we see the social injustice that has outraged the liberal conscience in every generation. In "Under Old Earth," where the suffocating perfection of utopia brings outbreaks of madness like that of the gentleman-suicides, "who gambled their lives—even more horribly, gambled sometimes for things worse than their lives—against different kinds of geophysics which real men had never experienced,"[28] we see again the future as nightmare that has haunted the literary imagination since Zamyatin and even before. It is significant that the role of Lady Alice More complements that of Lord Jestocost, for in "Under Old Earth," we learn that in her youth she was Santuna—lover of Sun-boy, a gentleman-suicide who became a threat to mankind when he "used the normal human appetitiousness for danger"[29] to tempt others with the too dangerous hypnotic musical communication of the utterly alien Douglas Ouyang planets.

Complementary problems demand complementary solutions: for mankind, freedom; for the underpeople, justice. Smith offers a synthesis of human values, but it is a pragmatic synthesis; for the Instrumentality is ever pragmatic, whether in its forgiveness of the rebellion in "Scanners Live in Vain" ("You don't think the Instrumentality would waste the scanners, do you?"[30]) or in its ruthless prosecution of the war against Raumsog, whose planet is decimated by atmospheric poisons and carcinogens. When, in "A Planet Named Shayol" (1961), the Lady Johanna Gnade shuts down a hellish prison world where prisoners have lived in endless torment while growing spare parts for organ banks, she has no interest in their desire for vengeful "justice:" those responsible have been *cured*. "Punishment is ended," she declares. "We will give you anything you wish, but not the pain of another."[31] As for their own destiny, "We will try to cure you and to make people of you again. But if you give up, we will not force you."[32] In *Norstrilia*, we learn that the Holy Insurgency is supporting the Rediscovery of Man and is equally pragmatic about it.

Norstrilia is the story of how Rod McBan, a youth of the world made rich by stroon, but kept plain in its life-style by astronomical import duties, actually *buys* Earth and travels there to escape death back home. Norstrilia is a world of harsh survival values, where those coming of age must pass a test of fitness, or die (*"We kill to live, and die to grow— That's the way the world must go!"*[33]). Eventually, he can return home safely, cured of the telepathic defect that called his fitness into question and able to inherit the Station of Doom and even forgive a short-lifer official who had sought his death. While on earth, however, he becomes involved with, among others, both Lord Jestocost and the E'Telekeli— the upshot of which is that the wealth represented by his purchase of a world is to be invested in a foundation to support cultural activities. "Men are evil when they are frightened or bored," says the E'Telekeli.

"They are good when they are happy and busy. I want you to give your money to provide games, sports, competitions, shows, music and a chance for honest hatred."[34]

Even hatred has its place in the scheme of things, for it is one of the expressions of vitality—the driving force of evolution. "If we hadn't been vital and greedy and lustful and yearning, if we hadn't had big thoughts and wanted bigger ones, we would have stayed animals, like all the little things back on Earth,"[35] says Folly in "Three to a Given Star" (1965), which was incorporated into *Quest of the Three Worlds* (1966). *Quest of the Three Worlds* centers on the spiritual odyssey of Casher O'Neill, exiled from the planet Mizzer when the reacculturation of the Rediscovery of Man brought a rebirth of ancient political passions and a coup against the rule of his corrupt uncle. Now he seeks justice against the tyranny that has taken hold of his world, "hoping in his innermost thoughts that 'justice' was not just another word for revenge."[36] Under the influence of T'Ruth, a turtle girl and a Christian, he undergoes a conversion, and he is able to use paranormal powers conferred by her to change the dictator Wedder. Wedder retains the same basic personality but is now: "More benign. More tolerant. More calm, more human. Even a little corrupt . . . "[37] So charity, too, has its place in the scheme of things.

Smith hints at some grand spiritual fulfillment of history, when men and underpeople will "pour into a common destiny,"[38] and his later works are filled with religious allusions. Like Pierre Teilhard de Chardin, he seems to have been attempting a synthesis of Christianity and evolution, of the eternal values of the *Tao* and the evolutionary values of science fiction as handed down by Wells. Where this would have ultimately led, we cannot tell; even Smith's extant notes reveal nothing of what was to come after the Rediscovery of Man,[39] although "Drunkboat" (1963) is addressed to an ostensible readership in a further future where the Instrumentality itself no longer exists. It is in "Drunkboat" that mankind discovers the new dimension of Space$_3$, which is later to be the source of a religious revelation given to the Robot, the Rat, and the Copt, referred to, but not detailed, in both *Norstrilia* and *Quest of the Three Worlds*. Neither in the devotional life of the E'Telekeli's daughter E'lamelanie, nor in Casher O'Neill's final renunciation of the world of action, however, can we perceive a synthesis on the philosophical level. Man's creation of the underpeople, for example, may be part of an unfolding divine evolutionary plan for augmentation of what Teilhard de Chardin called the noosphere, but we can never know for certain.

Smith's enduring achievement is the reconciliation of values in the existential world. In "The Ballad of Lost C'mell," for example, we see in Lord Jestocost a dedication as austere as that of Wells' New Samurai or Isaac Asimov's prime movers of the Second Foundation. For reasons of state, he must not try to consummate his love for C'mell, with whom he conspires to release secret data from the computer bank of the Bell to aid the cause of all the underpeople: "Their emotions could not come into it. The Bell mattered; justice mattered; the perpetual return of mankind to progress mattered."[40] Yet he values that love, and his last wish on his dying day is granted when he learns that she loved him, too: "More than death. More than life. More than time."[41] In *Norstrilia*, the rebirth of freedom and other human values is still tentative and uncertain, as revealed in two vignettes about a man exiled to Mars for the crime of publishing actual *news* in a newspaper, and a woman who must be mindwiped for having shared her unauthorized opinions about McBan with too many other people. Still, the pragmatic synthesis remains; we can sense that mankind has returned to ethical progress. Or, as the E'Telekeli puts it: "We're not ending time. We are just altering the material conditions of Man's situation for the present historical period. We want to steer mankind away from tragedy and self-defeat."[42]

THE UNBUILDER OF WALLS

There was a wall. It did not look important. It was built of uncut rocks roughly mortared. An adult could look right over it, and even a child could climb it. Where it crossed the roadway, instead of having a gate it degenerated into mere geometry, a line, an idea of boundary. But the idea was real. It was important. For seven generations, there had been nothing in the world more important than that wall.[43]

It is Shevek, the brilliant but frustrated physicist of Anarres, who crosses that wall in Ursula K. Le Guin's *The Dispossessed* (1974), a novel that has a good claim to being the most important work of science fiction of our generation—not necessarily the best, but nevertheless the most *important*. *The Dispossessed* remains a work of literary and philosophical synthesis without parallel in the genre. Le Guin (1929-) herself parallels Cordwainer Smith's role as a synthetist, even though the two are not usually bracketed by critics. She once revealed that Smith's "Alpha Ralpha Boulevard" influenced her decision to write sf;[44] like Smith's, her best work achieves a reconciliation of values that have too often been estranged in the ideological conflicts of our time. This is despite the apparent differences between her and Smith—their careers' only obvious similarities are relatively late starts, followed by rapid recognition. In terms of their contemporary loyalties, indeed, they might well be regarded as antithetical to one another. Smith was a professional soldier and very much of the Right in contemporary terms; Le Guin is a pacifist and very much of the Left. While Smith professed an orthodox Christianity, Le Guin's fundamental orientation is Taoist. While Smith never seems to have gone on record as to what his science fiction was "about," Le Guin has identified the theme of hers; "Marriage."[45]

Marriage? It sounds facetious, more appropriate for a reincarnation of Jane Austen than for a science fiction writer. Yet marriage, indeed, is what most of the works in the Hainish Cycle are about—"marriage," defined metaphorically, is Le Guin's approach to synthesis. Like Smith's epic of the Instrumentality, the Hainish Cycle is a future history, with distinct twists of its own. In her imagined universe, earth and a number of other worlds among the nearer stars were colonized ages ago by Hain, a world not unlike our own, although it is never seen directly. Earthmen thus find other worlds already inhabited by their own distant cousins— even the degenerate winged hominids of Rokanan in *Rocannon's World* (1966) and the hermaphrodites of *The Left Hand of Darkness* (1969) derive from ancient Hainish experiments in genetic engineering. When they return to bring succor to their long-lost colonies, lost for so long not even the memory of Hain remains, "They are moved by a guilt we don't even understand, despite all our crimes," says the ambassador to Urras of a ruined earth in *The Dispossessed*. "They are moved in all they do, I think, by the past, their endless past."[46] Once arrogant imperialists and soulless technicians, they have become cosmic altruists.

The expression of that altruism is the League of All Worlds, which seeks to bring universal peace and brotherhood to the scattered branches of mankind. It is the League which comes to the aid of the Athsheans in *The Word for World Is Forest* (1972). Having despoiled their own world, the Terrans have descended upon the planet they call New Tahiti like a plague of locusts to cut down the forests for timber that is virtually priceless on an earth where even Alaska has been turned into a desert. The yumens, as Athsheans call them, show as little mercy to the natives themselves as they do to the forest: "These yumens kill us as lightly as we kill snakes," says a wondering Selver. "The one who taught me said that they kill one another, in quarrels, and also in groups, like ants fighting."[47] Nothing like this kind of killing has ever been known among Athsheans, but that is changing now, for Selver has become a god, by bringing the idea of war out of his race's dream-time into real-time: "There is a wish to kill in them, and therefore I saw fit to put them to death."[48] Right in the midst of the uprising, there arrives a ship from earth, bearing a new device called the ansible, which puts worlds light-years apart into instant communication with one another. No longer is earth twenty-seven years away; in the course of its journey, the *Shackleton* has kept in contact with earth and other worlds, and history has been made during that journey. Lepennon, a Hainishman, and his Cetian counterpart Or, left earth as legates of their respective worlds. The League was established when they were nine years out; it has now existed for eighteen years. "Mr. Or and I are now Emissaries of the Council of the League, and so have certain powers and responsibilities we did not have when we left Earth,"[49] explains Lepennon.

Selver, whose own people followed him only when he was a god, finds the concept of government hard to comprehend, after Commander Yung of the *Shackleton* explains that the reason the exploitation of Athshe has ceased is that, "Your world has been placed under the League ban."[50]

"Well, you say that none of you shall cut the trees of Athshe: and all of you stop. And yet you live in many places. Now if a headwoman in Karach gave an order, it would not be obeyed by the people of the next village, and surely not by all the people in the world at once . . . "

"No, because you haven't one government over all. But we do—now—and I assure you its orders are obeyed. By all of us at once."[51]

It is no accident in Le Guin's future history that the Athsheans are natural anarchists. Although the League of All Worlds appears to be a force for good in its formative years, we already know that it will not always be so. In *Rocannon's World*, which was the first Hainish novel to appear although its setting is centuries later, the League has become a nascent tyranny. Feverishly preparing for the War to Come against alien invasion, it plagues primitive worlds like Formalhaut II with Technological Enhancement Missions and Control and Taxation Missions. For the feudal Angyar, ruling class among one of the three HILFs (High Intelligence Life Forms) catalogued by the League, the invasion threat means nothing—all they know is that "the Starlords had come again to collect their taxes . . . leaving the Angyar humiliated to the point of rebellion."[52]

Rebellion on a grander scale is brewing elsewhere, on an advanced world called Faraday, and Gaveral Rocannon, an ethnographer of Hainish descent, is caught in the middle of it when his mission on Fomalhaut II is destroyed in a nuclear attack to protect the secret of a rebel base on the unexplored southern continent. Rocannon, like Lepennon on Athshe 300 years before, is an idealist: it is his intervention that has had the world placed under interdict to protect it from taxation and technological forced development. Now he must undertake a hazardous and arduous overland journey to reach that rebel base and infiltrate it to broadcast a warning to the League over its ansible.

Fomalhaut II, the first of Le Guin's created worlds—"Semley's Necklace" (1964), incorporated into *Rocannon's World*, is one of her earliest stories—is romantic in the extreme, with archetypes borrowed from high fantasy: the Gdemiar, an industrious troglodytic race, recall J. R. R. Tolkien's dwarves, and the noble Angyar ride windsteeds. The plot is straight action adventure, of the sort Le Guin now disdains as a more conscious feminist and pacifist. Yet the theme of marriage is already there. For Rocannon has fallen in love, not just with the woman Ganye, but with a world: "Who are my people? I am not what I was. I have changed; I have drunk from the well in the mountains."[53] He agrees to remain for a while.

But it was for the rest of his life. When ships of the League returned to the planet, and Yahan guided one of the surveys south to Breygna to find him, he was dead. . . . So he never knew that the League had given that world his name.[54]

Marriage in the literal as well as the metaphorical sense recurs in *Planet of Exile* (1966). Again, centuries have passed. On a world known to the League as Gamma Draconis III, a Terran colony has been established for 600 years. But there is no more League; no ship has called in ages. Isolated from the rest of mankind, forbidden by the Cultural Embargo to disseminate their knowledge among the native Tevar, the colonials have turned inward, huddling in their last city:

Gradually, Year by Year for at least ten generations, their numbers had been dwindling; very gradually, but always there were fewer children born. They retrenched, they drew together. . . . They taught their children the old knowledge and the old ways, but nothing new.[55]

If the Alterrans have no future, the Tevar have no history, no sense of time as we know it: "Time to them was a lantern lighting a step before, a step behind—the rest was indistinguishable dark. Time was this day, this one day of the immense Year. They had no historical vocabulary; there was merely today and 'timepast.'"[56] Nevertheless, they have something in common with the Alterrans: an enemy, the Gaal—a warrior race moving southward now that the long winter of the world's Year (equal to *sixty* earth years) is closing in.

Only by embracing one another and making common cause can the two peoples hope to survive, and that embrace begins with a forbidden love affair between Jakob Agat, the Alterran assigned to negotiate alliance with the Tevar, and Rolery, granddaughter of the Tevar chieftain Wold. Despite the violation of taboo that involves, the Tevar are forced to take refuge in the Alterran city of Landin when their own Winter City is overrun by the barbarians. Fighting side by side, the two peoples successfully defend Landin against the besieging Gaal. But the greatest victory is *not* military: Rolery has become pregnant; the Alterrans have adapted to an alien world and can interbreed with the Tevar. Jakob Agat and his people can embrace their adopted world as home: "This was his fort, his world; these were his people. He was no exile here."[57] In *City of Illusions* (1967), we learn that the descendants of Alterrans and Tevar have become a hybrid people with a hybrid culture, who eventually rebuild civilization on the world they call Werel and begin to explore outward. Agad Ramarren, a descendant of Jakob and Rolery, is a navigator of the *Alterra* when it makes the 130-odd light-year journey to earth, only to be attacked and destroyed just outside the atmosphere. For the Shing, the invaders dreaded by the League so many centuries ago, now rule earth—an earth so remote in time, "that the Forest of archaic times, destroyed utterly during the era when men had made and kept their history, had grown up again."[58]

It is in this forest that Ramarren, his memory erased, awakens, to be adopted by the forest people of Zove's House and given the name Falk. Although they are kind to him, Falk yearns to learn the secret of his identity, and he sets out from the Eastern Forest across what was once called America to seek the city of Es Toch in the Rocky Mountains, even though it is a Shing city and he has been warned about the Shing. After a journey across a land of mutant animals and barbaric peoples, vaguely reminiscent of Cordwainer Smith's Wild, he is betrayed by a companion he met on the road and is imprisoned by the Shing. He makes the horrifying discovery that the Shing can *mindlie*: even their thoughts cannot be trusted. "Without trust, a man lives, but not a human life; without hope, he dies,"[59] and Falk has neither. The Shing want to restore his memory as Ramarren in order to learn the location of his homeworld, which would mean betraying it to the enemy, and he will not remember what he has learned as Falk. Yet he is able to defeat the Shing with a passive weapon: the Old Canon of Taoism:

> The way that can be gone
> is not the eternal Way.
> The name that can be named
> is not the eternal Name.[60]

Re-reading the same passage after the restoration of his Ramarren self, he is able to transcend the ordinary limits of identity and regain his Falk self as well: "He was Falk, and he was Ramarren. He was the fool and the wise man: one man twice born."[61] It is both gain and loss, for in escaping the Shing to bring the truth to Werel, Falk-Ramarren is at the same time *going* home and *leaving* home.

Such ambiguous journeys become a recurring motif in Le Guin's sf, as does the philosophy of Taoism. In *The Left Hand of Darkness*, Taoism is clearly one of the foundations of the Ekumen—an experiment in non-coercive unity among the worlds of mankind that arises after the Age of the Enemy. Genly Ai, its envoy to Gethen, arrives alone and unarmed; his mission depends entirely on the power of persuasion. The Ekumen is not a government, but "an attempt to reunify the mystical with the political."[62] he explains to the Commensals of Orgoreyn, one of the nations of Gethen. "It does not enforce laws; decisions are reached by council and consent, not by consensus or command."[63] Should it ever become a government, it will be reckoned a failure by its Hainish creators. Even in its present incarnation, he admits, it has been "mostly a failure; but its failure has done more good for humanity so far than the successes of its predecessors."[64] What does the Ekumen want of Gethen, in seeking its accession to the Ekumen? Communication and trade, not just in goods and artifacts, but also in ideas and techniques. Or, as Ai has put it earlier in an audience with Argaven XV, king of Karhide: "Material profit. Increase of knowledge. The augmentation of the complexity and intensity of the field of intelligent life. The enrichment of harmony and the greater glory of God. Curiosity. Adventure. Delight."[65]

But the mission of Genly Ai, the First Mobile on Gethen, is even more difficult than it might be on some other world. For in addition to the kind of conservative resistance and political intrigue he might encounter anywhere, there is the question of sex. Gethen is inhabited by a race that is both male and female—and neither. None of the familiar roles or rules can apply here; there is no sexual domination, no yin and yang dualism—only being and nonbeing, expressed in the term *shifgrethor*: the shadow an individual casts in the world. Gethenians are sexually active only during the brief phase of *kemmer*, when hormones in partners trigger opposite sexual responses—either partner can become a female, either can become pregnant. In *somer* phase, both are neuter—or are they? There are no absolute certainties, particularly in the social sphere. War is unknown on Gethen, but is it because of the lack of sexuality and sexual polarization most of the time, or simply because of the limited population and a harsh climate that diverts aggressive energies into the struggle against Nature? *The Left Hand of Darkness* is filled with such ambiguities, not the least of which is Genly Ai's own relationship with Estraven, a noble of Karhide who befriends his mission and is branded a traitor and exiled to Orgoreyn.

It is after his failure in Karhide than Ai himself tries again in Orgoreyn, which unlike the clannish society of Karhide, is evolving into a corporate state. But his message is rejected there, too; worse, he is charged with being an enemy agent and is sent to a labor camp. Estraven, at the risk of his own life, comes to his rescue, and together they set out on an epic journey across the eternal ice of the northern continent to Karhide, for the land border is too closely guarded. And it is on that journey that Ai must confront the essence of his mission: to establish a relationship of I and Thou, not We and They, with Gethen. It is the way of the Ekumen, whose "doctrine is just the reverse of the doctrine that the end justifies the means. It proceeds, therefore, by subtle ways, and slow ones, and queer, risky ones rather as evolution does . . ."[66] Ai is there to learn as well as teach; he is there to embrace the Other. And even after Estraven sacrifices his life to ensure the success of Ai's mission, he remains to some degree an enigma. He served mankind, Ai tells the repentant king.

As I spoke I did not know if what I said was true. True in part; an aspect of the truth. It would be no less true to say that Estraven's acts had risen out of pure personal loyalty. . . . Nor would that be the whole truth.[67]

Le Guin's first mature sf novel, full of touches like that, is also remarkable for cutting through the tangle of clichés that has so confused discussion of the fundamental issues facing mankind. Like, for example, the one about the thin "veneer" of civilization:

It can conceal a dozen fallacies at once. One of the most dangerous is that civilization, being artificial, is unnatural: that it is the opposite of primitiveness. . . . Of course, there is no veneer, the process is one of growth, and primitiveness and civilization are degrees of the same thing. If civilization has an opposite, it is war.[68]

In *The Dispossessed*, Le Guin returns to the source of such insights: the theory of ethical anarchism as expounded by Pyotr Kropotkin in *Mutual Aid* (1902). Kropotkin, unlike most utopian theorists, was a naturalist. His social theory was based on the premise that the survival of the fittest in evolution means the survival of the ethically fittest, those capable of working together for mutual survival and progress. On Urras, before the ansible, before the League, the same premise is the foundation for the philosophy of Odo, whom we meet in "The Day Before the Revolution" (1974), a prelude to *The Dispossessed* and the Hainish Cycle. The revolution of her time, although it seems to be sweeping the world, ends instead with the Odonians accepting exile to the desert satellite of Anarres, where Shevek begins his own struggle seven generations later.

In alternating chapters, we follow his life on Anarres, beginning in childhood, and his journey to Urras. The object of his work in temporal physics is a theoretical synthesis of sequency and simultaneity, and on that level alone, Le Guin's novel reveals its genius—both Shevek and his science are more compellingly believable than the scientists or the inventions in most hard sf. But *The Dispossessed* is, before all else, a *utopian novel* in which the emphasis properly belongs on both words. We are used to utopian lectures disguised as novels, and the disguises tend to be thin indeed. Yet we believe in Anarres, because we can believe in Shevek, and his partner Takver, and their friend Bedap, and all the other Anarresti who play a part in the story. Most utopias are populated by either saints or supermen; H. G. Wells' *In the Days of the Comet* (1905–6) and *Men Like Gods* (1923) suffer on that account. But the Anarresti show the kind of decency and heroism that even ordinary people are capable of: they are hairy Cetians, rather than Terrans, but they are *human*. It is the dystopian Urrasti, by contrast, who seem somehow unreal.

Anarres is a utopian world, but it is not a perfect one. It is poor in climate and resources, and even the necessities of life come hard. A drought brings terrible famine during the course of the novel, testing the solidarity of the Anarresti to the utmost; and we agonize with them as those stricken with hunger fight the temptation to loot food trains bound for areas where the hunger is even worse. Yet there is a spiritual struggle taking place, too, for in ethical as well as in other aspects of evolution, the struggle is never ending. The original Odonian ideals are calcifying into dogma, Zamyatin's "entropy of thought,"[69] as Shevek discovers when his temporal theory is denounced as heretical—blind obedience and conformism are undermining the spirit of free coopera-tion. While Anarres is a communal anarchy, without private property or social stratification, it was never intended to be a collectivistic anthill in which individual initiative and conscience are suppressed in the name of altruism; did not Odo herself warn "that nothing is so soon corrupted by power-seeking as altruism"?[70] *The Dispossessed* thus becomes a science fictional *bildungsroman*, in which Shevek must learn to defy authority in order to return to fundamental principles:

With the myth of the State out of the way, the real mutuality and reciprocity of society and the individual became clear. Sacrifice might be demanded of the individual, but never compromise: for though only the society could give security and stability, only the individual, the person, had the power of moral choice—the power of change, the essential function of life.[71]

Having found his philosophical roots, Shevek joins with others in forming a Syndicate of Initiative to challenge the unofficial bureaucracy and revive the true spirit of Odonianism, which recognizes the sanctity of "the individual's individuality, the work he can do best, therefore his best contribution to his society,"[72] which recognizes the balance that must be struck between private and social conscience. Le Guin is at her best in relating both social good and moral good to the temporal physics, the understanding of man in relation to time; that is Shevek's own vocation. A reforestation project in the desert, for example, "is in ac-cordance with the principle of Causative Reversibility, ignored by the Sequency School of Physics currently respectable on Anarres, but still an intimate, tacit element in Odonian thought."[73] On the other hand, it is sequency which underlies morality: "To break a promise is to deny the reality of the past; therefore it is to deny the hope of a real future."[74] And Shevek's quest for a synthesis of simultaneity of sequence can be seen also as a metaphor for the reconcilation of complementary ideals of being and becoming, of the Taoist and the Wellsian—a synthesis that had eluded Le Guin in *The Lathe of Heaven* (1971), with its gothic confrontation between a Wellsian scientist and a man whose dreams can change reality but knows the evil of even benevolent manipulation.

Most of Shevek's education takes place on Anarres, for the Urrasti have nothing to teach him. Le Guin's propertarians, like Ayn Rand's collectivists, tend to be so many clay pigeons in a shooting gallery; Urrasti physicists, whether from the state capitalist A-Io or the state socialist Thu, are all militarists and sexists to the core—there is neither an Oppenheimer nor a Sakharov to be found. Shevek *does* find the key to his synthesis in the works of the Terran Ainsetain and, after becoming rather mechanically involved in a local revolution, he has the Terrans disseminate to mankind the knowledge that will make possible the ansible and all that follows. Returning home with empty hands, he seems to feel that his mission to bring two worlds together has been a failure. And yet, in a sense, Anarres and its Odonian ideals have done so already, for they represent a synthesis of the values of both social justice and individual initiative that have been distorted in the cause of ideology, or forgotten altogether, on Urras. And in the Hainish ship *Davenant*, bearing him back to his homeworld, Shevek can even see the possibility of a greater cultural synthesis: "Its style had neither the opulence of Urras nor the austerity of Anarres, but struck a balance, with the effortless grace of long practice."[75]

But Le Guin no longer seems to see it. In *The Eye of the Heron* (1978), the complex philosophical issues of *The Dispossessed* are reduced to a confrontation between pacifists and stock macho feudalists, both exiled to the same world—a world which is hardly ever more than a stage set for their morality play. Even in *Always Coming Home* (1985), which Le Guin clearly sees as an advance in her thought, there seems to be a retreat. A collection of imaginary tales and folklore, rather than a novel, *Always Coming Home* centers on the Kesh, an ecologically conscious people who live in what is now the Napa Valley of California millenia after a holocaust. Combining the best traits of the American Indians and the Amish, but without the taint of patriarchy, they live in small villages, supported by a small-is-beautiful technology—even a world computer net. They use the land lightly, rather than possessing it, and their social and religious rituals emphasize sharing wealth and reverence for life— they believe even rocks have souls, and they apologize, like many Indians, to game animals they kill.

Their animism may seem quaint, but perhaps most people will always need religious reasons for doing what they ought to be doing anyway, out of enlightened concern for the welfare of human and other beings. Yet in *Always Coming Home*, there is none of the challenge of maintaining or renewing the ethical consciousness of a society: the only evils are external, as represented by the once-nomadic Condors who have turned to military conquest after becoming urbanized. They are so obnoxious—at once brutal *and* sexist *and* lazy *and* stupid—that it is hard to imagine how anyone could sympathize with them for a moment. Yet a woman of the Kesh actually goes to live with her Condor father's people, long enough to learn what was obvious to the readers from the start. It may all well be false sociology (the Mongols, for all their sins, became less warlike after settling down in cities), but worse is the false antithesis: here the only alternatives are the technocratic warfare state and a culture that, however attractive, seems also static, insular, and incurious.

No matter. In *The Dispossessed*, Le Guin has already shown us the kind of world in which we might overcome the alienation and self-division that have paralyzed ethical action, where social and even evolutionary experience can, as C. S. Lewis said of the literary experience itself, "[heal] the wound, without undermining the privilege, of individuality."[76]

EPILOGUE

It would be misleading, however attractive, to claim that science fiction as a whole has achieved a new synthesis. Indeed, one could well argue that sf is divided as never before: the very success of the genre, shown by its proliferation into new media as well as new markets, makes it impossible to impose any single set of standards, whether literary or ideological.

Star Trek (1966–9) and *Star Wars* (1977) brought to science fiction a mass audience undreamed of a few decades ago, yet that audience still remains primarily a film audience, indifferent to literary sf. Literary sf itself, however, has become fragmented. Most visible, obviously, are the best-sellers of Robert A Heinlein, Arthur C. Clarke, and Frank Herbert, which reach beyond the traditional sf audience; but even sf aimed at an sf audience comes in many varieties. Most prominent is what might be called the neoclassical school, exemplified by the lines of Del Rey, DAW, Baen, and other specialty publishers. Like most popular fiction, it tends to express established popular viewpoints; we have touched on the neoconservatism of Jerry Pournelle and his followers, but a consensus liberalism is at least equally represented in works ranging from *Star Trek* adaptations to Barry Longyear's *Manifest Destiny* (1980). Meanwhile, more consciously literary writers appeal to a more highbrow audience: Ian Watson's *The Embedding* (1973), Kate Wilhelm's *Where Late the Sweet Birds Sang* (1976), and Kim Stanley Robinson's *The Wild Shore* (1984) are all fine examples of an increasing literary sophistication in sf. What more ambitious science fiction writers have in common with neoclassical writers is a broad diversity of world views. Gregory Benford, for example, is fundamentally a Wellsian humanist in works like *Timescape* (1980), but Gene Wolfe, while exploiting the Wellsian vision of time in his monumental The Book of the New Sun pentalogy (1980–87), is committed to the Christian mythos (New Sun = New *Son*). And there are still niches for pure New Wave, radical feminist, and other ideological variants of science fiction.

Nevertheless, there seems to be a growing appreciation of the need for a synthesis on some level. In defending the post-New Wave writers of what New Wave author-critic Thomas M. Disch denounced as the "Labor Day Group,"[77] George R. R. Martin, author of *Dying of the Light* (1977) and *The Armageddon Rag* (1983), characterized the group as seeking "a fusion of . . . the concerns, the attitudes, and the dreams of the older science fiction and the literary concerns, especially for characterization and style, of the New Wave."[78] Some, although not all, of those in the Labor Day Group can also be characterized as Wellsian humanists in the tradition of Clarke, but with the infusion of new social and literary sensibilities, from the countercultural values apparent in John Varley's *The Persistence of Vision* (1978) to the influence of C. P. Snow and William Faulkner, respectively, in Benford's *Timescape* and *Against Infinity* (1983). In works of other Wellsian humanists, the need for a synthesis is approached more directly. Pamela Sargent's *Watchstar* (1980) is set in a future where there has been a complete divorce between the Rousselian pastoral culture of earth and the Wellsian technological civilization of space. Although Sargent tends to favor the Wellsian civilization, it is clear that both have suffered from their estrangement. C. J. Cherryh, in her Alliance-Union future history, similarly portrays the divergent and sometimes tragic evolution of two rival cultures, each of which has its distinct virtues and faults, which we see in their formative stages in *Downbelow Station* (1981) and *Cyteen* (1988).

Challenging the Wellsian humanist tradition is cyberpunk, a recent movement that combines the militant radicalism of the New Wave with the hard-science orientation of traditional science fiction. Cyberpunk, as its name suggests, is especially obsessed with the contemporary revolution in cybernetics and with the interface of man and machine. Perhaps its most common emblems are the implants which allow people to jack into computer nets directly, or to plug in modules that give them additional memories, skills, or even personalities. William Gibson's *Neuromancer* (1984), the most impressive first sf novel in many a year, was, if not the fountainhead of the movement, the catalyst for its development. Like other cyberpunks, Gibson (1948-) invokes the names of Thomas Pynchon, William S. Burroughs, and so on as primary influences on the movement;[79] but Raymond Chandler and John Varley seem more relevant. In *Neuromancer*, the atmosphere is reminiscent of that in Ridley Scott's film *Blade Runner* (1982). The oppressive social stratification, the domination of huge multinational corporations, the pervasive Japanese influence, and the punk underworld are all there. Gibson disclaims any influence by the film,[80] but the Chandleresque vision of the *film noir* was undoubtedly a strong influence on both. George Alec Effinger's *When Gravity Fails* (1986), a hard-boiled detective novel set in a Middle Eastern city that seems to owe more to Hollywood's image of *Casablanca* (1942) than to any real familiarity with the Arab world, is a more obvious example of the Chandleresque in cyberpunk. So is Richard Kadrey's *Metrophage* (1988), set in a decaying Los Angeles, which also recalls J. G. Ballard in its strikingly surreal images of the detritus of Western civilization.

"The sky above the port was the color of television, tuned to a dead channel."[81] Gibson's already classic opening line from *Neuromancer* has a lot to do with the world view of cyberpunk. It is the *artificial* that fascinates the movement, without a hint of the Rousselian sympathy for nature that is characteristic of most anti-Wellsian intellectuals. No matter that its social vision of the near future is so often grimly dystopian; cyberpunk sees technology as ultimately liberating—or, if not liberating, at least endlessly exciting. Even the advent of a "god" of the data matrix in *Neuromancer* seems more an occasion for wonder than for terror. It is the growing concentration of social and economic power, against which Gibson's outlaw protagonists carry on a fitful guerrilla warfare, that is truly menacing. The law of cyberspace, the consensual visual representation of the world data net that figures in Gibson's sf, is the law of the jungle. The outlook is even grimmer in Effinger's and Kadrey's works, in which protest and revolt seem utterly futile. But in John Shirley's *Eclipse* (1985), the first of a series, there is an organized resistance to the neo-fascist oligarchy that is attempting to impose its rule on the world during the confused aftermath of a Soviet invasion of Western Europe. Shirley's diabolical Second Alliance and his noble New Resistance recall the stereotypes of World War II movies, and the whole social and ideological conflict is too cut and dried—all other real or potential threats to peace and freedom, from totalitarian leftists to Muslim fundamentalists, have unaccountably vanished.

Even before cyberpunk was a recognized movement, however, Gibson, in collaboration with Bruce Sterling, had charted another direction for the movement in "Red Star, Winter Orbit" (1983). Here, the United States has given up on space, and the Soviet Union is about to. A few cosmonauts mount a futile resistance to the shutdown of their space station. When all seems lost, help arrives from an unexpected quarter—an exploring party of technopunks from the American solar power balloons, who have launched a shuttle on the cheap with surplus boosters hauled up into the stratosphere by cable. They may look weird, but they are as passionate about the possibilities of space as any old-time sf fan:

We can enlarge this thing, maybe build more. . . . It was our one chance to get out here on our own. Who'd want to live out here for the sake of some government, some army brass, a bunch of pen-pushers? You have to *want* a frontier, want it in your bones, right?[82]

Sterling (1954-), who has become the chief propagandist for cyberpunk, has taken a militant stance. His favorite catchphrase, "ideologically correct,"[83] would doubtless embarrass most contemporary Marxists. Yet his fiction is remarkably free of ideological stereotypes and clichés, and his invention (reminiscent of Varley's) leaves Shirley far behind.

In *Schismatrix* (1985), for example, Sterling develops a fascinating future history in which rival cultures—the technologically augmented Mechanists and the genetically altered Shapers—vie for dominance of human destiny in the space colonies, after the collapse of civilization back on earth. Complicating the struggle are crises of both internal and external origin, most notably the ecological collapse of some space habitats, and the sudden advent of the Investors—an alien race which seems at first benevolent in its intentions, but turns out to be rather less than that. Nevertheless, mankind seems to be moving toward some sort of ethical maturity, as witness the taboo on attacks against those fragile habitants that are now the only home and only hope of civilization:

> It was a deep and fundamental triumph. On the same deep level of the mind that held the constant fear, there was a stronger hope and confidence. It was a victory that belonged to everyone, a victory so thorough and so deep that it had vanished from sight, and belonged to that secret realm of the mind on which everything else is predicated.[84]

Sterling's novel itself has a philosophical depth that goes well beyond the usual parameters of cyberpunk to embrace such ideas as Ilya Prigogine's theory of the evolving complexity of human society and culture, and the possibility that diversity may actually be the true goal of evolution—the ideal of the Schismatrix is that of "a posthuman solar system, diverse yet unified, where tolerance would rule and every faction would have a share."[85]

Naturally, it does not turn out to be that simple, particularly for Abelard Lindsay, a Shaper partisan caught up in the ideological conflict in strange and often ugly ways, who eventually finds his escape from the worldly struggle in a transcendental denouement—almost a punk version of Arthur C. Clarke's *Childhood's End* (1953). But the theme of ideological conflicts taking strange new turns, and of the necessity for tolerance and accommodation, recurs in Sterling's *Islands in the Net* (1988), set on a near-future earth that has achieved nuclear disarmament but falls victim to a new wave of international terrorism by power-crazed fanatics. Michael Swanwick's delightful *Vacuum Flowers* (1987) brings a feminist consciousness to cyberpunk, while building on a situation similar to that in *Schismatrix*. Rebellious anarchists in the space colonies contend with both a corporate oligarchy and a hive-mind called the Comprise that has taken over earth; at the center of the conflict is Rebel Elizabeth Mudlark—a woman turned into a heroine by a hijacked plug-in persona originally intended for the mass consumer market. Swanwick seems to be reaching toward a synthesis of the values of humanistic anarchism and the Wellsian vision of traditional sf—the very synthesis Le Guin has forsworn in *Always Coming Home*.

Whether or not they achieve a true synthesis, the cyberpunks seem to know, better than most, what the war of the world views is about. But we are all too close to that conflict to know the outcome, in sf, or in the world. Perhaps we do live in the latter days of the Roman Empire; perhaps the apocalypse (nuclear or environmental) is at hand—in either case, such cultural phenomena as science fiction will be of interest only to scholars of some future civilization—if there ever *is* one. On the other hand, our contemporary crises, painful though they may be, are perhaps birth pangs rather than death throes; and what we have to say now might yet help our kind make the passage through them. It seems fashionable to deny that literature has any real effect on anyone, but we know better. Occasionally, as in the case of Harriet Beecher Stowe's *Uncle Tom's Cabin* (1852), the impact is direct and obvious. More often, as with the novels of Charles Dickens, it is more subtle and yet all the more profound: literature affects our imaginations, our sensibilities, even our very perceptions of ourselves and the world around us.

In our time of threat and promise, science fiction may be unique in that it tries to speak to both the head and the heart about the things that have always concerned us, but concern us more urgently now—from the place of man in nature to the relation between the individual and the community. But, like all literature, science fiction speaks to each of us individually, even as it speaks to our culture as a whole. It may never provide *the* answer to the global civil war, but perhaps it is enough if it can help each of us find his own answer. Although he used them in a different context, the words of Fletcher Pratt in his fantasy novel, *The Well of the Unicorn* (1948), seem appropriate here:

There is no peace but that interior in us.[86]

Notes

INTRODUCTION

1. Jack McKinney, *Genesis* (New York: Ballantine Books, 1987), p. 9.

2. Edgar Pangborn, *West of the Sun* (New York: Dell Books, 1966), p. 154.

3. Walter M. Miller and Martin H. Greenberg, eds., *Beyond Armageddon* (New York: Primus/Donald J. Fine, 1985), p. 15.

4. Ibid., p. 9.

5. C. P. Snow, *The Two Cultures and the Scientific Revolution* (New York: Cambridge University Press, 1961), p. 4.

6. Karel Capek, *R.U.R.*, trans. P. Selver (New York: Washington Square Press, 1969), Reader's Supplement, p. 10.

7. *Bartlett's Familiar Quotations*, 14th ed. (Boston: Little, Brown & Co., 1968), p. 573.

8. Ian Watson, *The Martian Inca* (New York: Ace Books, 1978), p. 69.

9. Ibid., p. 70.

10. Ibid., p. 235.

11. Ibid., p. 293.

12. Sam Moskowitz, personal conversation, May 1987; Lloyd Arthur Eshbach, remarks at Philadelphia sf convention, Nov. 5, 1988.

13. Donald A. Wollheim, *The Universe Makers* (New York: Harper & Row, 1971), p. 42.

14. C. S. Lewis, *Christian Reflections* (Grand Rapids, Mich.: William B. Eerdman's Publishing Co., 1967), p. 82.

15. Jack Williamson, "Scientifiction, Searchlight of Science," *Amazing Stories Quarterly*, (Fall 1928), p. 435.

16. H. G. Wells, *Seven Science Fiction Novels* (New York: Dover Publications, n.d.), pp. 814–15.

17. Jack Williamson, *People Machines* (New York: Ace Books, 1971), p. 187.

18. Jack Williamson, *Manseed* (New York: Ballantine Books, 1982), p. 216.

19. Lead-in for *Star Trek* television series (Paramount, 1966–69).

20. H. G. Wells, *3 Prophetic Novels* (New York: Dover Publications, n.d.), p. 228.

21. H. G. Wells, *The Shape of Things to Come* (London: Corgi Books, 1967), p. 291.

22. Ibid., p. 134.

23. Ibid., p. 315.

24. Ibid., p. 354.

25. Quoted in Norman Mackenzie and Jeanne Mackenzie, *H. G. Wells: A Biography* (New York: Simon and Schuster, 1973), p. 291.

26. J. R. R. Tolkien, *The Monsters and the Critics, and Other Essays* (Boston: Houghton Mifflin Co., 1984), pp. 150–51.

27. George Orwell, *The Road to Wigan Pier* (New York: Berkley Books, 1961), pp. 161, 163.

28. Mark Hillegas, *The Future as Nightmare: H. G. Wells and the Anti-Utopians* (New York: Oxford University Press, 1967), p. 59.

29. Quoted in Hillegas, *The Future as Nightmare*, pp. 59–60.

30. Ibid., p. 87.

31. Robert A. Heinlein, *The Past through Tomorrow* (New York: G. P. Putnam's Sons, 1967), p. 200.

32. Ibid., p. 205.

33. Arthur C. Clarke, *The Lost Worlds of 2001* (New York: New American Library, 1972), p. 35.

34. Lester del Rey, *The World of Science Fiction, 1926–76: The History of a Subculture* (New York: Ballantine Books, 1979), pp. 345–46.

35. Miles J. Breuer, M.D., "The Future of Scientifiction," *Amazing Stories Quarterly* (Summer 1929), p. 291.

36. John W. Campbell, Jr., *The Best of John W. Campbell* (New York: Ballantine Books, 1976), p. 40.

37. Laurence Manning, *The Man Who Awoke* (New York: Ballantine Books, 1975), p. 77.

38. Ibid., p. 158.

39. Ibid.

40. Ibid., p. 77.

41. Quoted in Hillegas, *The Future as Nightmare*, p. 58.

42. Stanley G. Weinbaum, *A Martian Odyssey and Other Science Fiction Tales* (Westport, Conn.: Hyperion Press, 1974), pp. xxvii–xxviii.

43. C. J. Cherryh, interview in *Locus*, April 1987, p. 5.

44. Daryl Lane, William Vernon, and David Carson, eds., *The Sound of Wonder* (Phoenix, Ariz.: Oryx Press, 1985), vol. 1, p. 48.

CHAPTER 1

1. Arthur C. Clarke, *The City and the Stars* (New York: New American Library, 1987), p. 241.

2. Ibid., p. 240.

3. Arthur C. Clarke, *Childhood's End* (New York: Ballantine Books, 1967), p. 4.

4. Ibid., p. 205.

5. H. G. Wells, *Things to Come,* screenplay (Boston: Gregg Press, 1975), p. 141.

6. Arthur C. Clarke, *The Songs of Distant Earth* (New York: Ballantine Books pb ed., 1987), p. 302.

7. Arthur C. Clarke, *Profile of the Future* (New York: Warner Books, 1985), p. 95.

8. Arthur C. Clarke, *The Nine Billion Names of God* (New York: Harcourt Brace Jovanovich, 1967), p. 60.

9. Ibid., p. 265.

10. Ibid., p. 270.

11. Ibid., p. 238.

12. Arthur C. Clarke, *The Deep Range* (New York: Harcourt Brace Jovanovich, pb ed., n.d.), p. 89.

13. Ibid., p. 183.

14. Ibid., p. 194.

15. Ibid., p. 197.

16. Ibid., p. 238.

17. Clarke, *The Songs of Distant Earth,* p. 122.

18. Ibid., p. 61.

19. Ibid., p. 62.

20. Ibid., p. 93.

21. Arthur C. Clarke, *The Fountain of Paradise* (New York: Harcourt Brace Jovanovich, 1979), p. 9.

22. Clarke, *The Songs of Distant Earth,* p. 143.

23. Ibid., p. 258.

24. Clarke, *The Nine Billion Names of God,* p. 277.

25. Arthur C. Clarke, *Imperial Earth* (New York: Harcourt Brace Jovanovich, 1976), p. 292.

26. Ibid., p. 184.

27. Arthur C. Clarke, *Earthlight* (New York: Ballantine Books, 1966), p. 155.

28. Clarke, *The City and the Stars,* p. xi.

29. Ibid., p. 26.

30. Ibid., p. 27.

31. Ibid., p. 108.

32. Ibid., p. 143.

33. Ibid., p. 135.

34. Ibid., p. 237.

35. Ibid.

36. Ibid., p. 253.

37. Isaac Asimov, *Second Foundation* (New York: Avon Books, 1964), p. 92.

38. Isaac Asimov, *In Memory Yet Green* (Garden City, N.Y.: Doubleday & Co., 1979), p. 311.

39. Ibid., p. 167.

40. Ibid., p. 212.

41. H. G. Wells, *The Shape of Things to Come* (London: Corgi Books, 1967), p. 131.

42. Ibid., p. 262.

43. Isaac Asimov, *Foundation* (New York: Avon Books, 1966), p. 17.

44. Isaac Asimov, *The Currents of Space* (Greenwich, Conn.: Fawcett Books, 1971), p. 66.

45. Ibid.

46. Ibid., p. 62.

47. Ibid., p. 61.

48. Ibid., p. 62.

49. Ibid., p. 187.

50. Asimov, *In Memory Yet Green*, p. 600.

51. Asimov, *The Stars Like Dust* (New York: Lancer Books, 1963), p. 57.

52. Ibid., p. 58.

53. Asimov, *Foundation*, p. 107.

54. Ibid., p. 198.

55. Isaac Asimov, *Foundation and Empire* (New York: Avon Books, 1966), p. 30.

56. Ibid., p. 81.

57. Asimov, *Second Foundation*, p. 62.

58. Ibid., p. 67.

59. Ibid., p. 187.

60. Isaac Asimov, *I, Robot* (Greenwich, Conn.: Fawcett Books, 1970), p. 191.

61. Ibid., p. 192.

62. Isaac Asimov, *The End of Eternity* (Greenwich, Conn.: Fawcett Books, 1971), p. 185.

63. Ibid., p. 187.

64. Isaac Asimov, *Nightfall and Other Stories* (Greenwich, Conn.: Fawcett Books, 1970), p. 59.

65. Isaac Asimov, *Foundation's Edge* (Garden City, N.Y.: Doubleday & Co., 1982), pp. 344–45.

66. Isaac Asimov, *Robots and Empire* (New York: Ballantine Books, 1986), p. 467.

67. Ibid., p. 354.

68. Isaac Asimov, *The Naked Sun* (Greenwich, Conn.: Fawcett Books, 1972), pp. 215–16.

69. Isaac Asimov, *Foundation and Earth* (Garden City, N.Y.: Doubleday & Co., 1986), p. 29.

70. Ibid., pp. 226–27.

CHAPTER 2

1. C. S. Lewis, *That Hideous Strength* (New York: The Macmillan Company, 1965), p. 338.

2. Roger Lancelyn Green and Walter Hooper, *C. S. Lewis: A Biography* (New York: Harcourt Brace Jovanovich, 1974), p. 164.

3. C. S. Lewis, *On Stories, and Other Essays on Literature* (New York: Harcourt Brace Jovanovich, 1982), pp. 71–72.

4. Green and Hooper, *C. S. Lewis*, p. 163.

5. C. S. Lewis, *Christian Reflections* (Grand Rapids, Mich.: William B. Eerdman's Publishing Co., 1967), p. 82.

6. Ibid., p. 88.

7. C. S. Lewis, *Letters of C. S. Lewis* (New York: Harcourt, Brace & World, 1966), p. 296.

8. C. S. Lewis, *The Abolition of Man* (New York: The Macmillan Company, 1965), p. 84.

9. Mark Hillegas, *The Future as Nightmare: H. G. Wells and the Anti-Utopians* (New York: Oxford University Press, 1967), p. 137.

10. Green and Hooper, *C. S. Lewis*, p. 220.

11. Lewis, *Letters of C. S. Lewis*, p. 167.

12. C. S. Lewis, *Out of the Silent Planet* (New York: The Macmillan Company, 1965), p. 35.

13. Ibid., p. 75.

14. Ibid., pp. 136–37.

15. Ibid., p. 100.

16. C. S. Lewis, *Perelandra* (New York: The Macmillan Company, 1965), p. 91.

17. Lewis, *That Hideous Strength*, p. 42.

18. Ibid., p. 221.

19. R. A. Lafferty, *Past Master* (New York: Ace Books, 1968), p. 31.

20. Walter M. Miller, Jr., *The Science Fiction Stories of Walter M. Miller, Jr.*, (Boston: Gregg Press, 1978) p. 47.

21. Ibid., p. 62.

22. Ibid.

23. Ibid., p. 63.

24. Ibid., p. 174.

25. Ibid., p. 175.

26. Ibid., p. 185.

27. Ibid., p. 188.

28. Walter M. Miller, Jr., *A Canticle for Leibowitz* (New York: Bantam Books, 1961), pp. 183–84.

29. Ibid., p. 245.

30. Ibid., p. 246.

31. Brian W. Aldiss, *The Saliva Tree* (London: Sphere Books, 1968), p. 7.

32. Quoted in Frederik Pohl and Frederick Pohl IV, *Science Fiction Studies in Film* (New York: Ace Books, 1981), p. 86.

33. Ibid.

34. Brian W. Aldiss, *Billion Year Spree* (New York: Schocken Books, 1974), p. 8.

35. Ibid., p. 29.

36. Brian W. Aldiss and Harry Harrison, eds., *Hell's Cartographers* (London: Futura Publications Ltd., 1976), p. 201.

37. Aldiss, *The Saliva Tree*, p. 23.

38. Ibid., p. 85.

39. Brian W. Aldiss, *Starship* (New York: Avon Books, 1969), p. 162.

40. Brian W. Aldiss, *The Dark Light-Years* (New York: New American Library, 1964), p. 99.

41. Brian W. Aldiss, *Frankenstein Unbound* (Greenwich, Conn.: Fawcett Books, 1975), p. 55.

42. Ibid., p. 127.

43. Ibid., pp. 127–28.

44. Brian W. Aldiss, *Barefoot in the Head* (New York: Avon Books, 1981), p. 68.

45. Ibid., p. 69.

46. Ibid., p. 142.

47. Ibid., p. 206.

48. Ibid., p. 209.

49. Brian W. Aldiss, *The Malacia Tapestry* (New York: Berkley Books, 1985), p. 130.

50. Brian W. Aldiss, *Helliconia Spring* (New York: Atheneum, 1982), p. 55.

51. Ibid., p. 255.

52. Brian W. Aldiss, *Helliconia Summer* (New York: Atheneum, 1983), p. 24.

53. Ibid., p. 379.

54. Brian W. Aldiss, *Helliconia Winter* (New York: Atheneum, 1985), p. 280.

CHAPTER 3

1. Clifford D. Simak, "The World of the Red Sun," in: Isaac Asimov, ed., *Before the Golden Age* (Garden City, N.Y.: Doubleday & Co., 1974), p. 208.

2. Interview in Paul Walker, ed., *Speaking of Science Fiction* (Oradell, N.J.: Luna Publications, 1978), p. 63.

3. Ibid.

4. Simak, "The World of the Red Sun," in: Asimov, *Before the Golden Age*, p. 222.

5. Clifford D. Simak, *Strangers in the Universe* (New York: Berkley Books, 1968), pp. 112–13.

6. Clifford D. Simak, *City* (New York: Ace Books, 1973), p. 168.

7. Ibid., p. 207.

8. Ibid., p. 211.

9. Clifford D. Simak, *Ring Around the Sun* (New York: Avon Books, 1967), p. 167.

10. Ibid., p. 128.

11. Clifford D. Simak, *Project Pope* (New York: Ballantine Books, 1981), p. 244.

12. Ibid., p. 157.

13. Clifford D. Simak, *Cosmic Engineers* (New York: Paperback Library, 1964), p. 26.

14. Ibid., p. 72.

15. Ibid., p. 83.

16. Ibid., p. 84.

17. Ibid., p. 146.

18. Ibid., p. 147.

19. Ibid., p. 159.

20. Ibid., p. 111.

21. Clifford D. Simak, *Time and Again* (New York: Ace Books, n.d.), p. 158.

22. Ibid., p. 32.

23. Ibid., p. 193.

24. Ibid., p. 256.

25. Ibid., p. 248.

26. Clifford D. Simak, *Way Station* (New York: Macfadden Books, 1964), p. 68.

27. Ibid., p. 69.

28. Ibid.

29. Ibid., p. 123.

30. Ibid., p. 31.

31. Ibid., p. 30.

32. Ibid., p. 86.

33. Ibid., p. 90.

34. Ibid., p. 38.

35. Ibid., p. 132.

36. Ibid., p. 175.

37. Ibid., p. 185.

38. Theodore Sturgeon, *Sturgeon Is Alive and Well* (New York: Berkley Books, 1971), p. 168.

39. Theodore Sturgeon, *Godbody* (New York: New American Library, 1987), p. 5.

40. Theodore Sturgeon, *A Way Home* (New York: Pyramid Books, 1956), p. 122.

41. Ibid., p. 123.

42. Ibid., p. 124.

43. Ibid., p. 129.

44. Ibid.

45. Ibid., p. 133.

46. Ibid., p. 9.

47. Theodore Sturgeon, *The Golden Helix* (New York: Dell Publishing Co., 1980), p. 228.

48. Ibid., p. 259.

49. Ibid., p. 228.

50. Ibid., p. 92.

51. Theodore Sturgeon, *More Than Human* (New York: Ballantine Books, 1953), p. 115.

52. Ibid., p. 172.

53. Ibid., pp. 177–78.

54. Ibid., p. 183.

55. Ibid.

56. Ibid., p. 186.

57. Harlan Ellison, ed., *Dangerous Visions* (New York: Berkley Books, 1972), p. 412.

58. Ibid., p. 416.

59. Theodore Sturgeon, *The Synthetic Man* (New York: Pyramid Books, 1957), p. 38.

60. Sturgeon, *Sturgeon Is Alive and Well*, p. 10.

61. Ibid., p. 87.

62. Ibid., p. 94.

63. Ibid., p. 179.

CHAPTER 4

1. Robert A. Heinlein, *Starship Troopers* (New York: Berkley Books, 1968), p. 147.

2. Ibid.

3. Ibid.

4. Robert A. Heinlein, *Beyond This Horizon* (New York: New American Library, n.d.), p. 28.

5. Ibid., p. 97.

6. Heinlein, *Starship Troopers*, p. 95.

7. Robert A. Heinlein, *Expanded Universe* (New York: Grosset & Dunlap, 1980), p. 332.

8. Heinlein, *Beyond This Horizon*, p. 100.

9. Ibid., p. 157.

10. Robert A. Heinlein, *Have Space Suit—Will Travel* (New York: Charles Scribner's Sons, 1958), p. 9.

11. Robert A. Heinlein, *Tunnel in the Sky* (New York: Charles Scribner's Sons, 1955), p. 21.

12. Ibid., p. 223.

13. Ibid., p. 228.

14. Introduction to Theodore Sturgeon, *Godbody* (New York: New American Library, 1987), pp. 5–6.

15. Heinlein, *Starship Troopers*, p. 144.

16. Robert A. Heinlein, *The Moon Is a Harsh Mistress* (New York: G.P. Putnam's Sons, 1966), p. 35.

17. Ibid., p. 178.

18. Ibid., p. 383.

19. Robert A. Heinlein, *Citizen of the Galaxy* (New York: Charles Scribner's Sons, 1957), p. 214.

20. Ibid., p. 301.

21. Algis Budrys, *Rogue Moon* (Greenwich, Conn.: Fawcett Books, 1960), pp. 116–17.

22. Ibid., p. 10.

23. Ibid., p. 116.

24. Ibid., pp. 153–54.

25. Tom Godwin, "The Cold Equations," in: Robert Silverberg, ed., *Science Fiction Hall of Fame* (New York: Avon Books, 1971), p. 569.

26. Raymond Z. Gallun, *The Best of Raymond Z. Gallun* (New York: Ballantine Books, 1978), p. 38.

27. Ibid., p. 148.

28. Ibid., pp. 306–7.

29. Ibid., p. 309.

30. Henry Kuttner, *Clash by Night* (Feltham, Middlesex, U.K.: Hamlyn Publishing Group, 1980), p. 53.

31. Ibid., p. 67.

32. Kuttner, *Fury* (New York: Lancer Books, n.d.), p. 12.

33. Ibid., p. 222.

34. Kuttner, *The Best of Henry Kuttner* (New York: Ballantine Books, 1975), p. 49.

35. Ibid., p. 36.

36. Ibid., p. 60.

37. Ibid., p. 61.

38. Lester del Rey, *The Best of Lester del Rey* (New York: Ballantine Books, 1978), p. 219.

39. Ibid., p. 256.

40. Ibid., p. 265.

41. Ibid., p. 139.

42. Ibid., p. 151.

43. Lester del Rey, *Mortals and Monsters* (New York: Ballantine Books, 1965), p. 173.

44. Ibid., p. 185.

45. Ibid., p. 188.

46. Ibid.

47. Lester del Rey, *The Eleventh Commandment* (Evanston, Ill.: Regency Books, 1962), p. 154.

48. Algis Budrys, *Budrys' Inferno* (New York: Berkley Books, 1963), p. 37.

49. Algis Budrys, *Unexpected Dimension* (New York: Ballantine Books, 1960), p. 91.

50. Budrys, *Rogue Moon*, p. 174.

51. Ibid., p. 176.

CHAPTER 5

1. J. G. Ballard, *The Burning World* (New York: Berkley Books, 1964), p. 17.

2. Quoted in Colin Greenland, *The Entropy Exhibition: Michael Moorcock and the British 'New Wave' in Science Fiction* (London: Rutledge & Kegan Paul, 1983), p. 69.

3. Ibid., pp. 72–73.

4. Ibid., p. 74.

5. Michael Moorcock, editorial, *New Worlds* 142 (May-June 1964), pp. 2–3.

6. Greenland, *The Entropy Exhibition*, p. 49.

7. J. G. Ballard, editorial, *New Worlds* 118 (May 1962), pp. 2–3.

8. Quoted in Greenland, *The Entropy Exhibition*, p. 51.

9. Ibid.

10. Ibid., p. 37.

11. Thomas M. Disch, *The Genocides* (New York: Berkley Books, 1965), p. 141.

12. *Bartlett's Familiar Quotations*, 14th ed. (New York: Little, Brown & Co., 1968), p. 709.

13. Thomas M. Disch, ed., *The Ruins of Earth* (New York: Berkley Books, 1971), p. 5.

14. Thomas M. Disch, *Fun with Your New Head* (New York: New American Library, 1972), p. 144.

15. Ibid.

16. Thomas M. Disch, *Camp Concentration* (New York: Avon Books, 1971), p. 72.

17. Ibid., p. 175.

18. Thomas M. Disch, *334* (New York, Avon Books, 1974), p. 15.

19. Ibid., p. 197.

20. Ibid., p. 242.

21. Ibid., p. 41.

22. Ibid., p. 265.

23. John T. Sladek, "The Poets of Milgrove, Iowa," *New Worlds* 168, (Nov. 1966), pp. 87–88.

24. Barry N. Malzberg, *Beyond Apollo* (New York: Pocket Books, 1974), p. 141.

25. J. G. Ballard, *Empire of the Sun* (New York: Washington Square Press, 1985), p. 190.

26. Quoted in Greenland, *The Entropy Exhibition*, p. 96.

27. J. G. Ballard, *The Wind from Nowhere* (New York: Berkley Books, 1962), p. 142.

28. J. G. Ballard, *The Drowned World* (New York: Berkley Books, 1962), pp. 13–14.

29. Ibid., p. 20.

30. Ibid., pp. 64–65.

31. Ibid., p. 115.

32. Ibid., p. 158.

33. Ballard, *The Burning World*, p. 29.

34. Ibid., p. 11.

35. Ibid., pp. 102–3.

36. Ibid., p. 160.

37. J. G. Ballard, *The Crystal World* (New York: Berkley Books, 1967), p. 13.

38. Ibid., p. 59.

39. Ibid., p. 73.

40. Ibid., p. 74.

41. Ibid., p. 79.

42. Ibid., p. 106.

43. Ibid., p. 154.

44. J. G. Ballard, *Terminal Beach* (New York: Berkley Books, 1964), p. 149.

45. J. G. Ballard, *The Atrocity Exhibition* (London: Triad/Panther Books, 1979), p. 107.

46. Ibid., p. 93.

47. Ibid., back cover review blurbs.

48. J. G. Ballard, "Mythmaker of the 20th Century," NW 142, May-June 1964, p. 121.

49. Peter Nicholls, ed., *The Science Fiction Encyclopedia* (Garden City, N.Y.: Doubleday & Co., 1979), p. 97.

50. Ibid., pp. 15–16.

51. Kurt Vonnegut, Jr., *The Sirens of Titan* (New York: Dell Books, 1966), p. 301.

52. Michael Moorcock, *The Cornelius Chronicles* (New York: Avon Books, 1977), p. 141.

53. Ibid., p. 469.

54. Greenland, *The Entropy Exhibition*, p. 182.

55. Samuel R. Delany, *Stars in My Pocket Like Grains of Sand* (New York: Bantam Books, 1984), p. 194.

56. Samuel R. Delany, *The Complete Nebula Award-Winning Fiction* (New York: Bantam Books, 1986), p. 405.

57. Michael Moorcock, review, NW 214, Autumn 1978, p. 47.

58. Samuel R. Delany, *The Einstein Intersection* (New York: Ace Books, 1967), p. 78.

59. Ibid., p. 79.

60. Samuel R. Delany, *The Fall of the Towers* (New York: Ace Books, 1970), p. 50.

61. Ibid., p. 46.

62. Ibid., p. 383.

63. Ibid., p. 370.

64. Samuel R. Delany, *Nova* (New York: Bantam Books, 1969), p. 116.

65. Ibid., p. 123.

66. Ibid., p. 101.

67. Ibid.

68. Samuel R. Delany, *Dhalgren* (New York: Bantam Books, 1975), pp. 879–81.

69. Ibid., pp. 15–16.

70. Samuel R. Delany, *The Jewel-Hinged Jaw: Notes on the Language of Science Fiction* (Elizabeth, N.Y.: Dragon Press, 1977), pp. 239–308.

71. Samuel R. Delany, *Triton* (New York: Bantam Books, 1976), p. 221.

72. Ibid., p. 117.

73. Ibid., p. 116.

74. Ibid., p. 71.

75. Ibid., p. 1.

76. Delany, *Stars in My Pocket Like Grains of Sand*, p. 86.

77. Ibid., p. 136.

78. Norman Spinrad, *Bug Jack Barron* (New York: Avon Books, 1969), p. 93.

CHAPTER 6

1. Harlan Ellison, ed., *Dangerous Visions* (New York: Berkley Books, 1972), p. 186.

2. Ibid.

3. Robert A. Heinlein, "On the Writing of Speculative Fiction," in Lloyd Arthur Eshbach, ed., *Of Worlds Beyond* (Reading, Pa.: Fantasy Press, 1947), pp. 13ff.

4. Harlan Ellison, *The Beast That Shouted Love at the Heart of the World* (New York: Avon Books, 1969), p. 25.

5. Ibid., p. 34.

6. Ibid., p. 212.

7. Ibid., p. 210.

8. Ibid., p. 213.

9. Harlan Ellison, "Croatoan," in Terry Carr, ed., *The Best Science Fiction of the Year #5* (New York: Ballantine Books, 1976), p. 149.

10. Ellison, *The Beast That Shouted Love at the Heart of the World*, pp. 219–20.

11. Ibid., p. 237.

12. Frederik Pohl and Frederik Pohl IV, *Science Fiction Studies in Film* (New York: Ace Books, 1981), p. 240.

13. Ibid.

14. Basil Davenport, ed., *The Science Fiction Novel: Imagination and Social Criticism* (Chicago: Advent Books, 1964), pp. 109–10.

15. Ellison, *Dangerous Visions*, p. 52.

16. Harlan Ellison, ed., *Again, Dangerous Visions* (New York: New American Library, 1973), vol. 1, p. 287.

17. Ibid., vol. 1, p. 331.

18. Robert Silverberg, *Thorns* (New York: Ballantine Books, 1967), p. 222.

19. Harlan Ellison, *Approaching Oblivion* (New York: Bluejay Books, 1985), p. 22.

20. Ibid., p. 20.

21. Ibid., p. 19.

22. Harlan Ellison, *Alone against Tomorrow* (New York: Collier Books, 1971), p. 144.

23. Harlan Ellison, *Deathbird Stories* (New York: Bluejay Books, 1983), pp. 16–17.

24. Ellison, *Alone against Tomorrow*, p. 32.

25. Larry Niven and Jerry Pournelle, *The Mote in God's Eye* (New York, Simon and Schuster, 1974), p. 20.

26. Ellison, ed., *Again, Dangerous Visions*, vol. 1, p. 271.

27. Ibid., p. 278.

28. Ibid., p. 276.

29. William Shakespeare, *Hamlet*, act II, sc. II, lines 306–7.

30. Ibid., act I, sc. II, line 146.

31. C. L. Moore, personal conversation, 1979.

32. *Startling Stories*, Fall 1945, p. 112.

33. Leigh Brackett, *Eric John Stark: Outlaw of Mars* (New York: Ballantine Books, 1982), p. 174.

34. For example, Peter Nicholls, ed., *The Science Fiction Encyclopedia* (Garden City, N.Y.: Doubleday & Co., 1979), p. 661.

35. Ellison, ed., *Again, Dangerous Visions*, vol. 1, p. 267.

36. Joanna Russ, *The Female Man* (New York: Bantam Books, 1975), p. 195.

37. Ibid., p. 12.

38. James Tiptree, Jr., *Star Songs of an Old Primate* (New York: Ballantine Books, 1978), p. 224.

39. Ibid., p. 211.

40. Suzy McKee Charnas, *Walk to the End of the World* (New York: Ballantine Books, 1974), p. 39.

41. Ibid., p. 193.

42. Ibid.

43. Suzy McKee Charnas, *Motherlines* (New York: G. P. Putnam's Sons, 1978), p. 103.

44. Suzette Haden Elgin, *Native Tongue* (New York: DAW Books, 1984), p. 22.

45. Joan Slonczewski, *A Door into Ocean* (New York: Avon Books, 1987), p. 286.

46. Ibid., p. 50.

47. Ibid., p. 406.

48. Pamela Sargent, *The Shore of Women* (New York: Bantam Books, 1987), p. 471.

CHAPTER 7

1. Ivan Yefremov, *Andromeda*, trans. George Hanna (Moscow: Progress Publishers, 1980), p. 223.

2. Ibid., p. 163.

3. Alexei Tolstoi, *The Garin Death Ray*, trans. George Hanna (Moscow: Foreign Languages Publishing House, [1957]), p. 223.

4. Ibid., author's note, p. 6.

5. Darko Suvin, *The Utopian Tradition of Russian Science Fiction* (Modern Humanities Research Association/ W. S. Maney & Son Ltd., n.d.) p. 152.

6. Patrick L. McGuire, *Red Stars: Political Aspects of Soviet Science Fiction* (Ann Arbor, Mich.: UMI Research Press, 1985), p. 14.

7. Vladimir Nemtsov, *Oskolok Solntsa* (Moscow: Sovietsky Pisatel, 1955), p. 3.

8. Vladimir Nemtsov, *Oskolok Solntsa* (Moscow: Detskaya Literatura, 1978), p. 14.

9. Vladimir Nemtsov, *Kogda Priblizhayutsya Dali* (Moscow: Sovietsky Pisatel, 1975), p. 3.

10. Ibid., pp. 5–6.

11. Darko Suvin, *Russian Science Fiction, 1956–1974, a Bibliography* (Elizabethtown, N.Y.: Dragon Press, 1975), p. 43.

12. Nemtsov, *Oskolok Solntsa* (1978), p. 77.

13. Vladimir Nemtsov, *Tri Zhelaniya* (Moscow: Detskaya Literatura, 1967), p. 375.

14. Ibid., p. 380.

15. Ibid., p. 572.

16. Nemtsov, *Kogda Priblizhayutsya Dali*, p. 73.

17. Anatoly Dneprov, "The Island of the Crabs," in: Darko Suvin, ed., *Other Worlds, Other Seas* (New York: Berkley Books, 1972), p. 210.

18. Anatoly Deprov, "Siema," in *The Heart of the Serpent* [no editor given] (Moscow: Foreign Languages Publishing House, 1960), p. 164.

19. Sever Gansovsky, "A Day of Wrath," in: *Path into the Unknown* [no editor given] (New York: Dell Books, 1968), p. 87.

20. McGuire, *Red Stars*, p. 16.

21. Ibid., 18–19.

22. Yefremov, *Andromeda*, p. 67.

23. Mark Hillegas, *The Future as Nightmare: H. G. Wells and the Anti-Utopians* (New York: Oxford University Press, 1967), pp. 176–78.

24. Yefremov, *Andromeda*, p. 396.

25. Ibid., p. 253.

26. Ibid., p. 58.

27. Ibid., p. 185.

28. Ibid., p. 285.

29. Ibid., p. 62.

30. Genrikh Altov and Valentina Zhuravlyova, *Ballad of the Stars*, trans. Roger DeGaris (New York: Macmillan Publishing Co., 1982), p. 221.

31. Ibid., p. 236.

32. McGuire, *Red Stars*, pp. 31–32, 37–38, 43, 47–48, 53–54.

33. Vadim Shefner, "A Modest Genius," in: Franz Rottensteiner, ed., *The View from Another Shore* (New York: The Seabury Press, 1973), p. 222.

34. Quoted by Michael Kandel in introduction to Stanislaw Lem, *Mortal Engines*, trans. Michael Kandel (New York: Avon/Bard Books, 1982), p. x.

35. Mikhail Yemtsev (Emtsev) and Yeremei (Eremei) Parnov, *World Soul*, trans. Antonina W. Bouis (New York: Macmillan Publishing Co., 1978), p. 90.

36. Arkady Strugatsky and Boris Strugatsky, *Roadside Picnic/Tale of the Troika*, trans. Antonina W. Bouis (New York: Macmillan Publishing Co., 1977), p. 145.

37. Arkady Strugatsky and Boris Strugatsky, *Space Apprentice*, trans. Antonina W. Bouis (New York: Macmillan Publishing Co., 1981), p. 78.

38. Ibid., p. 149.

39. Ibid., p. 190.

40. Ibid., p. 231.

41. McGuire, *Red Stars*, p. 70.

42. Arkady Strugatsky and Boris Strugatsky, *The Final Circle of Paradise*, trans. Leonid Renen (New York: DAW Books, 1976), p. 53.

43. Ibid., pp. 171–72.

44. Arkady Strugatsky and Boris Strugatsky, *Noon: 22nd Century*, trans. Patrick L. McGuire (New York: Macmillan Publishing Co., 1978), p. 88.

45. Ibid., p. 276.

46. Arkadi Strugatsky and Boris Strugatski, *Hard to Be a God*, trans. Wendayne Ackerman (New York: Seabury Press, 1973), p. 35.

47. Ibid., p. 197.

48. Ibid.

49. Ibid., p. 198.

50. Arkady Strugatsky and Boris Strugatsky, *Prisoners of Power*, trans. Helen Saltz Jacobson (New York: MacMillan Publishing Co., 1977), p. 63.

51. Ibid., p. 174.

52. Ibid., p. 286.

53. Suvin, *Russian Science Fiction, 1956–1974*, pp. 43, 48, 49.

54. Arkady Strugatsky and Boris Strugatsky, *Far Rainbow/The Second Invasion from Mars*, trans. Gary Kern (New York: Macmillan Publishing Co., 1979), p. 131.

55. Ibid.

56. Ibid., p. 60.

57. Arkady Strugatsky and Boris Strugatsky, *Beetle in the Anthill,* trans. Antonina W. Bouis (New York: Macmillan Publishing Co., 1980), p. 170.

58. Arkady Strugatsky and Boris Strugatsky, *The Snail on the Slope,* trans. Alan Meyers (New York: Bantam Books, 1980), p. 227.

59. Ibid., p. 52.

60. Ibid., pp. 242–43.

CHAPTER 8

1. John Brunner, *The Long Result* (New York: Ballantine Books, 1965), p. 95.

2. Ibid., p. 54.

3. Ibid., p. 25.

4. Ibid., p. 95.

5. Ibid.

6. John Brunner, *Stand on Zanzibar* (New York: Ballantine Books, 1969), p. 77.

7. Ibid., p. 442.

8. Ibid., p. 627.

9. Ibid., p. 646.

10. John Brunner, *The Sheep Look Up* (New York: Ballantine Books, 1973), p. 56.

11. John Brunner, *Total Eclipse* (New York, DAW Books, 1975), p. 186.

12. Frederik Pohl, *The Way the Future Was* (New York: Ballantine Books, 1978), p. 120.

13. "Our Questionnaire," *Soviet Literature,* Feb. 1984, p. 155.

14. Frederik Pohl, *Chernobyl* (New York: Bantam Books Inc, 1987), p. 260.

15. Frederik Pohl, column (not traced, but purport confirmed in personal conversation, Nov. 1, 1988).

16. Frederik Pohl, ed., *Nightmare Age* (New York: Ballantine Books, 1970), p. 2.

17. Ibid., p. 1.

18. Frederik Pohl, *Pohlstars* (New York: Ballantine Books, 1984), p. 164.

19. Frederik Pohl, *Jem* (New York: St. Martin's, 1979), pp. 34–35.

20. Ibid., p. 85.

21. Ibid., p. 121.

22. Ibid., p. 312.

23. Ibid., p. 351.

24. George Orwell, *A Collection of Essays by George Orwell* (Garden City, N.Y.: Doubleday & Co.-Anchor Books, 1954), p. 59.

25. Ibid., p. 111.

26. Frederik Pohl, *Gateway* (New York: St. Martin's, 1977), p. 15.

27. Frederik Pohl, *The Age of the Pussyfoot* (New York: Ballantine Books, 1969), pp. 196–97.

28. Frederik Pohl, *Syzygy* (New York: Bantam Books, 1982), p. 247.

29. Ayn Rand, *Atlas Shrugged* (New York: New American Library, n.d.), p. 993.

30. Ayn Rand, "Anthem," *Famous Fantastic Mysteries,* June 1953.

31. Barbara Branden, *The Passion of Ayn Rand* (Garden City, N.Y.: Doubleday & Co., 1986), p. 413.

32. Ayn Rand, *The Romantic Manifesto* (Cleveland: World Publishing Co., 1969), p. 94ff.

33. Ibid., p. 161ff.

34. Ibid., p. 22.

35. Rand, *Atlas Shrugged*, p. 626.

36. Ibid., p. 434.

37. Ayn Rand, *Anthem* (New York: New American Library, 1961), pp. 122–3.

38. Rand, *Atlas Shrugged*, p. 1063.

39. Ibid., p. 165.

40. Ibid., p. 983.

41. Mark Hillegas, *The Future as Nightmare: H. G. Wells and the Anti-Utopians* (New York: Oxford University Press, 1967), p. 59.

42. L. Neil Smith, *The Probability Broach* (New York: Ballantine Books, 1980), p. 283.

43. J. Neil Schulman, *Alongside Night* (New York: Crown Publishers, 1979), p. 70.

44. J. Neil Schulman, *The Rainbow Cadenza* (New York: Simon and Schuster, 1983), p. 75.

45. Ibid., p. 247.

CHAPTER 9

1. Cordwainer Smith [pseud. Paul M. A. Linebarger], *The Best of Cordwainer Smith* (New York: Ballantine Books, 1975), p. 283.

2. Ibid., pp. 284–85.

3. Yevgeny Zamyatin, *A Soviet Heretic*, ed. and trans. Mirra Ginsburg (Chicago: University of Chicago Press, 1970), p. 82.

4. Ibid., pp. 286–88.

5. Smith, *The Best of Cordwainer Smith*, pp. 52–53.

6. Ibid., p. 53.

7. Ibid.

8. Ibid., p. 58.

9. Personal conversation with Genevieve Linebarger, 1970; other background material from Cordwainer Smith papers, University of Kansas, Lawrence, Kans.; Tony Lewis, *Concordance to Cordwainer Smith* (Cambridge, Mass.: NESFA Press, 1984).

10. Unpublished manuscript (1961) of "War No. 81-Q" at University of Kansas, Lawrence, Kans., p. 1.

11. Cordwainer Smith, *Norstrilia* (New York: Ballantine Books, 1975), p. 211.

12. Ibid., p. 272.

13. Cordwainer Smith, unpublished partial draft, "Where is the Which of the What-She-Did?" (University of Kansas collection), p. 1.

14. Cordwainer Smith, *The Instrumentality of Mankind* (New York: Ballantine Books, 1979), p. 29.

15. Ibid., p. 39.

16. Ibid., p. 1.

17. Smith, *The Best of Cordwainer Smith*, p. 211.

18. Smith, *The Instrumentality of Mankind*, p. 14.

19. Smith, *The Best of Cordwainer Smith*, p. 122.

20. Ibid., p. 211.

21. Ibid., p. 162.

22. Sandra Miesel, "I Am Joan & I Love You," in Andrew Porter, ed., *Exploring Cordwainer Smith* (New York: Algol Press, 1975), pp. 24–28.

23. Smith, *The Best of Cordwainer Smith*, p. 137.

24. Ibid., p. 205.

25. Ibid., p. 150.

26. Ibid., p. 207.

27. Ibid., p. 318.

28. Ibid., pp. 210–11.

29. Ibid., p. 255.

30. Ibid., p. 37.

31. Ibid., p. 376.

32. Ibid.

33. Smith, *Norstrilia*, p. 6.

34. Ibid., p. 249.

35. Cordwainer Smith, *Quest of the Three Worlds* (New York: Ballantine Books, 1978), p. 160.

36. Ibid., p. 1.

37. Ibid., p. 126.

38. Smith, *Norstrilia*, p. 247.

39. Cordwainer Smith papers, University of Kansas, Lawrence, Kans., esp. notebook, 1965–6.

40. Smith, *The Best of Cordwainer Smith*, p. 330.

41. Ibid., p. 337.

42. Smith, *Norstrilia*, p. 241.

43. Ursula K. Le Guin, *The Dispossessed* (New York: Harper & Row, 1974), p. 1.

44. Paul Walker, ed., *Speaking of Science Fiction* (Oradell, N.J., Luna Publications, 1978), p. 34.

45. Ursula K. Le Guin, introduction to *Planet of Exile* (New York: Harper & Row, 1978), p. xii.

46. Le Guin, *The Dispossessed*, p. 307.

47. Ursula K. Le Guin, *The Word for World Is Forest* (New York: Berkley Publishing Corp., 1976), p. 43.

48. Ibid.

49. Ibid., p. 77.

50. Ibid., p. 185.

51. Ibid., p. 186.

52. Ursula K. Le Guin, *Rocannon's World* (New York: Ace Books, 1966), p. 10.

53. Ibid., pp. 135–36.

54. Ibid., p. 136.

55. Le Guin, *Planet of Exile*, p. 32.

56. Ibid., p. 82.

57. Ibid., p. 140.

58. Ursula K. Le Guin, *City of Illusions* (New York: Ace Books, 1967), p. 14.

59. Ibid., p. 125.

60. Ibid., p. 127.

61. Ibid., p. 139.

62. Ursula K. Le Guin, *The Left Hand of Darkness* (New York: Ace Books, 1969), p. 132.

63. Ibid.

64. Ibid.

65. Ibid., p. 37.

66. Ibid., p. 245.

67. Ibid., p. 276.

68. Ibid., p. 101.

69. Zamyatin, *A Soviet Heretic*, p. 108.

70. Ursula K. Le Guin, *The Wind's Twelve Quarters* (New York: Harper & Row, 1975), p. 296.

71. Le Guin, *The Dispossessed*, p. 293.

72. Ibid.

73. Ibid., p. 41.

74. Ibid., p. 199.

75. Ibid., p. 336.

76. C. S. Lewis, *An Experiment in Criticism* (Cambridge: Cambridge University Press, 1969), p. 140.

77. Thomas M. Disch, review column, *The Magazine of Fantasy and Science Fiction* (Feb. 1981), pp. 40–47.

78. Daryl Lane, William Vernon, and David Carson, eds., *The Sound of Wonder* (Phoenix, Ariz: Oryx Press, 1985), vol. 2, p. 193.

79. William Gibson, interview, *Science Fiction Eye* (Winter 1987), pp. 6–17; See also Bruce Sterling interview, pp. 27–42.

80. Ibid., p. 14.

81. William Gibson, *Neuromancer* (New York: Ace Books, 1984), p. 3.

82. William Gibson, *Burning Chrome* (New York: Ace Books, 1987), p. 102.

83. For example, introduction to Bruce Sterling, ed., *Mirrorshades: The Cyberpunk Anthology* (New York: Arbor House, 1986), p. xiii.

84. Bruce Sterling, *Schismatrix* (New York: Ace Books, 1986), p. 80.

85. Ibid., p. 133.

86. Fletcher Pratt, *The Well of the Unicorn* (New York: Ballantine Books, 1976), p. 388.

Bibliography

As in *Foundations of Science Fiction* and *Great Themes of Science Fiction*, the bibliography here documents editions cited in the notes and, wherever necessary, *first-year* (not necessarily *first*) book editions or original magazine publications. In some cases, paperback (pb), mass-market, or first U.S. edition came out in the same year as hardcover (hc), limited edition, or foreign versions. Serializations appearing in the same year as first book editions are not cited except in the case of title changes. Magazine abbreviations are as follows:

AMZ	*Amazing Stories*
ASF	*Astounding/Analog Science Fiction*
FAN	*Fantastic Stories*
F&SF	*The Magazine of Fantasy and Science Fiction*
FUT	*Future*
GAL	*Galaxy Science Fiction*
IF	*Worlds of If*
INF	*Infinity*
NW	*New Worlds*
PLA	*Planet Stories*

SS	*Startling Stories*
WOT	*Worlds of Tomorrow*
WS	*Wonder Stories/Thrilling Wonder Stories*

FICTIONAL WORKS, INCLUDING CRITICAL EDITIONS AND COLLECTIONS

Ahern, Jerry. *Total War* (New York: Zebra Books, 1981).

Aldiss, Brian W. *Barefoot in the Head* (New York: Avon Books, 1981; London: Faber & Faber Ltd., 1969). Incorporates segments from "Just Passing Through" (*Impulse*, Feb. 1967) and "Multi-Value Motorway" (NW 174, Aug. 1967) through "Ouspenski's Astrobahn" (NW 186, Jan. 1969).

————. *The Dark Light-Years* (New York: New American Library, 1964).

————. *Enemies of the System* (New York: Avon Books, 1981; London: Jonathan Cape, 1978).

————. *Frankenstein Unbound* (Greenwich, Conn.: Fawcett Books, 1975; London: Jonathan Cape, 1973).

————. *Greybeard* (St. Alban's, U.K.: Panther Books, 1968; London: Faber & Faber, 1964).

————. *Helliconia Spring* (New York: Atheneum, 1982).

————. *Helliconia Summer* (New York: Atheneum, 1983).

————. *Helliconia Winter* (New York: Atheneum, 1985).

————. *Life in the West* (London/Dallas, Pa.: Corgi Books, 1982; London: Weidenfeld & Nicholson, 1980).

————. *The Malacia Tapestry* (New York: Berkley Books, 1985; New York: Harper & Row, 1976).

————. *Report on Probability A* (New York: Avon Books, 1981; London: Faber & Faber, 1968; NW 171, Mar. 1967).

————. *The Saliva Tree* (London: Sphere Books, 1968; London: Faber & Faber, 1966). Incl. "The Saliva Tree" (F&SF, Sept. 1965).

————. *Starship* (New York: Avon Books, 1969; as *Non-Stop*, London: Faber & Faber, 1958).

Altov, Genrikh, and Valentina Zhuravlyova. *Ballad of the Stars*. Trans. Roger DeGaris (New York: Macmillan Publishing Co., 1982). Incl. "Ballad of the Stars," trans. from "Ballada o Zvezdakh" (*Znanie-Sila* 8–10, 1960).

Ambler, Eric. *A Coffin for Demetrios* (New York: Alfred A. Knoff, 1939).

Arlen, Michael. *Man's Mortality* (Garden City, N.Y.: Doubleday, Doran, 1933).

Asimov, Isaac. *The Caves of Steel* (Greenwich, Conn.: Fawcett Books, 1972; Garden City, N.Y.: Doubleday & Co., 1954; GAL, Oct.-Dec. 1953).

————. *The Currents of Space* (Greenwich, Conn.: Fawcett Books, 1971; Garden City, N.Y.: Doubleday & Co., 1952; ASF, Oct.-Dec. 1952).

————. *The End of Eternity* (Greenwich, Conn.: Fawcett Books, 1971; Garden City, N.Y.: Doubleday & Co., 1955).

————. *Foundation* (New York: Avon Books, 1966; New York: Gnome Press, 1951). Incorporates "Foundation" (ASF, May 1942), "Bridle and Saddle" (ASF, June 1942), "The Big and the Little" (ASF, Aug. 1944).

————. *Foundation and Earth* (Garden City, N.Y.: Doubleday & Co., 1986).

———. *Foundation and Empire* (New York: Avon Books, 1966; New York: Gnome Press, 1952). Incorporates "Dead Hand" (ASF, Apr. 1945) and "The Mule" (ASF, Nov.-Dec. 1945).

———. *Foundation's Edge* (Garden City, N.Y.: Doubleday & Co., 1982).

———. *I, Robot* (Greenwich, Conn.: Fawcett Books, 1970; Garden City, N.Y.: Doubleday & Co., 1950). Incl. "The Evitable Conflict" (ASF, June 1950).

———. *The Naked Sun* (Greenwich, Conn.: Fawcett Books, 1972; Garden City, N.Y.: Doubleday & Co., 1957; ASF, Oct.-Dec. 1956).

———. *Nightfall and Other Stories* (Greenwich, Conn.: Fawcett Books, 1970; Garden City, N.Y.: Doubleday & Co., 1969). Incl. "Green Patches" (as "Misbegotten Missionary," GAL, Nov. 1950).

———. *Pebble in the Sky* (New York: Bantam Books, 1957; Garden City, N.Y.: Doubleday & Co., 1950).

———. *Robots and Empire* (New York: Ballantine Books, 1986; Garden City, N.Y.: Doubleday & Co., 1985).

———. *The Robots of Dawn* (Garden City, N.Y.: Doubleday & Co., 1983).

———. *Second Foundation* (New York: Avon Books, 1964; New York: Gnome Press, 1953). Incorporates "Now You See It . . ." (ASF, Jan. 1948) and " . . . And Now You Don't" (ASF, Nov. 1949-Jan. 1950).

———. *The Stars Like Dust* (New York: Lancer Books, 1963; Garden City, N.Y.: Doubleday & Co., 1951; as *Tyrann*, GAL, Jan.-Mar. 1951).

Ballard, J. G. *The Atrocity Exhibition* (London: Triad/Panther, 1979; London, Jonathan Cape, 1970). Incorporates "The Assassination of John Fitzgerald Kennedy Considered as a Downhill Motor Race" (*Ambit,* 1966), "Why I want to Fuck Ronald *Reagan*" (*Ronald Reagan: The Magazine of Poetry,* Summer 1968), "Love and Napalm: Export U.S.A." (*The Running Man,* Summer 1968).

———. *Billenium* (New York: Berkley Books, 1962). Incl. "Billenium" (NW 112, Nov. 1961).

———. *The Burning World* (New York: Berkley Books, 1964; as *The Drought,* London: Jonathan Cape, 1965).

———. *The Crystal World* (New York: Berkley Books, 1967; London: Jonathan Cape, 1966).

———. *The Drowned World* (New York: Berkley Books, 1966, 1962).

———. *Empire of the Sun* (New York: Washington Square Press, 1985; New York: Simon & Schuster, 1984).

———. *Terminal Beach* (New York: Berkley Books, 1964). Incl. "The Terminal Beach" (NW 140, Mar. 1964), "The Subliminal Man" (NW 126, Jan. 1963).

———. *The Wind from Nowhere* (New York: Berkley Books, 1966, 1962; as *Storm Wind,* NW 110–111, Sept.-Oct. 1961).

Barjavel, René. *Ashes, Ashes.* Trans. Damon Knight (Garden City, N.Y.: Doubleday & Co., 1967), from *Ravage* (Paris: Editions Denoel, 1943).

Belyayev, Aleksandr. *Vlastelin Mira* [*The Master of the World*] in *Uzdrannye Nauchno-Fantasticheskie Proizvedeniya,* tom. 3 (Moscow: Molodaya Gvardia, 1957); serialized *Vokrug Sveta,* 1929.

Benford, Greg. *Against Infinity* (New York: Pocket/Timescape Books, 1983).

———. *Timescape* (New York: Simon & Schuster, 1980).

Bester, Alfred. *The Stars My Destination* (New York: Bantam Books, 1970; as *Tiger!*

Tiger!, London: Sidgwick & Jackson, 1956; as *The Stars My Destination*, GAL, Oct. 1956-Jan. 1957).

Bishop, Michael. *Beneath the Shattered Moons* (New York: DAW Books, 1977; as *And Strange at Ectaban the Trees*, New York: Harper & Row, 1976).

———. *Blooded on Arachne* (New York: Pocket/Timescape Books, 1982). Incl. "The White Otters of Childhood" (F&SF, July 1973).

Bloch, Robert. *Psycho* (New York: Simon and Schuster, 1959).

———. "A Toy for Juliette." See Ellison, Harlan, ed., *Dangerous Visions*.

Bova, Ben. "Brillo." See Ellison, Harlan, ed., *Partners in Wonder*.

———. "Zero Gee." See Ellison, Harlan, ed., *Again, Dangerous Visions*.

Brackett, Leigh. *Eric John Stark: Outlaw of Mars* (New York: Ballantine Books, 1982). Incorporates *People of the Talisman* (New York: Ace Books, 1964), exp. from "Black Amazon of Mars" (PLA, Mar. 1951).

Brin, David. *Startide Rising* (New York: Bantam Books, 1983).

Brunner, John. *The Jagged Orbit* (New York: Ace Books, 1969).

———. *The Long Result* (New York: Ballantine Books, 1965).

———. *The Sheep Look Up* (New York: Ballantine Books, 1973; Garden City, N.Y.: Doubleday & Co., 1972).

———. *Stand on Zanzibar* (New York: Ballantine Books, 1969; Garden City, N.Y.: Doubleday & Co., 1968).

———. *Total Eclipse* (New York: Daw Books, 1975; Garden City, N.Y.: Doubleday & Co., 1974).

———. *The Wrong End of Time* (Garden City, N.Y.: Doubleday & Co., 1971).

Budrys, Algis. *Budrys' Inferno* (New York: Berkley Books, 1963). Incl. "Between the Dark and the Daylight" (as by David G. Hodgkins, INF, Oct. 1958).

———. *Rogue Moon* (Greenwich, Conn.: Fawcett Books, 1960).

———. *Unexpected Dimension* (New York: Ballantine Books, 1960). Incl. "The Burning World" (INF, July 1957).

Bulychev, Kir. et al. *Earth and Elsewhere*. Trans. Roger DeGaris (New York: Macmillan Pubishing Co., 1985). Incl. Arkady Strugatsky and Boris Strugatsky, "The Way to Amalteia," from *Put Na Amalteyu* (Moscow: Molodaya Gvardia, 1960); Sever Gansovsky, "A Part of the World," from "Chast Etogo Mira," *NF Almanakh* 14 (Moscow: Znanie, 1974).

Burroughs, William S., *Nova Express* (New York: Grove Press, 1964).

Campbell, John W., Jr. *The Best of John W. Campbell* (New York: Ballantine Books, 1976). Incl. "Twilight" (ASF, Nov. 1934).

Capek, Karel. *R.U.R.* Trans. P. Selver (New York: Washington Square Press, 1969), from *R.U.R.* (Prague: Aventinum, 1921).

Champagne, Maurice. *La Vallée Mysterieuse* [The Mysterious Valley] (Paris: Delagrave, 1915; serialized, 1914).

Charnas, Suzy McKee. *Motherlines* (New York: G. P. Putnam's Sons, 1978).

———. *Walk to the End of the World* (New York: Ballantine Books, 1974).

Cherryh, C. J. *Cyteen* (New York: Warner Books, 1988).

———. *Downbelow Station* (New York: DAW Books, 1981).

Clarke, Arthur C. *Childhood's End* (New York: Ballantine Books, 1967, reset from first, 1953 edition).

———. *The City and the Stars* (New York: New American Library, 1987); New

York: Harcourt Brace, 1956). Rev. from *Against the Fall of Night* (New York: Gnome Press, 1953; SS, Nov. 1948).

———. *The Deep Range* (New York: Harcourt Brace Jovanovich, Pb, n.d.; Harcourt, Brace & World, hc, 1957).

———. *Earthlight* (New York: Ballantine Books, 1966, 1955).

———. *The Fountains of Paradise* (New York: Harcourt Brace Jovanovich, 1979).

———. *Imperial Earth* (New York: Harcourt Brace Jovanovich, 1976; rev. from London: Victor Gollancz, 1975).

———. *The Nine Billion Names of God* (New York: Harcourt Brace Jovanovich, pb, 1967; hb, 1957). Incl. "Rescue Party" (ASF, May 1946), "Transience" (SS, July 1949), " 'If I Forget Thee, O Earth' " (FUT, Sept. 1951), "The Star" (INF, Nov. 1955).

———. *Rendezvous with Rama* (New York: Harcourt, Brace & World, 1973).

———. *The Songs of Distant Earth* (New York: Ballantine Books pb, 1987; hc, 1986).

———. *2001: a Space Odyssey* (New York: New American Library, 1968).

———. *2010: Odyssey Two* (New York: Ballantine Books, hc, 1982).

Coblentz, Stanton A. *The Sunken World* (Los Angeles: Fantasy Publishing Co., 1948; AMZ Quarterly, Summer 1928).

Compton, D. G. *The Silent Multitude* (New York: Ace Books, 1968; London: Hodder & Staughton, 1967).

Delany, Samuel R. *Babel–17* (New York: Ace Books, 1965).

———. *The Complete Nebula Award-Winning Fiction* (New York: Bantam Books, 1986). Incl. *A Fabulous, Formless Darkness* (a.k.a. *The Einstein Intersection*), "Time Considered as a Helix of Semi-Precious Stones" (Donald A. Wollheim, and Terry Carr, eds., *World's Best Science Fiction*, 1969, New York: Ace Books, 1969, rev. from NW 185, Dec. 1968).

———. *Dhalgren* (New York: Bantam Books, 1975).

———. *Driftglass* (New York: New American Library, 1972; Garden City, N.Y.: Doubleday & Co., 1971). Incl. "The Star Pit" (WOT, Feb. 1967), "Aye and Gomorrah" (Harlan Ellison, ed., *Dangerous Visions*, Garden City, N.Y.: Doubleday & Co., 1967), "Driftglass" (IF, June 1967); "Cage of Brass" (IF, June 1968).

———. *The Einstein Intersection* (New York: Ace Books, 1967).

———. *The Fall of the Towers* (New York: Ace Books, 1970). Incl. *Out of the Dead City* (London: Sphere Books, 1968, rev. from *Captives of the Flame*, New York: Ace Books, 1963), *The Towers of Toron* (London: Sphere Books, 1968, rev. from New York: Ace Books, 1964), *City of a Thousand Suns* (London: Sphere Books, 1969, rev. from New York: Ace Books, 1965).

———. *The Jewels of Aptor* (New York: Ace Books, 1968; rev. and exp. from New York: Ace Books, 1962).

———. *Nova* (New York: Bantam Books, 1969; Garden City, N.Y.: Doubleday & Co., 1968).

———. *Stars in My Pocket Like Grains of Sand* (New York: Bantam Books, hc, 1984).

———. *Triton* (New York: Bantam Books, 1976).

Delany, Samuel R., with Howard V. Chaykin. *Empire* (New York: Berkley-Windhover, 1978).

del Rey, Lester. *The Best of Lester del Rey* (New York: Ballantine Books, 1978). Incl. "Helen O'Loy" (ASF, Dec. 1938), "For I Am a Jealous People" (*Star Short Novels*, New York: Ballantine Books, 1954), "The Years Draw Nigh" (ASF, Oct. 1951).

———. *The Eleventh Commandment* (Evanston, Ill.: Regency Books, 1962).

———. *Mortals and Monsters* (New York: Ballantine Books, 1965). Incl. "Recessional" (as "Forgive Us Our Debts," FUT, May 1952).

Dick, Philip K. "Faith of Our Fathers." See Ellison, Harlan, ed., *Dangerous Visions*.

Disch, Thomas M. *Camp Concentration* (New York: Avon Books, 1971; London: Rupert Hart-Davis, 1968; NW 173–6, July-Oct. 1967).

———. *Fun with Your New Head* (New York: New American Library, 1972; London: Rupert Hart-Davis, 1968). Incl. "Descending" (FAN, July 1964), "Moondust, the Smell of Hay and Dialectical Materialism" (F&SF, Aug. 1967), "Thesis on Social Forms and Social Controls in the U.S.A." (FAN, Jan. 1964), "Casablanca" (NW, Oct. 1968).

———. *The Genocides* (New York: Berkley Books, 1965).

———. *On Wings of Song* (New York: St. Martin's, 1979).

———. *334* (New York: Avon Books, 1974; London: MacGibbon Kee, 1972). Incorporates shorter works, incl. "The Problem of Creativeness," (F&SF, Apr. 1967), "Angouleme" (NW 202, Sept. 1971), "334" (NW 205, June 1972).

Disch, Thomas M. ed. *The New Improved Sun* (New York: Harper & Row, 1975). Incl. Disch, "Pyramids for Minnesota" (*Harper's*, Jan. 1974).

———. *The Ruins of Earth* (New York: Berkley Books, 1972; New York: Harper & Row, 1971).

Dneprov, Anatoly [pseud. A. P. Mitskevitch]. "Glinyanyi Bog" ["Clay God"]. See Strugatsky, Arkady, and Boris Strugatsky, *Strana Bagrovykh Tuch*.

———. "Interview with a Traffic Policeman," trans. not given, in Darko Suvin, ed., *Other Worlds, Other Seas* (New York: Berkley Books, 1972; New York: Random House, 1970), from "Intervyu s regulirovshchikem ulichnogo dvizheniya" (*Fantastika* 1965, no. 1, Moscow: Molodaya Gvardia).

———. "The Island of the Crabs," trans. not given, in Darko Suvin, ed., *Other Worlds, Other Seas* (New York: Berkley Books, 1972; New York: Random House, 1970), from "Kraby idut po ostrovu" (*Doroga V Eto Parsekov*, Moscow: Molodaya Gvardia, 1959).

———. "Siema." Trans. N. Grishin. In *The Heart of the Serpent* (Moscow: Foreign Languages Publishing House, 1960), from "Siema" (*Doroga v Eto Parsekov* Moscow: Molodaya Gvardia, 1959).

Döblin, Alfred. *Berge, Meere und Giganten* [*Mountains, Seas and Giants*] (Berlin: S. Fischer, 1924).

———. *Berlin Alexanderplatz, The Story of Franz Biberkopf*, trans. Eugene Jolas (New York: Frederick Ungar, 1984), from *Berlin Alexanderplatz, die geschichte vom Franz Biberkopf* (Berlin: S. Fischer, 1929).

Dos Passos, John. *U.S.A.* (New York: The Modern Library, 1939). Incorporates *The 42nd Parallel* (New York and London: Harper Bros., 1930), *1919* (New York: Harcourt, Brace & Co, 1932), *The Big Money* (New York: Harcourt, Brace & Co., 1936).

Dostoyevsky, Fyodor. *The Brothers Karamazov*, trans. Constance Garrett (New York: New American Library, 1957) from 1879–80 Russian text.

———. *Crime and Punishment*, trans. Sidney Monas (New York: New American Library, 1968), from 1866 Russian text.

Drake, David. *Hammer's Slammers* (New York: Ace Books, 1979).

Drury, Allen. *Advise and Consent* (Garden City, N.Y.: Doubleday & Co., 1959).

Effinger, George Alec. *When Gravity Fails* (New York: Arbor House, 1986).

Elgin, Suzette Haden. *The Judas Rose* (New York: DAW Books, 1987).

———. *Native Tongue* (New York: DAW Books, 1984).

Elliott, Jeffrey, M., ed. *Kindred Spirits: An Anthology of Gay and Lesbian Science Fiction Stories* (Boston: Alyson, 1984).

Ellison, Harlan. *Alone Against Tomorrow* (New York: Collier Books, 1971). Incl. "I Have No Mouth, and I Must Scream" (IF, Mar. 1967); " 'Repent, Harlequin!' Said the Ticktockman" (GAL, Dec. 1965).

———. *Approaching Oblivion* (New York: Bluejay Books, 1985; New York: Walker, 1974). Incl. "Silent in Gehenna" (Ben Bova, ed., *The Many Worlds of Science Fiction*, New York: E. P. Dutton Co., 1971).

———. *The Beast That Shouted Love at the Heart of the World* (New York: Avon Books, 1969). Incl. "The Beast That Shouted Love at the Heart of the World" (GAL, June 1968), "Along the Scenic Route" (as "Dogfight on 101," AMZ, Sept. 1969), "Shattered Like a Glass Goblin" (Damon Knight, ed., *Orbit 4*, New York: Berkley Books, 1968), "A Boy and His Dog" (exp. from NW 189, Apr. 1969).

———. "Croatoan." In Terry Carr, ed. *The Best Science Fiction of the Year #5*, (New York: Ballantine Books, 1976); F&SF, May 1975.

———. *Deathbird Stories* (New York: Bluejay Books, 1983; New York: Harper & Row, 1975). Incl. "Paingod" (FAN, June 1964), "The Whimper of Whipped Dogs" (Thomas M. Disch, ed., *Bad Moon Rising*, New York: Harper & Row, 1973), "Pretty Maggie Moneyeyes" (*Knight*, 1967).

———. *Partners in Wonder* (New York: Avon Books, 1972; New York: Walker, 1971). Incl. "Brillo," with Ben Bova (ASF, Aug. 1970), "The Human Operators," with A. E. Van Vogt (F&SF, Jan. 1971).

Ellison, Harlan, ed. *Again, Dangerous Visions* (New York: New American Library, 1973, two volumes; Garden City, N.Y.: Doubleday & Co., 1972). Incl. Ursula K. Le Guin, "The Word for World Is Forest"; Joanna Russ, "When It Changed"; Kurt Vonnegut, Jr., "The Big Space Fuck"; Bernard Wolfe, "The Bisquit Position"; Ben Bova, "Zero Gee"; Richard A. Lupoff, "With the Bentfin Boomer Boys on Little Old New Alabama."

———. *Dangerous Visions* (New York: Berkley Books, 1972; Garden City, N.Y.: Doubleday & Co., 1967). Incl. Ellison, "The Prowler in the City at the Edge of the World"; Robert Bloch, "A Toy for Juliette"; Robert Silverberg, "Flies"; Philip José Farmer, "Riders of the Purple Wage"; Philip K. Dick, "Faith of Our Fathers"; Theodore Sturgeon, "If All Men Were Brothers, Would You Let One Marry Your Sister?"; Norman Spinrad, "The Carcinoma Angels"; Samuel R. Delany, "Aye, and Gomorrah."

———. *Medea, Harlan's World* (Huntington Woods, Mich.: Phantasia Press, 1985).

Farmer, Philip José. *Image of the Beast* (Hollywood, Calif.: Essex House, 1968).

———. "Riders of the Purple Wage." See Ellison, Harlan, ed., *Dangerous Visions*.

Forster, E. M. *The Infinite Moment, and Other Stories* (New York: Harcourt, Brace & Co., 1928). Incl. "The Machine Stops" (*Oxford and Cambridge Review*, 1909).

Gallun, Raymond Z. *The Best of Raymond Z. Gallun* (New York: Ballantine Books, 1978). Incl. "Old Faithful" (ASF, Dec. 1934), "Godson of Almarlu" (ASF, Oct. 1936), "The Restless Tide" (*Marvel Stories*, Nov. 1951).

Gansovsky, Sever. "A Day of Wrath," trans. not given, in *Path into the Unknown* (New York: Dell Books, 1968), from "Den Gneva" (*NF Almanakh*, vol. 1, Moscow: Znanie, 1964).

———. "A Part of the World." See Bulychev, Kir, et al., *Earth and Elsewhere*.

Gearhart, Sally Miller. *The Wanderground* (Watertown, Mass.: Persephone Press, 1980). Incorporates shorter works, original places and dates of publication not given.

Gibson, William. *Burning Chrome* (New York: Ace Books, 1987; New York: Arbor House, 1986). Incl. "Red Star, Winter Orbit," with Bruce Sterling (*Omni*, July 1983).

———. *Count Zero* (New York: Arbor House, 1986).

———. *Mona Lisa Overdrive* (New York: Bantam Books, 1988).

———. *Neuromancer* (New York: Ace Books, 1984).

Godwin, Tom. "The Cold Equations." In Robert Silverberg, ed. *The Science Fiction Hall of Fame* (New York: Avon Books, 1971; Garden City, N.Y.: Doubleday & Co, 1970; ASF, Aug. 1954).

Grigoriev, Vladimir. "The Horn of Plenty." Trans. Mirra Ginsburg. Mirra Ginsburg, ed. *The Ultimate Threshhold* (New York: Holt, Rinehart and Winston, 1970), from "Rog Izobiliya," *Fantastika 1964* (Moscow: Molodaya Gvardia, 1964).

Hamilton, Edmond. *The Best of Edmond Hamilton* (New York: Ballantine Books, 1977). Incl. "The Man Who Evolved" (WS, Apr. 1931).

———. *Crashing Suns* (New York: Ace Books, 1965). Incl. "Crashing Suns" (Weird Tales, Aug.-Sept. 1928), "Within the Nebula" (*Weird Tales*, May 1929).

———. *The Star Kings* (New York: Paperback Library, 1967; New York: Frederick Fell, 1949; AMZ, Sept. 1947).

Harrison, M. John. "The Ash Circus" (NW, 189, Apr. 1969).

Heinlein, Robert A. *Beyond This Horizon* (New York: New American Library, n.d.; Los Angeles, Fantasy Publishing Co., 1948; ASF, Apr.-May 1942, as by Anson MacDonald).

———. *Citizen of the Galaxy* (New York: Charles Scribner's Sons, 1957).

———. *Double Star* (Garden City, N.Y.: Doubleday & Co., 1956).

———. *Farmer in the Sky* (New York: Charles Scribner's Sons, 1950).

———. *Farnham's Freehold* (New York: New American Library, 1965; New York: G. P. Putnam's Sons, 1964).

———. *Have Space Suit—Will Travel* (New York: Charles Scribner's Sons, 1958).

———. *The Moon Is a Harsh Mistress* (New York: G. P. Putnam's Sons, 1966; IF, Dec. 1965-Apr. 1966).

———. *Orphans of the Sky* (New York: New American Library, 1965; London: Victor Gollancz, 1963. Incl. "Universe" (ASF, May 1941).

————. *The Past through Tomorrow* (New York: G. P. Putnam's Sons, 1967). Future History stories, incl. "Requiem" (ASF, Jan. 1940), "Coventry" (ASF, July 1940).

————. *The Puppet Masters* (Garden City, N.Y.: Doubleday & Co., 1951).

————. *Starship Troopers* (New York: Berkley Books, 1968; New York: G. P. Putnam's Sons, 1959; as *Starship Soldier*, F&SF, Oct.-Nov. 1959).

————. *Stranger in a Strange Land* (New York: G. P. Putnam's Sons, 1961).

————. *Tunnel in the Sky* (New York: Charles Scribner's Sons, 1955).

Held, S. S. *The Death of Iron*. Trans. Fletcher Pratt (WS, Sept.-Nov. 1932), from *La Mort de La Fer* (Paris: 1931).

Hubbard, L. Ron. *Battlefield Earth* (New York: St. Martin's, 1983).

————. *Fear and Typewriter in the Sky* (New York: Gnome Press, 1951). Incl. "Typewriter in the Sky" (UNK, Nov.-Dec. 1940).

————. *Final Blackout* (North Hollywood, Calif.: Leisure Books, 1970; Providence, R.I.: Hadley, 1948; ASF, Apr.-June 1940).

————. *Mission Earth*, series of 10 novels, from *The Invaders Plan* (1985) through *The Doomed Planet* (1987), all Los Angeles, Calif.: Bridge Publications.

Huxley, Aldous. *Brave New World* (Garden City, N.Y.: Doubleday, Doran & Co., 1932).

Joyce, James. *Finnegans Wake* (New York: The Viking Press, 1939).

Kadrey, Richard. *Metrophage* (New York: Ace Books, 1988).

Kazantsev, Aleksandr. *Arktichesky Most [Arctic Bridge]* (Moscow: Molodaya Gvardia, 1946).

————. *Lunnaya Doroga [The Road To The Moon]* (Moscow: Geografiz, 1960).

Kornbluth, C[yril] M. *The Syndic* (Garden City, N.Y.: Doubleday & Co., 1953).

Kuttner, Henry. *The Best of Henry Kuttner* (New York: Ballantine Books, 1975). Incl. "Two-Handed Engine" (F&SF, Aug. 1955).

————. *Clash by Night* (Feltham, U.K.: Hamlyn Publishing Group, 1980). Incl. "Clash by Night" (as by Lawrence O'Donnell, ASF, Mar. 1943).

————. *Fury* (New York: Lancer Books, n.d.; New York: Grosset and Dunlap, 1950; as by Lawrence O'Donnell, ASF, May-July 1947).

Lafferty, R. A. "Ishmael into the Barrens." In Robert Silverberg, ed., *Four Futures* (New York: Hawthorne Books, 1971).

————. *Past Master* (New York: Ace Books, 1968).

Lagin, Lazar. *Patent A.V.* (Moscow: Sovietsky Pisatel, 1948).

Laumer, Keith. *Dinosaur Beach* (New York: Charles Scribner's Sons, 1971).

Lee, Harper. *To Kill a Mockingbird* (Philadelphia: J. B. Lippincott Co., 1960).

Le Guin, Ursula K. *Always Coming Home* (New York: Harper & Row, 1985). Incorporates some short works from 1984, such as "The Trouble with the Cotton People" (*Missouri Review*, vol. 7, no. 2).

————. *City of Illusions* (New York: Ace Books, 1967).

————. *The Dispossessed* (New York: Harper & Row, 1974).

————. *The Eye of the Heron* (New York: Harper & Row, 1983; London: Victor Gollancz, 1982; Virginia Kidd, ed., *Millenial Women*, New York: Dell Publishing Co., 1979; New York: Delacorte Press, 1978).

————. *The Lathe of Heaven* (New York: Charles Scribner's Sons, 1971).

————. *The Left Hand of Darkness* (New York: Ace Books, 1969).

————. *Planet of Exile* (New York: Harper & Row, 1978; New York: Ace Books, 1966).

————. *Rocannon's World* (New York: Ace Books, 1966). Incorporates "The Dowry of Angyar" (AMZ, Sept. 1964).

————. *The Wind's Twelve Quarters* (New York: Harper & Row, 1975). Incl. "The Day before the Revolution" (GAL, Aug. 1974): "Semley's Necklace" (retitled from "The Dowry of Angyar,").

————. *The Word for World Is Forest* (New York: Berkley Publishing Corp., 1976; Harlan Ellison, ed., *Again, Dangerous Visions*, Garden City, N.Y.: Doubleday & Co., 1972).

Lem, Stanislaw. *Mortal Engines*. Trans. Michael Kandel (New York: Avon/Bard Books, 1982; New York: The Seabury Press, 1977), from various collections in Polish.

————. *Oblok Magellana [The Magellan Nebula]* (Prague, 1955).

Lewis, C. S. *Out of the Silent Planet* (New York: Macmillan Co., 1965; London: Lane, 1938).

————. *Perelandra* (New York: Macmillan Co., 1965; London: Lane, 1943).

————. *The Screwtape Letters* (London: Bles, 1942).

————. *That Hideous Strength* (New York: Macmillan Co., 1965; London: Lane, 1945).

Longyear, Barry. *Manifest Destiny* (New York: Berkley Books, 1980).

Lupoff, Richard A. "With the Bentfin Boomer Boys on Little Old New Alabama." See Ellison, Harlan, ed., *Again, Dangerous Visions*.

McKinney, Jack. *Genesis* (New York: Ballantine Books, 1987).

Malzberg, Barry N. *Beyond Apollo* (New York: Pocket Books, 1974; New York: Random House, 1972).

————. *The Falling Astronauts* (New York: Ace Books, 1975).

———— [pseudo K. M. O'Donnell] *Universe Day*. (New York: Avon Books, 1971).

Manning, Laurence. *The Man Who Awoke* (New York: Ballantine Books, 1975). Incorporates series from WS, Mar.-Aug. 1933.

Martin, George R. R. *The Armageddon Rag* (New York: Pocket Books, 1983).

————. *Dying of the Light* (New York: Simon and Schuster, 1977).

Meredith, Richard C. *The Sky Is Filled with Ships* (New York: Ballantine Books, 1969).

Miller, Walter M., Jr. *A Canticle for Leibowitz* (New York: Bantam Books, 1961; Philadelphia: J. B. Lippincott Co., 1959). Incorporates "A Canticle for Leibowitz" (F&SF, Apr. 1955), "And the Light Is Risen" (F&SF, Aug. 1956), "The Last Canticle" (F&SF, Feb. 1957).

————. *The Science Fiction Stories of Walter M. Miller, Jr.* (Boston: Gregg Press, 1978). Incl. "Crucifixus Etiam" (ASF, Feb. 1953), "The Big Hunger" (ASF, Oct. 1952).

Miller, Walter M., Jr., and Martin H. Greenberg, eds. *Beyond Armageddon* (New York: Primus/Donald J. Fine, 1985).

Mitchell, Margaret. *Gone with the Wind* (New York: The Macmillan Company, 1936).

Moorcock, Michael. *The Black Corridor* (New York: Ace Books, 1969).

————. *The Cornelius Chronicles* (New York: Avon Books, 1977). Incorporates *The*

Final Programme (New York: Avon Books, 1968; in turn incorporates "Preliminary Data," NW 153, Aug. 1965; "Further Information," NW 157, Dec. 1965; and "Phase Three," NW 160, Mar. 1966), *A Cure for Cancer* (New York: Holt, Rinehart and Winston, 1971; NW 188–91, Mar.-June, 1969), *The English Assassin* (New York: Harper & Row, 1972); *The Condition of Muzak* (London: Allison & Busby, 1977).

———. *The Ice Schooner* (New York: Berkley Books, 1969).

———. *Stormbringer* (London: Jenkins, 1965).

Moorcock, Michael, ed. *New Worlds, An Anthology* (London: Fontana Paperbacks, 1983). Incl. Pamela Zoline, "The Heat Death of the Universe" (NW 173, July 1967) and other fiction and nonfiction from *New Worlds* chosen by Moorcock himself as the best of the British New Wave.

Moore, Ward. *Greener Than You Think* (New York: Sloane, 1947).

Morris, Janet, with David R. Drake. *Active Measures* (New York: Baen Books, 1985).

Nemtsov, Vladimir. *Kogda Priblizhayutsya Dali* [*When Distances Approach*] (Moscow: Sovietsky Pisatel, 1975).

———. *Oskolok Solntsa* [*A Splinter of the Sun*] (Moscow: Sovietsky Pisatel, 1955; slightly revised, Moscow: Detskaya Literatura, 1978).

———. *Syem Tsvetov Radugi* [*The Seven Colors of the Rainbow*] (Moscow: Molodaya Gvardia, 1950).

———. *Tri Zhelaniya* [*Three Wishes*] (Moscow: Detskaya Literatura, 1967). Incl. *Zolotoe Dno* [*Golden Bottom*] (Moscow: Detgiz, 1949; *Tekhnika-Molodezhi*, 1948, nos. 3–12).

Niven, Larry. *The Long Arm of Gil Hamilton* (New York: Ballantine Books, 1976). Incl. "Death by Ecstasy" (as "The Organleggers," GAL, Jan. 1969).

Niven, Larry, and Jerry Pournelle. *Footfall* (New York: Ballantine Books, hc, 1985).

———. *Lucifer's Hammer* (Chicago: Playboy Press, 1977).

———. *The Mote in God's Eye* (New York: Simon and Schuster, 1974).

———. *Oath of Fealty* (New York: Simon and Schuster, 1981).

Norman, John. *Captives of Gor* (New York: Ballantine Books, 1972).

———. *Nomads of Gor* (New York: Ballantine Books, 1969).

Pangborn, Edgar. *West of the Sun* (New York: Dell Books, 1966; Garden City, N.Y.: Doubleday & Co., 1953).

Pohl, Frederik. *The Age of the Pussyfoot* (New York: Ballantine Books, 1969; GAL, Oct. 1965-Feb. 1966).

———. *Alternating Currents* (New York: Ballantine Books, 1956). Incl. "Happy Birthday, Dear Jesus" (new to collection).

———. *Chernobyl* (New York: Bantam Books, hc, 1987).

———. *Gateway* (New York: St. Martin's, 1977; GAL, Nov.-Dec. 1976).

———. *Jem* (New York: St. Martin's, 1979; GAL, Nov. 1978-July 1980).

———. *The Merchants' War* (New York: St. Martin's, 1984).

———. *Pohlstars* (New York: Ballantine Books, 1984). Incl. "Rem the Rememberer" (written 1974, first published in collection).

———. *Syzygy* (New York: Bantam Books, 1982).

———. *The Years of the City* (New York: Timescape Books, 1984).

Pohl, Frederik, and C[yril] M. Kornbluth. *Search the Sky* (New York: Ballantine Books, 1954).

———. *The Space Merchants* (New York: Ballantine Books, 1953; as *Gravy Planet*, GAL, June-Aug. 1952).

Pohl, Frederik, ed. *Nightmare Age* (New York: Ballantine Books, 1970).

Pournelle, Jerry. *The Mercenary* (New York: Pocket Books, 1977). Incorporates series from "Peace with Honor" (ASF, May 1971) to "Sword and Sceptre" (ASF, May-June 1973).

———. *West of Honor* (New York: Pocket Books, 1978; rev. from New York: Laser Books, 1976).

Pratt, Fletcher. *The Well of the Unicorn* (New York: Ballantine Books, 1976; as by George U. Fletcher, New York: Sloane, 1948).

Rand, Ayn. *Anthem* (New York: New American Library, 1961; Los Angeles: The Pamphleteers, 1946; rev. from London: Cassell, 1938).

———. *Atlas Shrugged* (New York: New American Library, n.d.; New York: Random House, 1957).

———. *The Fountainhead* (Indianapolis: Bobbs- Merrill, 1943).

———. *We the Living* (New York: New American Library, 1968; rev. from New York: Macmillan, 1936).

Robinson, Kim Stanley. *The Wild Shore* (New York: Ace Books, 1984).

Rousseau, Victor. *The Messiah of the Cylinder* (Westport, Conn.: Hyperion Press, 1974; reprint of Chicago: A. C. McClurg & Co., 1917).

Russ, Joanna. *The Female Man* (New York: Bantam Books, 1975).

———. "When It Changed." See Ellison, Harlan, ed., *Again, Dangerous Visions*.

Russell, Eric Frank. " . . . And Then There Were None." In Frederik Pohl and Carol Pohl, eds., *Science Fiction: The Great Years* (New York: Ace Books, 1973); ASF, June 1951.

Sargent, Pamela. *The Shore of Women* (New York: Bantam Books, 1987).

———. *Watchstar* (New York: Pocket Books, 1980).

Sargent, Pamela, ed. *Women of Wonder* (New York: Random House, 1975). First in a series.

Schachner, Nat. "Revolt of the Scientists" (WS, Apr. 1933).

Schulman, J. Neil. *Alongside Night* (New York: Crown Publishers, 1979).

———. *The Rainbow Cadenza* (New York: Simon and Schuster, 1983).

Sheckley, Robert. *Untouched by Human Hands* (New York: Ballantine Books, 1954). Incl. "Seventh Violin" (GAL, Apr. 1953).

Shefner, Vadim. "A Modest Genius." Trans. Matthew J. O'Connell, in Frank Rottensteiner, ed., *The View from Another Shore* (New York: Seabury Press, 1973), from "Skromnyi Genii," in Shefner's *Zapozdalyi Strelok* (Leningrad: Sovietsky Pisatel, 1968).

Shelley, Mary. *Frankenstein* (Indianapolis: Bobbs-Merrill Co., 1974; as anon., London: Lackington, Hughes, 1818).

———. *The Last Man* (Lincoln: University of Nebraska Press, 1965; London: Henry Colborn, 1826).

Shirley, John. *Eclipse* (New York: Bluejay Books, 1985).

Silverberg, Robert. "Flies." See Ellison, Harlan, ed., *Again, Dangerous Visions*.

———. *Thorns* (New York: Ballantine Books, 1967).

Simak, Clifford D. *All Flesh Is Grass* (Garden City, N.Y.: Doubleday & Co., 1965).

————. *A Choice of Gods* (New York: Berkley Books, 1973; New York: G. P. Putnam's Sons, 1972).

————. *City* (New York: Ace Books, 1973, reset from 1958; New York: Gnome Press, 1952). Incorporates series, incl. "Desertion" (ASF, Nov. 1944), "Paradise" (ASF, June 1946) "Hobbies" (ASF, Nov. 1946), "Aesop" (ASF, Dec. 1947).

————. *Cosmic Engineers* (New York: Paperback Library, 1964; New York: Gnome Press, 1950; ASF, Feb.-Apr. 1939).

————. *Project Pope* (New York: Ballantine Books, 1981).

————. *Ring Around the Sun* (New York: Avon Books, 1967; New York: Simon and Schuster, 1952).

————. *Strangers in the Universe* (New York: Berkley Books, 1968; New York: Simon and Schuster, 1956). Incl. "The Answers" (William M. Sloane, ed., *Stories for Tomorrow*, New York: Funk & Wagnall's, 1954), "Shadow Show" (F&SF, Nov. 1953).

————. *Time and Again* (New York: Ace Books, n.d.; New York: Simon and Schuster, 1952; as *Time Quarry*, GAL, Oct.-Dec. 1950).

————. *Way Station* (New York: Macfadden Books, 1964; Garden City, N.Y.: Doubleday & Co., 1963; as *Here Gather the Stars*, GAL, June-Aug. 1963).

————. "The World of the Red Sun." In Isaac Asimov, ed., *Before the Golden Age* (Garden City, N.Y.: Doubleday & Co., 1974); WS, Dec. 1931.

Siodmak, Curt. *Donovan's Brain* (New York: Alfred A. Knopf, 1943).

Sladek, John T. "The Poets of Milgrove, Iowa" (NW 168, Nov. 1966).

Slonczewski, Joan. *A Door into Ocean* (New York: Avon Books, 1987; New York: Arbor House, 1986).

Smith, Cordwainer. (New York: Arbor House, 1986) [pseud. Paul M. A. Linebarger]. *The Best of Cordwainer Smith* (New York: Ballantine Books, 1975). Incl. "Scanners Live in Vain" (*Fantasy Book* no. 6, 1950), "The Lady Who Sailed *The Soul*" (GAL, June 1960), "The Game of Rat and Dragon" (GAL, Oct. 1955), "The Burning of the Brain" (IF, Oct. 1958), "Golden the Ship Was—Oh! Oh! Oh!" (AMZ, Apr. 1959), "The Dead Lady of Clown Town" (GAL, Aug. 1964), "Under Old Earth" (GAL, Feb. 1966), "Alpha Ralpha Boulevard" (F&SF, June 1961), "The Ballad of Lost C'mell" (GAL, Oct. 1962), "A Planet Named Shayol" (GAL, Oct. 1961).

————. *The Instrumentality of Mankind* (New York: Ballantine Books, 1979). Incl. "No, No, Not Rogov!" (IF, Feb. 1959), "Mark Elf" (*Saturn*, May 1957), "War No. 81-Q" (*The Adjutant*, June 1928), "When the People Fell" (GAL, Apr. 1959), "Drunkboat" (AMZ, October 1963), "The Queen of the Afternoon," completed by Genevieve Linebarger (GAL, Apr. 1978).

————. *Norstrilia* (New York: Ballantine Books, 1975). Excerpts, with bridge material, appeared as "The Boy Who Bought Old Earth" (GAL, Apr. 1964), "The Store of Heart's Desire" (IF, May 1964), *The Planet Buyer* (New York: Pyramid Books, 1964), *The Underpeople* (New York: Pyramid Books, 1968).

————. *Quest of the Three Worlds* (New York: Ballantine Books, 1978; New York: Ace Books, 1966). Incorporates Casher O'Neill series, from "On the Gem Planet" (GAL, Oct. 1963) through "Three to a Given Star" (GAL, Oct. 1965).

————. Unpublished papers, University of Kansas, Lawrence, Kans. Incl. 1961 revision of "War No. 81-Q," early drafts of sf stories such as "The Ballad of Lost C'mell," and notes for unwritten stories.

Smith, Edward E. *Spacehounds of IPC* (New York: Berkley Books, 1983; Reading, Pa.: Fantasy Press, 1947; AMZ, July-Sept. 1931).

Smith, L. Neil. *The Gallatin Divergence* (New York: Ballantine Books, 1985).

———. *The Probability Broach* (New York: Ballantine Books, 1980).

———. *Tom Paine Maru* (New York: Ballantine Books, 1984).

———. *The Venus Belt* (New York: Ballantine Books, 1981).

———. *The Wardove* (New York: Berkley Books, 1986).

Snegov, Sergel, *Lyudi Kak Bogi (Men Like Gods)* in *Ellinski Sekret* (Leningrad: Lenizdat, 1966).

Spinrad, Norman. *Bug Jack Barron* (New York: Avon Books, 1969; NW 178–182, Dec.-Jan. 1967/8-July 1968).

———. "The Carcinoma Angels." See Ellison, Harlan, ed., *Dangerous Visions*.

———. *Little Heroes* (New York: Bantam Books Inc., 1987).

Stapledon, Olaf. *Last and First Men* and *Star Maker* (New York: Dover Publications, 1968). Incl. *Last and First Men* (London: Methuen, 1931), *Star Maker* (London: Methuen, 1937).

Steele, Curtis. *Scourge of the Invisible Death* (New York: Dimedia, 1980; *Operator No. 5*, Nov. 1935).

Sterling, Bruce. *Islands in the Net* (New York: Arbor House, 1988).

———. *Schismatrix* (New York: Ace Books, 1986; New York: Arbor House, 1985).

Sterling, Bruce, ed. *Mirrorshades: The Cyberpunk Anthology* (New York: Arbor House, 1986).

Stevenson, Robert Louis. "The Strange Case of Dr. Jekyll and Mr. Hyde." In Damon Knight, ed., *A Century of Great Science Fiction Short Novels* (New York: Delacorte Press, 1964); London: Longman's Green, 1886.

Stine, Hank. *Season of the Witch* (Hollywood, Calif.: Essex House, 1968).

Stowe, Harriet Beecher. *Uncle Tom's Cabin; or, Life among the Lowly* (Boston: J. P. Jewett & Co., 1852).

Strugatsky, Arkady, and Boris Strugatsky. *Beetle in the Anthill*. Trans. Antonina W. Bouis (New York: Macmillan Co., 1980), from *Zhuk v Muraveineke* (*Znanie-Sila*, 1979–80).

———. *Definitely Maybe*. Trans. Antonina W. Bouis (New York: Macmillan Co., 1978), from *Za Milliard Let do Kontsa Sveta* [*A Billion Years before the End of the World*] (*Znanie-Sila*, 1976–7, nos. 9–12, 1).

———. *Escape Attempt*. Trans. Roger DeGaris (New York: Macmillan Co., 1982). Incl. "Escape Attempt" from "Popytka k Begstvu" (*Fantastika* 1962, Moscow: Molodaya Gvardia): "The Kid from Hell" from "Paren iz Preispodnei" (*Nezrimyi Most*, Leningrad: Detskaya Literatura, 1976); "Space Mowgli" from "Malysh" ["The Boy"] (Leningrad: Detskaya Literatura, 1973).

———. *Far Rainbow/The Second Invasion from Mars*. Trans. Gary Kern (New York: Macmillan Co., 1979). Incl. "Far Rainbow" from *Dalekaya Raduga* (*Novaya Signalnaya*, Moscow: Znanie, 1963).

———. *The Final Circle of Paradise*. Trans. Leonid Renen (New York: DAW Books, 1976), from *Khishchnye Veshchi Veka* [*Predatory Things of the Age*] (Moscow: Molodaya Gvardia, 1965).

————. [Strugatski]. *Hard to Be a God*. Trans. (from German Version, pub. data not known) Wendayne Ackerman (New York: Seabury Press, 1973), from *Trudno Byt Bogom*, in *Dalekaya Raduga* (Moscow: Molodaya Gvardia, 1964).

————. *Noon: 22nd Century*. Trans. Patrick L. McGuire (New York: Macmillan Co., 1978), from *Polden, XXII Vek* (Moscow: Detskaya Literatura, 1967), rev. and exp. from *Polden, 22-i Vek* (Moscow: Detgiz, 1962). Incorporates stories from "Almost the Same" (*Ural* no. 6, 1961) to "Strantstvyushchikh i pyteshestvuyushchikh" ["Pilgrims and Wayfarers"] (*Fantastika* 1963, Moscow: Molodaya Gvardia).

————. *Prisoners of Power*. Trans. Helen Saltz Jacobson (New York: Macmillan Co., 1977), from *Obitaeymi Ostrov* [*Inhabited Island*] (Moscow: Detskaya Literatura, 1971), rev. and exp. from *Neva*, 1969, nos. 1–3.

————. *Roadside Picnic/Tale of the Troika*. Trans. Antonina W. Bouis (New York: Macmillan Co., 1977). Incl. *Roadside Picnic*, from "Piknik na Obochine" (*Avrora*, 1972, nos. 7–10).

————. *The Snail on the Slope*. Trans. Alan Meyers (New York: Bantam Books, 1980), from Estonian edition of 1972 (data not given). Incorporates "Ulitka na Sklone" (*Ellinski Sekret*, Leningrad: Lenizdat, 1966), "Pepper" (*Baikal*, 1968, nos. 1–2).

————. *Space Apprentice*. Trans. Antonina W. Bouis (New York: Macmillan Co., 1981), from *Stazhori* [The Probationers] (Moscow: Molodaya Gvardia, 1962).

————. *Strana Bagrovykh Tuch* [*The Land of Crimson Clouds*] (Moscow: Detskaya Literatura, 1969). Incl. *Strana Bagrovykh Tuch* (Moscow: Detgiz, 1959); Anatoly Dneprov, "Glinyanyi Bog" ["Clay God"] (*Mir Priklyucheny Almanakh* no. 9, Moscow: Detgiz, 1964).

————. *The Time Wanderers*. No Trans. given (New York: Richardson & Steirman, 1986), from *Volny Gasiet Veter* [*The Wave Extinguishes the Wind*] (*Znanie-Sila*, 1985–6, nos. 6–12, 1–3).

————. "The Way to Amalteia." See Bulchev, Kir, et al., *Earth and Elsewhere*.

Sturgeon, Theodore. *Godbody* (New York: New American Library, 1987; New York: Donald I. Fine, 1986).

————. *The Golden Helix* (New York: Dell Publishing Co., 1980; Garden City, N.Y.: Doubleday & Co., 1979). Incl. "The Man Who Lost the Sea" (F&SF, Oct. 1959), "The Skills of Xanadu" (GAL, July 1956).

————. "If All Men Were Brothers, Would You Let One Marry Your Sister?" See Ellison, Harlan, ed., *Dangerous Visions*.

————. *More Than Human* (New York: Ballantine Books, 1953). Incorporates "Baby Is Three" (GAL, Oct. 1952).

————. *Sturgeon Is Alive and Well* (New York: Berkley Books, 1971). Incl. "Slow Sculpture" (GAL, Feb. 1970), "Brownshoes," as "The Man Who Learned Loving" (*Knight*, 1969).

————. *The Synthetic Man* (New York: Pyramid Books, 1957; as *The Dreaming Jewels*, New York: Greenberg, 1950).

————. *A Way Home* (New York: Pyramid Books, 1956; New York: Funk & Wagnall's, 1955). Incl. "Thunder and Roses" (ASF Nov. 1947), "Unite and Conquer" (ASF, Oct. 1948).

Suvin, Davko, ed., *Other Worlds, Other Seas* (New York: Berkley Books, 1972; New York: Random House, 1970). See entries for Dneprov, Anatoly.

Swanwick, Michael. *Vacuum Flowers* (New York: Ace Books, 1988, New York: Arbor House, 1987).

Tiptree, James, Jr. [pseud. Alice Sheldon]. *Out of the Everywhere* (New York: Ballantine Books, 1981). Incl. "Your Faces, O My Sisters! Your Faces Filled of Light!" (Vonda McIntire and Susan Anderson, eds., *Aurora: Beyond Equality*, Greenwich, Conn.: Fawcett Books, 1976).

————. *Star Songs of an Old Primate* (New York: Ballantine Books, 1978). Incl. "Houston, Houston, Do You Read?" (Vonda McIntire and Susan Anderson, eds., *Aurora: Beyond Equality*, Greenwich, Conn.: Fawcett Books, 1976).

————. *Warm Worlds and Otherwise* (New York: Ballantine Books, 1975). Incl. "The Women Men Don't See" (F&SF, Dec. 1973), "All the Kinds of Yes" (as "Filomena & Greg & Rikki-Tikki & Barlow & the Alien" in Robert Silverberg, ed., *New Dimensions II*, Garden City, N.Y.: Doubleday & Co., 1972).

Tolstoi, Alexei [Aleksei], *The Garin Death Ray*. Trans. George Hanna (Moscow: Foreign Languages Publishing House, n.d.), from *Giperboloid Inzhenera Garina [Engineer Garin's Hyperboloid]*. Moscow, Sovietsky Literatura, 1937; revised from Moscow, Sovietsky Literatura, 1933; Moscow, Gosizdat, 1927; serialized, Krasnaya Nov, no. 7, 1925, no's. 4–9, 1926).

Van Vogt, A. E. "The Human Operators." See Ellison, Harlan, *Partners in Wonder*.

————. *The Weapon Makers* (New York: Tempo Books, 1970; New York: Greenberg, 1952; rev. from Providence, R.I.: Hadley, 1947; ASF, Feb.-Apr. 1943).

————. *The World of Null-A* (New York: Berkley Books, 1970; rev. from *The World of Ā*, New York: Simon and Schuster, 1948; rev. from ASF, Aug.-Oct. 1945).

Varley, John. *The Persistence of Vision* (New York: Dial, 1978).

Verne, Jules. *Master of the World/Robur the Conqueror*. Trans. not given (New York: Ace Books, n.d.), from *Robur le conquerant* (Paris: Hetzel, 1886) and *Maitre du monde* (Paris: Hetzel, 1904).

Voiskunsky, Yevgeny, and Isai Lukodyanov. "The Black Pillar." Trans. not given. In *The Molecular Cafe* (Moscow: Mir, 1963), from "Chernyi Stolb" in *Chernyi Stolb* (Moscow: Znanie, 1962).

————. *Plesk Zvezdnynkh Morei [The Splash of Starry Seas]* (*Fantastika* 1967; Moscow: Molodaya Gvardia).

Vonnegut, Kurt, Jr. "The Big Space Fuck." See Ellison, Harlan, ed., *Again, Dangerous Visions*.

————. *Cat's Cradle* (New York: Dell Publishing Co., 1965; New York: Holt, Rinehart and Winston, 1963).

————. *The Sirens of Titan* (New York: Dell Publishing Co., 1966, reprinted 1959).

————. *Slaughterhouse Five: or, The Children's Crusade* (New York: Delacorte, 1969).

Watson, Ian. *The Embedding* (St. Alban's, U.K.: Granada Publishing Ltd., 1980; London: Victor Gollancz, 1973).

————. *The Martian Inca* (New York: Ace Books, 1978; New York: Charles Scribner's Sons, 1977).

Weinbaum, Stanley G. *A Martian Odyssey and Other Science Fiction Tales* (Westport, Conn.: Hyperion Press, 1974). Incl. autobiographical introduction.

Wells, H. G. *A Modern Utopia* (Lincoln: University of Nebraska Press, 1967; London: Chapman & Hall, 1905; *Fortnightly Review*, Oct. 1904-Apr. 1905).

———. *Seven Science Fiction Novels* (New York: Dover Publications, n.d.). Incl. *The Time Machine* (London: William Heinemann, 1895), *The Island of Dr. Moreau* (London: William Heinemann, 1896), *The Invisible Man* (London: C. Arthur Pearson, 1897), *The War of the Worlds* (London: William Heinemann, 1898; *Pearson's Magazine*, Apr.-Dec., 1897), *The First Men in the Moon* (London: George Newnes, 1901; *The Strand*, Dec. 1900-Aug. 1901), *The Food of the Gods* (London: Macmillan & Co., 1904; *Pearson's Magazine*, Dec. 1903-June 1904), *In the Days of the Comet* (London: Macmillan & Co., 1906; *Daily Chronicle*, 1905–6).

———. *The Shape of Things to Come* (London: Corgi Books, 1967; London: Hutchinson, 1933).

———. *Things to Come* (Boston: Gregg Press, 1975; reprint, with added critical material, from London: Cresset, 1935).

———. *3 Prophetic Novels* (New York: Dover Publications, n.d.). Incl. *When the Sleeper Wakes* (London: Harper & Bros., 1899; *The Graphic*, 1898–9).

———. *28 Science Fiction Stories* (New York: Dover Publications, n.d.). Incl. *Men Like Gods* (London: Cassell & Co., 1923), "The Star" (*The Graphic*, Christmas 1897), "A Story of the Days to Come" (*Pall Mall Magazine*, 1897), "A Dream of Armageddon" (*Black and White*, 1901).

Wilhelm, Kate. *Where Late the Sweet Birds Sang* (New York: Pocket Books, 1977; New York: Harper & Row, 1976).

Williamson, Jack. *The Legion of Space* (New York: Pyramid Books, 1967; Reading, Pa.: Fantasy Press, 1947; ASF, Apr.-Sept. 1935).

———. *Manseed* (New York: Ballantine Books, 1982).

———. *People Machines* (New York: Ace Books, 1971). Incl. "Breakdown" (ASF, Jan. 1942).

Wilson, Richard. *The Girls from Planet 5* (New York: Ballantine Books, 1955).

Wolfe, Bernard. "The Bisquit Position." See Ellison, Harlan, ed., *Again, Dangerous Visions*.

Wolfe, Gene. *The Citadel of the Autarch*. Book of the New Sun Series. (New York: Simon and Schuster, 1983).

———. *The Claw of the Conciliator*. Book of the New Sun Series. (New York: Simon and Schuster, 1981).

———. *The Shadow of the Torturer*. Book of the New Sun Series. (New York: Simon and Schuster, 1980).

———. *The Sword of the Lictor*. Book of the New Sun Series. (New York: Simon and Schuster, 1982).

———. *The Urth of the New Sun*. Book of the New Sun Series. (New York: Tor, 1987).

Wright, S. Fowler. *The World Below* (London: Collins, 1929). Incorporates *The Amphibians* (London: Merton, 1925).

Yefremov, Ivan. *Andromeda*. Trans. George Hanna (Moscow: Progress Publishers, 1980; Moscow: Foreign Languages Publishing House, 1959), from

Tumannost Andromedy (Moscow: Molodaya Gvardia, 1958). Serialized in *Tekhnika-Molodezhi*, 1957.

————. *Chas Byka* [*The Hour of the Bull*] (Moscow: Molodaya Gvardia, 1970).

Yemtsev [Emtsev], Mikhail, and Yeremei [Eremei] Parnov. *World Soul*. Trans. Antonina W. Bouis (New York: Macmillan Co., 1978), from *Dusha Mira* (in *Uvravneniya c Blednogo Neptuna* [*The Pale Neptune Equation*] (Moscow: Molodaya Gvardia, 1964).

Zahn, Timothy. *Cobra* (New York: Baen Books, 1985).

Zamyatin, Yevgeny. *We*. Trans. Mirra Ginsburg (New York: Viking Press, 1972), from *Mwy* (New York: Chekhov Publishing House, 1952), from 1920 manuscript.

Zoline, Pamela. "The Heat Death of the Universe." See Moorcock, Michael, ed., *New Worlds*.

NONFICTIONAL WORKS

Aldiss, Brian W. *Billion Year Spree* (New York: Schocken Books, 1974; Garden City, N.Y.: Doubleday & Co., 1973).

Aldiss, Brian W., and Harry Harrison, eds. *Hell's Cartographers* (London: Futura Publications Ltd., 1976; London: Weidenfeld and Nicholson, 1975).

Asimov, Isaac. *In Memory Yet Green* (Garden City: N.Y.: Doubleday & Co., 1979).

Ballard, J. G. editorial, NW 118, May 1962.

————. "Myth-Maker of the 20th Century," NW 142, May-June 1964.

Barr, Marlene, Richard Law, and Ruth Salvaggio. *Suzy McKee Charnas, Joan Vinge, Octavia Butler, Starmont Reader's Guide 23* (Mercer Island, Wash.: Starmont Books, 1986).

Barron, Neal, ed. *Anatomy of Wonder*. 2d ed. (New York and London: R. R. Bowker Co., 1981).

Bartlett's Familiar Quotations. 14th ed. (Boston: Little, Brown & Co., 1968).

Bleiler, Everett F., ed. *Science Fiction Writers: Critical Studies of the Major Authors from the Early Nineteenth Century to the Present Day* (New York: Charles Scribner's Sons, 1982).

Branden, Barbara. *The Passion of Ayn Rand* (Garden City, N.Y.: Doubleday & Co., 1986).

Breuer, Miles J., M.D., "The Future of Scientifiction" (AMZ Quarterly, Summer 1929).

Brigg, Peter. *J. G. Ballard: Starmont Reader's Guide 26* (Mercer Island, Wash.: Starmont Books, 1985).

Bugliosi, Vincent, and Curt Gentry. *Helter Skelter* (New York: Norton, 1974).

Cherryh, C. J. Interview in *Locus*, April 1987.

Clareson, Thomas J., ed. *SF: The Other Side of Realism* (Bowling Green, Ohio: Bowling Green University Popular Press, 1971).

Clarke, Arthur C. *The Lost Worlds of 2001* (New York: New American Library, 1972).

————. *Profiles of the Future*. Rev. ed. (New York: Warner Books, 1985; New

York: Holt, Rinehart and Winston, 1984 [original version, London: Victor Gollancz, 1962]).

Cole, W. R. *A Checklist of Science Fiction Anthologies* (Brooklyn, N.Y.: privately printed, 1964).

Collins, Michael R. *Brian W. Aldiss: Starmont Reader's Guide 28* (Mercer Island, Wash.: Starmont Books, 1986).

Contento, William. *Index to Science Fiction Anthologies and Collections, 1951–1976* (Boston: G. K. Hall, 1978).

———. *Index to Science Fiction Anthologies and Collections, 1977–1983* (Boston: G. K. Hall, 1984).

Davenport, Basil, ed. *The Science Fiction Novel: Imagination and Social Criticism* (Chicago: Advent Books, 1964).

Day, Donald B. *Index to the Science Fiction Magazines, 1926–1950* (Portland, Oreg.: Perri Press, 1952).

Delany, Samuel R. *The American Shore: Meditations of a Tale of Science Fiction by Thomas M. Disch—"Angouleme"* (Elizabethtown, N.Y.: Dragon Press, 1978).

———. *The Jewel-Hinged Jaw: Notes on the Language of Science Fiction* (Elizabethtown, N.Y.: Dragon Press, 1977).

———. *The Motion of Light in Water* (New York: Arbor House, 1987).

del Rey, Lester. *The World of Science Fiction, 1926–76: The History of a Subculture* (New York: Ballantine Books, 1979).

Disch, Thomas M. Review column; F&SF, Feb. 1981.

Eshbach, Lloyd Arthur, ed. *Of Worlds Beyond* (Chicago: Advent Books, 1964; Reading, Pa.: Fantasy Press, 1947). Incl. Robert A. Heinlein, "On the Writing of Speculative Fiction."

Franklin, H. Bruce. *Robert A. Heinlein: America as Science Fiction* (New York: Oxford University Press, 1980).

Gibson, William. Interviews, *Science Fiction Eye*, Winter 1987.

Green, Roger Lancelyn, and Walter Hooper. *C. S. Lewis: A Biography* (New York: Harcourt Brace Jovanovich, 1974).

Greenland, Colin. *The Entropy Exhibition: Michael Moorcock and the British 'New Wave' in Science Fiction* (London: Rutledge & Kegan Paul, 1983).

Gunn, James E. *Alternate Worlds: The Illustrated History of Science Fiction* (Englewood Cliffs, N.J.: Prentice-Hall, 1975).

Haining, Peter, ed. *The H. G. Wells Scrapbook* (New York: Clarkson N. Potter, 1978). Incl. "The Man of the Year Million" (*Pall Mall Gazette*, 1893).

Hammond, J. R. *Herbert George Wells: An Annotated Bibliography* (New York and London: Garland Publishing, 1977).

Hardy, Phil, ed. *Science Fiction: The Complete Film Sourcebook* (New York: Morrow, 1984).

Heinlein, Robert A. *Expanded Universe* (New York: Grosset & Dunlap, 1980).

Hillegas, Mark. *The Future as Nightmare: H. G. Wells and the Anti-Utopians* (New York: Oxford University Press, 1967).

Hubbard, L. Ron. "Dianetics: The Evolution of the Science" (ASF, May 1950).

Koestler, Arthur. *The Act of Creation* (New York: Macmillan Co., 1964).

Kropotkin, Petr [Pyotr]. *Mutual Aid* (Boston: Extending Horizons Books, n.d.; first edition, New York: McClure, Phillips & Co., 1902).

Lane, Daryl, William Vernon and David Carson, eds. *The Sound of Wonder* (Phoenix, Ariz.: Oryx Press, 1985, two volumes). Incl. interviews with C. J. Cherryh, George R. R. Martin.

Lewis, C. S. *The Abolition of Man* (New York: Macmillan Co., pl, 1965b; hc, 1947; London: Oxford University Press, 1943).

————. *The Allegory of Love: A Study on Medieval Tradition* (New York: Oxford University Press, 1936.

————. *An Experiment in Criticism* (Cambridge: Cambridge University Press, 1969).

————. *Christian Reflections* (Grand Rapids, Mich.: William B. Eerdman's Publishing Co., 1967). Incl. "The Funeral of a Great Myth."

————. *Letters of C. S. Lewis*, ed., with a memoir, by W. H. Lewis (New York: Harcourt, Brace & World, 1966).

————. *On Stories, and Other Essays on Literature* (New York: Harcourt Brace Jovanovich, 1982). Incl. "A Reply to Professor Haldane" (undated).

Lewis, Tony. *Concordance to Cordwainer Smith* (Cambridge, Mass.: NESFA Press, 1984).

McGuire, Patrick L. *Red Stars: Political Aspects of Soviet Science Fiction* (Ann Arbor, Mich.: UMI Research Press, 1985).

Mackenzie, Norman, and Jeanne Mackenzie. *H. G. Wells: A Biography* (New York: Simon & Schuster, 1973).

Metcalf, Norman. *The Index of Science Fiction Magazines, 1951–65* (El Cerrito, Calif.: J. Ben Stark, 1968).

Moorcock, Michael. Editorial, NW 142, May–June 1964.

————. Review Column, NW 214, Autumn 1978.

Moskowitz, Sam. *Seekers of Tomorrow* (Cleveland: World Publishing Co., 1966).

New England Science Fiction Association. *Index to the Science Fiction Magazines, 1966–70* (West Hanover, Mass.: Halliday Lithograph Corp., 1971).

————. *Index to the Science Fiction Magazines and Original Anthologies*. Bound volume of annual and biennial indexes (West Hanover, Mass.: privately printed/NESFA Press, 1973–1982, for listings 1971–81).

Nicholls, Peter, ed. *The Science Fiction Encyclopedia* (Garden City, N.Y.: Doubleday & Co., 1979).

Orwell, George. *A Collection of Essays by George Orwell* (Garden City, N.Y.: Anchor Books, 1954). Incl. "Charles Dickens" (original year of publication given as 1939).

————. *The Road to Wigan Pier* (New York: Berkley Books, 1961; London: Victor Gollancz, 1937).

Pohl, Frederik. *The Way the Future Was* (New York: Ballantine Books, hc, 1978).

Pohl, Frederik, and Frederik Pohl IV. *Science Fiction Studies in Film* (New York: Ace Books, 1981).

Porter, Andrew, ed. *Exploring Cordwainer Smith* (New York: Algol Press, 1975). Incl. Sandra Miesel, "I Am Joan & I Love You."

Rand, Ayn. *Capitalism: The Unknown Ideal* (New York: New American Library, 1966).

————. *The New Left: The Anti-Industrial Revolution* (New York: New American Library, 1971).

————. *The Romantic Manifesto* (Cleveland: World Publishing Co., 1969).

————. *The Virtue of Selfishness: A New Concept of Egoism* (New York: New American Library, 1965).

Rottensteiner, Franz. *The Science Fiction Book* (New York: New American Library, 1975).

Smith, Curtis C., ed. *Twentieth Century Science Fiction Writers.* 2d ed. (Chicago and London: St. James Press, 1986).

Snow, C. P. *The Two Cultures and the Scientific Revolution* (New York: Cambridge University Press, 1961).

Soviet Literature, Feb. 1984.: "Our Questionnaire" [sf authors' responses].

Sterling, Bruce. Interview, *Science Fiction Eye*, Winter 1987.

Suvin, Darko. *Metamorphoses of Science Fiction: On the Poetics and History of a Literary Genre* (New Haven, Conn.: Yale University Press, 1979).

————. *Russian Science Fiction, 1956–1974: A Bibliography* (Elizabethtown, N.Y.: Dragon Press, 1976).

————. *The Utopian Tradition of Russian Science Fiction* (Modern Humanities Research Association/W. S. Maney & Son Ltd., n.d.). Pamphlet reprint of essay (*The Modern Language Review*, Jan. 1971).

Tolkien, J. R. R. *The Monsters and the Critics, and Other Essays* (Boston: Houghton Mifflin Co., 1984). Incl. "On Fairy Stories" from *Essays Presented to Charles Williams* (London: Oxford University Press, 1947), rev. from 1939 lecture.

Tymm, Marshall B., ed. *The Science Fiction Reference Book* (Mercer Island, Wash.: Starmont House, 1981).

Versins, Pierre. *Encyclopedie de l'utopie, des voyages extraordinaires et de la science fiction* (Lausanne: Editions L'Age d'Homme, 1973).

Walker, Paul, ed. *Speaking of Science Fiction* (Oradell, N.J.: Luna Publications, 1978). Incl. interviews with Clifford D. Simak, Ursula K. Le Guin.

Weedman, Jane Branham. *Samuel R. Delany: Starmont Reader's Guide 10* (Mercer Island, Wash.: Starmont Books, 1982).

Wells, H. G. "The Man of the Year Million." See Haining, Peter, *The H. G. Wells Scrapbook*.

————. *The Outline of History* (London: George Newnes, 1920).

Wells, H. G., G. P. Wells, and Julian Huxley. *The Science of Life* (London: Amalgamated Press, 1930).

Williamson, Jack. *H. G. Wells: Critic of Progress* (Baltimore: Mirage Press, 1973).

————. "Scientifiction, Searchlight of Science," AMZ Quarterly, Fall 1928.

Wollheim, Donald A. *The Universe Makers* (New York: Harper & Row, 1971).

Zamyatin, Yevgeny. *A Soviet Heretic*. Ed. and trans. Mirra Ginsburg (Chicago: University of Chicago Press, 1970). Incl. "On Synthetism" (1922), "On Literature, Revolution, Entropy and Other Matters" (1923). "H. G. Wells" (1922).

FILM AND TELEVISION WORKS

(Studio in parentheses; P = producer; D = director; S = scriptwriter).

"The Architects of Fear," episode of *The Outer Limits*. United Artists (1963). P: Ben Brady. D: Byron Haskin. S: Meyer Dolinsky.

The Avengers, television series. ABC/Thames Television (1961–69). P,D,S: Various.

Billy Liar. Vic Films (1963). P: Joe Janni. D: John Schlesinger S: Keith Waterhouse, Willis Hall (from Waterhouse's novel and their play).

Birth of a Nation. Epoch (1915). P: D. W. Griffith, Harry E. Aitken. D: D. W. Griffith. S: D. W. Griffith, Frank E. Woods (from Thomas Dixon Jr.'s *The Clansman*).

Blade Runner. The Ladd Company (1982). P: Harve Bennett. D: Ridley Scott. S: Hampton Fancher, David Peoples (from Philip K. Dick's *Do Androids Dream of Electric Sheep?*).

A Boy And His Dog. LQJaf Films (1975). P: Alvy Moore. D: L. Q. Jones. S: L. Q. Jones (From Harlan Ellison's novella).

Brazil. Universal (1985). P: Arnon Milchan. D: Terry Gilliam. S: Terry Gilliam, Tom Stoppard, Charles McKeown.

Casablanca. Warner Bros. (1942). P: Hal B. Wallis. D: Michael Curtiz. S: Howard Koch (from Murray Bennett and Jean Allison's *Everybody Comes to Rick's*).

Empire of the Sun. Warner Bros. (1987). P: Steven Spielberg, Kathleen Turner. D: Steven Spielberg. S: Tom Stoppard (from J. G. Ballard's novel).

Forbidden Planet. MGM (1956). P: Nicholas Nayfack. D: Fred M. Wilcox. S: Cyril Hume.

Gone with the Wind. MGM (1939). P: David O. Selznick. D: Victor Fleming. S: Sidney Howard (from Margaret Mitchell's novel).

Heart Like a Wheel. Aurora (1983). P: Charles Rovin. D: Jonathan Kaplan. S: Ken Friedman.

Invasion of the Body Snatchers. Walter Wanger Prods (1956). P: Walter Wanger. D: Don Siegel. S: Daniel Mainwaring (from Jack Finner's *The Body Snatchers*).

The Last Valley. ABC/Season/Seamaster (1971). P, D, S: James Clavell (from the novel by J. B. Pick).

Mad Max. Kennedy-Miller (1979). P: Byron Kennedy. D: George Miller. S: George Miller, James McCasland.

Psycho. Shamley (1960). P, D: Alfred Hitchcock. S: Joseph Stefano (from the novel by Robert Bloch).

The Road Warrior. Kennedy-Miller Enterprises (1981). P: Byron Kennedy. D: George Miller. S: George Miller, Terry Hayes, Brian Hannant.

Robotech, television series. Harmony Gold USA (1985). P: Ahmed Agrama, Carl Macek. D: Robert Barron. S: various. Adapted in part from *Super Dimension Fortress Macross* (Tatsunogo, 1982).

Star Trek, television series. Paramount (1966–9). P: Gene Roddenberry. D, S: various.

Star Wars. 20th Century Fox (1977). P: Gary Kurtz. D: George Lucas. S: George Lucas (from the story by George Lucas).

The Thing. Winchester (1951). P: Howard Hawks. D: Christian Nyby. S: Charles Lederer (from John W. Campbell's "Who Goes there?").

Things to Come. London Films (1936). P: Alexander Korda. D: William Cameron Menzies. S: H. G. Wells (from Wells' *The Shape of Things to Come*).

2001: A Space Odyssey. MGM (1968). P, D: Stanley Kubrick. S: Stanley Kubrick and Arthur C. Clarke (inspired by Clarke's "The Sentinel").

Index

About the Author

JOHN J. PIERCE is associate editor of *Private Label* magazine. He is the author of *Foundations of Science Fiction* (Greenwood Press, 1987) and *Great Themes of Science Fiction* (Greenwood Press, 1987), the companion volumes to this, the final book in the "Study in Imagination and Evolution" series. Mr. Pierce is a contributor to *The New Encyclopedia of Science Fiction* (1988) and *Twentieth Century Science Fiction Writers* (1986), author of various articles appearing in science fiction periodicals, and science fiction reviewer for *Rave Reviews*.